Spindletop Unwound

Roger L. Shaffer

Republic of Texas Press

Library of Congress Cataloging-in-Publication Data

Shaffer, Roger L. (Roger Lee), 1941-.
  Spindletop unwound / Roger L. Shaffer.
     p.   cm.
  Includes bibliographical references and index.
  ISBN 1-55622-550-4 (pb)
  1. Trials--Texas.   2. McFadden family.   3. Humphries family.
  4. Petroleum industry and trade--Texas--Beaumont Region.
  5. Inheritance and succession--Texas--Beaumont Region. I. Title.
  KF228.M388S53   1997
  364.15'23'09764145—dc21   97-12739
                                   CIP

ISBN 1-55622-550-4
10 9 8 7 6 5 4 3 2 1
9707

All inquiries for volume purchases of this book should be addressed to Wordware Publishing, Inc., at 2320 Los Rios Boulevard, Plano, Texas 75074. Telephone inquiries may be made by calling:

(972) 423-0090

Oct 1850

I certify these to be 64 pages & a piece of free inhabitance & done as near in acordance with my oath as I could do it the people was hard to get along with

H Swearingen A M

Contents

Daddy's Always Told Us That

Sorting It Out: Greed And Grasping

Acknowledgements

Out of the morass of myths, legends, and plain prevarications surrounding Spindletop, I was fortunate enough to find clear-thinking Jim Petty. His assistance is greatly appreciated.

The Texas General Land Office and the clerks of the courts of Harris, Harrison, Panola, Shelby, and especially Jefferson Counties, were all very courteous and helpful. It was a thrill to be able to actually hold in my own hands original Humphries documents over one hundred and fifty years old. Houston's Clayton Library and Beaumont's public library were very helpful too. Cathy Romano, of the Records and Briefs section of the United States Supreme Court Library, was particularly helpful with locating W.T. Weir's Jurisdictional Statement.

I am grateful for the generosity of the Panola and Harrison County Historical Societies. Christy Marino, Curator of the Spindletop/Gladys City Boomtown Museum, was especially helpful. (So was the nice East Texas policewoman patrolling U.S. 59 who gave me a friendly warning, instead of a ticket, as I scurried a bit too fast out of Nacogdoches headed for Panola County.)

My family deserves special thanks: for my son Roger's insights, assistance in legal analysis, and proofreading skills; for my wonderful daughter Jeanne Rivera's support and proofreading skills (how she remembers all those grammar rules is beyond me); for my father Al Shaffer's enthusiastic support of this project (he still can't get over the outrageousness of the Medders); for my sister Joanna Armstrong's graphic design skills and encouragement; my Texas sister Suzanne Miskin's legal analysis, general support, and taxi

ix

service trekking around Jefferson County, Beaumont, and the Pelham Humphries League. And most especially, my wife Peggy deserves special thanks. Putting up with me day to day is hard enough, but slogging through the woods in a cold November rain to find the elusive Pulaski and Humphries Bluff was above and beyond the call of duty.

Finally, I wish to publicly thank my editor and friend, Mary Elizabeth Goldman, for her support and early confidence in this project.

Preface

The preposterousness of nearly a hundred years of litigation over a single tract of land, the enormous sums of money involved, and especially the colorful characters make this a fun story to tell. But to fully understand the logic (or lack thereof) of the many lawsuits, court decisions, and legal documents, a smattering of legal explanation is useful. I have tried to make that as painless as possible. As a lawyer, the normal urge was to write this story in the style of a legal brief or law review article. You know, using lots of legalese and hundreds of footnotes. While I admit to giving in to a few footnotes, for the most part, I would like to think I successfully resisted.

I have not been particularly neutral, unbiased, or kind towards some of the lawyers and characters involved in the Spindletop story. However, as a social scientist, a lawyer (one of three lawyers in my family—surely that gives me some license), and a former homicide investigator, I couldn't resist offering my opinion on some of the events and human motivations. The opinions are mine. Reasonable people may differ.

I am convinced that a historian could easily spend a lifetime researching Spindletop and the Humphries claims. The temptation to get lost in the minutia of the story is great. I confess to wandering a bit, too.

A Cast of Characters

The Killing

8:00 p.m., Monday, August 18, 1986
Highway 73 near the M Half Circle Ranch, Jefferson County, Texas.

Jefferson County is located in the southeast corner of Texas. The county is primarily low coastal land and the Gulf of Mexico is its southern border. Much of the county is still rural and supports ranching.

The M Half Circle Ranch is on Texas Highway 73 about twenty miles south of Beaumont and some twenty miles west of Port Arthur. Running east and west, 73 becomes a sparsely populated two-lane highway when it leaves Port Arthur and heads towards Winnie, just inside neighboring Chambers County. The ranch is on the north side of 73, between Labelle and Wilford Roads. The entrance is marked by a roadside mailbox with "M Half Circle Ranch" lettered on it and two reflectors on its post. A single-lane road leads from 73 north into the property. A few car lengths off the highway, a locked gate keeps unwanted visitors out. Other than an occasional car passing on 73, the area is deserted.

Ranch entrance

It was getting dark as Joe and Marie Perkins drove the pickup towards the ranch. At fifty-six, Joe was still quite capable of causing himself women trouble. He had already been married and divorced several times in the past few years, and, now that she knew about Rosine, Marie wanted out. On top of that, he and Rosine had argued. His threat had angered her, and her temper scared him. His job as her ranch hand was through, and he knew he would be lucky if that was the worst of it.

Joe Perkins

2600 Ashley Avenue, Beaumont, Texas.

When Rosine thought of the McFaddin Family, just like the "G" in God, the "F" in Family was always capitalized. With a hundred years of Family money, power, and social position, W.P.H. McFaddin's granddaughter was accustomed to having things her way. Rosine was a woman of action and one definitely to be reckoned with. She had no patience with those who opposed her and little control over her fierce temper.

Rosine McFaddin Wilson
photo courtesy of the *Beaumont Enterprise*

Rosine was angry. Once Joe Perkins had been a solution. After all, at seventy, her husband, Will, was eleven years older than she. They did not share a bedroom, and he had lots of medical problems. Now Joe was a problem. It was bad enough that people were talking. Worse yet, a new, better funded and much more sophisticated Humphries attack was underway. Now they had a real genealogist! Well, the Humphries weren't going to get any help from Joe Perkins. Family interests must always be protected.

Will was not home yet. Making her decision, Rosine left a note and, taking a pistol from the closet, got into her Cadillac to find Joe.

8:30 p.m., M Half Circle Ranch.

It was dark when the Cadillac's headlights picked up the reflectors on the mailbox post and Rosine turned onto the ranch road. The pickup was stopped on the highway side of the gate, headed towards 73. She saw Joe lock the gate and get behind the wheel.

Recognizing the Cadillac, Joe sat in the pickup and waited for her. The pickup took up most of the single lane, and Rosine drove partially off the road to get next to Joe. She pulled up driver's side to driver's side, just a few feet apart from each other. Their windows were down. Rosine picked up her pistol and fired a shot into Joe's chest. In shock and disbelief Joe gasped, "Son of a bitch, she shot me!" He gunned the pickup and sped out of the ranch road, getting away from her and the gun. Blood was already starting to soak his shirt as he turned right on 73 towards Winnie.

Rosine felt better. Turning the Cadillac around, she headed east on 73 and started back to Beaumont. In the darkness and the excitement, she hadn't noticed Marie sitting in the passenger seat of the pickup.

Westbound 73 between M Half Circle Ranch and Wilford Road.

Joe had to stop. He was losing blood and couldn't breathe. Marie ran around to the driver's side, moved him over and

Wilford Road, north off State Highway 73

drove the remaining mile or so to the home of Leo and Joyce Brown on Wilford Road. They called for the Winnie Fire Department's ambulance while Joe lay bleeding in the pickup. He was dead before the ambulance arrived.

Wilford Road home of Leo and Joyce Brown

2600 Ashley Avenue.

As Marie and the Browns waited on Wilford Road for the ambulance, Rosine arrived back home. While she was confident that no one had seen her shoot Joe, she still felt it was prudent to get rid of the gun.

9:25 p.m., Brown residence, Wilford Road just off Highway 73.

Richie W. Droddy, a Jefferson County sheriff's deputy, arrived at the Brown's house on Wilford Road. Joe Perkins lay dead from the gunshot wound. Marie told Deputy Droddy that Rosine McFaddin Wilson killed Joe. Jack Cravy, Jefferson County's Precinct 4 justice of the peace and coroner, was called to the scene. Cravy pronounced Joe dead and ordered an autopsy. The sheriff knew the investigation of a McFaddin accused of murder in Jefferson County was going to require careful handling.

Tuesday, August 19, 1986, Beaumont.

Satisfied that she was now back in control, Rosine was in a bank trustee's meeting when sheriff's sergeants Jay White and John Gowling found her and informed her of Joe's death. She made no attempt to disguise her annoyance that they had dared to interrupt her important meeting because of a dead ranch hand. She managed to ask if he had died of a heart attack. Since Rosine was adamant about continuing her meeting, the deputies left when she agreed to meet with them at the sheriff's office when she was through.

Later that day she came to the sheriff's office with Will. That proved to be a mistake. Sergeant Gowling interviewed Will apart from Rosine while Sergeant White, one of Jefferson County's female deputies, spoke with Rosine. Rosine continued to deny all knowledge of the incident. She said that she had played bridge and done some shopping between 4 and 7 p.m. on Monday, and that she had not left home after that. It was then that Sergeant White told Rosine of Marie's story about Rosine shooting Joe at the ranch Monday evening.

Knowing her gun would never be found and that it was just Marie Perkin's word against a McFaddin, Rosine stuck to her own story. She said she couldn't understand why Marie would lie like that. She suggested that Marie must have it in for them because Joe had been fired. Then, ever the resourceful opportunist, Rosine saw a way to misdirect the investigation. "You need to check out Marie Perkins," she said. "She's getting a divorce and was about to leave her husband. I guess now she's got an instant divorce." If it wasn't for Will and her note, it might have worked.

As Rosine was in one room denying she had been at the ranch and shifting the investigative focus towards Marie, in the other room Will was telling Sergeant Gowling that when he came home Monday evening he found Rosine's note saying she was going to the ranch. Despite her lie and Marie's statement, Rosine was a McFaddin and the sheriff's office didn't arrest her. Still, now that she was caught in a lie, Rosine had a problem.

Wednesday, August 20, 1986.

Rosine needed a new story and a way out of this mess. When she couldn't solve a problem by her direct personal action, even Rosine looked for help. By Wednesday afternoon she was ready. Accompanied by her lawyer, Lum Hawthorn, a noted Beaumont criminal attorney, Rosine told Sergeant White the shooting had been accidental. She didn't think she had hit Joe. It was because she was so surprised when they told her Joe was dead, that she panicked and denied she was at the ranch that night. The sheriff decided to continue the investigation. But Justice of the Peace Jack Cravy thought the preferential treatment of a McFaddin had gone on long enough.

Jack Cravy
photo courtesy of the *Beaumont Enterprise*

Monday, August 25, 1986.

Arrested on a warrant issued by Jack Cravy, Rosine was brought before him to be arraigned on the charge of murder. He set bond at $25,000. She paid the bond and was released.

Rosine wasn't having a good week. That Friday, the 29th, there was another Humphries story in the paper. It had a particularly irritating quote from a Humphries heir saying that the McFaddins had "been driving my Mercedes Benz for too long."

Thursday, September 4, 1986, Beaumont.

The Jefferson County Grand Jury was not persuaded by the accidental shooting story. Following a session lasting until 12:30 a.m. Thursday, they indicted Rosine for first degree murder.

In the Beginning

When today's Texas was still part of Mexico, under a plan to populate the area brought about through the efforts of Stephen Austin, colonization laws entitled certain early settlers to land grants from the government. Qualified heads of families got a *first class headright*, consisting of both a league of land (4,428 acres) for ranching and a labor of land (177.1 acres) for farming. Throughout history, perhaps because man is a territorial animal, the urge to acquire land and the compulsion to defend it has been an awesome motivating force—a force equal to and often intertwined with another basic human motivation, greed.

September 27, 1834
Town of San Augustine, State of Coahuila and Texas, Mexico.

Colonist William Humphries applies for his headright league. His petition, assigned number 118 and written with a flourishing hand in the officially required Spanish, is approved, and Arthur Henrie is authorized to survey Humphries' league. For reasons not clear now, Humphries' first name is recorded as "Pelham" rather than William. Unable to read or write, he does not recognize the error and signs the petition by making his mark.

February 14, 1835
Town of Nacogdoches, State of Coahuila and Texas, Mexico

The survey having been properly concluded, Citizen Jorge Antonio Nixon, Special Commissioner of the Supreme Government of the State of Coahuila and Texas, issues a title of possession to the surveyed league in the name of "Pelham" Humphries.

The Pelham Humphries league is located along the west bank of the Neches River, a few miles south of present-day Beaumont. Surveyor Henrie describes the league as containing eight labors of arable land and the remainder pasture. Although not described in the survey, the league includes roughly one-third of a geologic formation now recognized as a salt dome. While only about thirty feet high and perhaps a mile at its widest point, it was nonetheless a significant prominence above the otherwise low and flat coastal plane. Originally called "Big Hill" by the locals, the area came to be called "Spindletop."

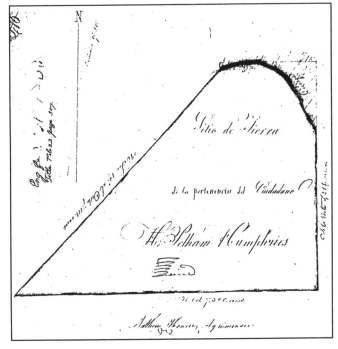

Original Pelham Humphries survey.

October 6, 1835
Town of San Augustine, State of Coahuila and Texas, Mexico

The error of Humphries' title of possession being issued in the name of "Pelham," rather than William, is recognized. To correct the error, William executes a power of attorney as follows:

I do hereby constitute and appoint Wm. Inglish my agent to take a title out of the Commissioners office in Nacogdoches and to alter from Pilham to William my true and propper name San Agustin Oct 6. 1835

his

William x Umphreys

mark

It may have been that Mr. Inglish was confused about which document was which, since they were all written in Spanish. Perhaps someone else had a hand in the matter. But, for whatever reason, the title of possession was not changed from Pelham to William, his "true and propper name." Instead, it was Humphries' original petition for the league that was altered to read "William" instead of "Pelham."

December 1883

There was plenty of recorded activity on the title after William's misdirected power of attorney to Inglish. Between September 27, 1834, and January 10, 1901, Jefferson County records show more than twenty deeds on all or portions of the Pelham Humphries league. In 1883 W.P.H. McFaddin became the owner of record.

10:00 a.m. January 10, 1901, Beaumont, Texas

Drilling under a lease from McFaddin, Wiess and Kyle (a partnership with the husbands of W.P.H.'s first cousins), and Anthony Lucas, drawn to the project by Beaumont's own oil guru, Pattillo Higgins, brought in America's first oil "gusher" on the Humphries' league section of Big Hill. For nine days, until a way was devised to cap it, a six-inch stream of oil shot more than a hundred feet into the air.

The Lucas gusher at Spindletop, January 10, 1901. This is the discovery well that heralded the age of liquid fuel and made Texas an oil state.
Photo courtesy Texas Mid-Continent Oil & Gas Assn.

As the news spread, Spindletop's gusher drew people like California's gold rush and the Klondike. Beaumont's population exploded. Forty thousand new people arrived, seemingly overnight, seeking their fortune in oil. Trading in oil leases was furious and the Texas oil industry leaped into life. From that single gusher, the Spindletop field grew to more than three hundred wells in record time. In some cases, the derricks were so close to each other that a man could actually step from one derrick floor to another.

Spindletop attracted big names and big money. The Mellon family invested over five million. Oil giants Gulf and Texaco started at Spindletop. Howard Hughes Sr.

began his billion dollar oil-tool dynasty after drilling at Spindletop.

As was to be expected, the mass of people and money at Spindletop also drew drunks, hookers, brawlers, killers, liars, and cheats. Just staying alive was tough. Beaumont's chief of police advised people to "tote" guns to protect themselves and to "tote 'em in your hands...so everybody can see you're loaded." Because of the rampant schemes designed to separate oil-hungry newcomers from their money, the descriptive term "swindletop" became popular.

In some cases the derricks were so close to each other that a man could actually step from one derrick floor to another. Photo circa 1903.

In addition, Humphries' heirs began what has become a ninety-year attack, asserting ownership rights to the Pelham Humphries league and the past oil revenues. The Humphries have been tenacious but the McFaddins and the oil companies have traditionally been better financed and are tough fighters themselves.

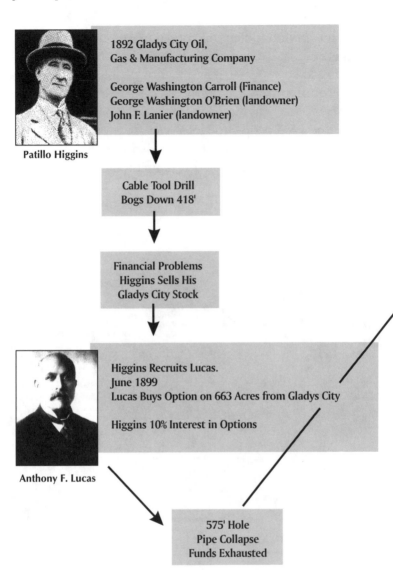

Patillo Higgins

1892 Gladys City Oil,
Gas & Manufacturing Company

George Washington Carroll (Finance)
George Washington O'Brien (landowner)
John F. Lanier (landowner)

Cable Tool Drill
Bogs Down 418'

Financial Problems
Higgins Sells His
Gladys City Stock

Higgins Recruits Lucas.
June 1899
Lucas Buys Option on 663 Acres from Gladys City

Higgins 10% Interest in Options

Anthony F. Lucas

575' Hole
Pipe Collapse
Funds Exhausted

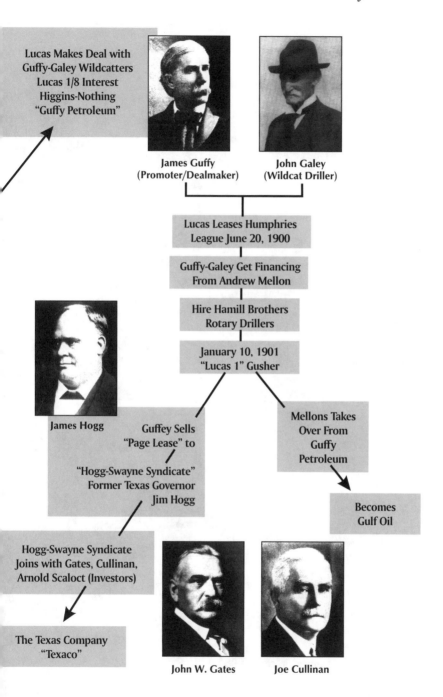

Lucas Makes Deal with
Guffy-Galey Wildcatters
Lucas 1/8 Interest
Higgins-Nothing
"Guffy Petroleum"

James Guffy
(Promoter/Dealmaker)

John Galey
(Wildcat Driller)

Lucas Leases Humphries
League June 20, 1900

Guffy-Galey Get Financing
From Andrew Mellon

Hire Hamill Brothers
Rotary Drillers

January 10, 1901
"Lucas 1" Gusher

James Hogg

Guffey Sells
"Page Lease" to

"Hogg-Swayne Syndicate"
Former Texas Governor
Jim Hogg

Mellons Takes
Over From
Guffy
Petroleum

Becomes
Gulf Oil

Hogg-Swayne Syndicate
Joins with Gates, Cullinan,
Arnold Scaloct (Investors)

The Texas Company
"Texaco"

John W. Gates

Joe Cullinan

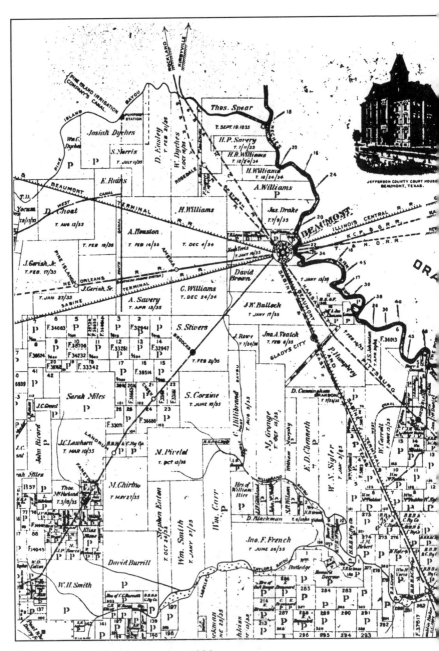

Higgins' Jefferson County map, circa 1898

Top, Pelham
Humphries league,
1994

Left, wooden oil
tank on the Pelham
Humphries league
at Spindletop. A
remnant from the
past.

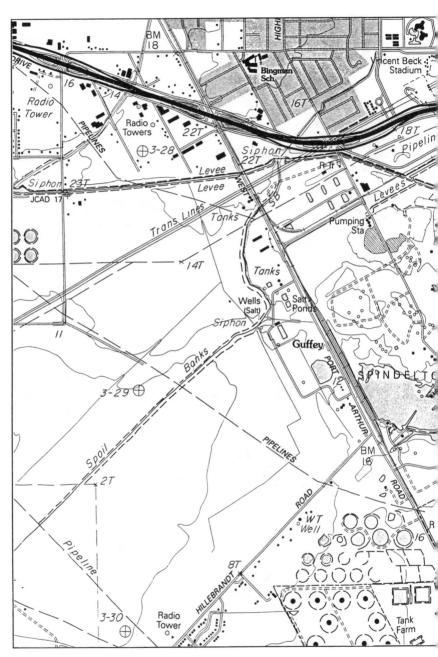

Spindletop today

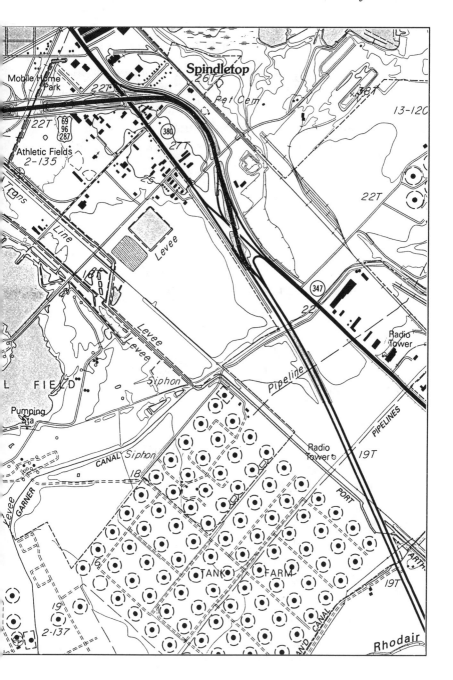

Gunfight at Nacogdoches

For the past fifty years most of the Humphries' claims to the land and the oil revenues at Spindletop have generally relied on their kinship to "Pelham" Humphries. Brown Peregoy, the one-time head of various Humphries associations, recites their position like a religious mantra:

Pelham Humphries was a bounty hunter for the Mexican government;

On September 5, 1835, Pelham was killed in a gunfight at the Hawthorne boarding house in Nacogdoches;

Pelham was killed on the orders of William McFaddin just when Pelham was about to arrest McFaddin for cattle rustling;

McFaddin escaped arrest and laid claim to Pelham's league of land for his cattle operation;

Being unmarried and having no children of his own, Pelham's only heirs were his brother "William" Humphries, his sister Betsie Janie Humphries, and a half brother, Elisha V. Humphries Jr.;

Peregoy and his group of heirs are the descendants of Pelham's brother William Humphries;

William's name was added to the original Spanish title as part of a fraud to take the land away from Pelham;

William Humphries' true heirs never sold their interest in the Spindletop league, and all deeds, including those to "W.P.H. McFaddin," are fraudulent;

In furtherance of the conspiracy to defraud the true Humphries' heirs, the initials "W.P.H." in front of the McFaddin name stand for the adopted name "William Pelham Humphries" McFaddin took to make people think he had a connection to Pelham Humphries.

Finally, there is an escrow account with the oil money that belongs to Spindletop's true owners—William Humphries' heirs.

As might be expected, the estimated amount in escrow increases as time goes by. The 1947 lawsuit against the McFaddins and the oil companies brought by Peregoy's uncle L.B. Glover sought a modest 500 million. To his credit, despite a 1986 article estimating the escrow account at "trillions" of dollars, Peregoy showed great restraint in asking for a mere 200 billion in his 1989 lawsuit.

If Peregoy's analysis is correct, to share in the benefits of "Uncle Pel's" league at Spindletop, proof of each potential heir's actual lineage to Pelham's brother William Humphries is necessary. For this daunting task, Brown Peregoy sought professional assistance.

July 1984

James W. Petty is a respected genealogist headquartered in Salt Lake City. After being contacted by Peregoy, then serving as the head of the Pelham Humphries Heirs Association, Jim Petty's intellectual and academic curiosity was piqued. He entered into a contract to do the research necessary for association members.

Family Values

Early September 1986, Salt Lake City, Utah

Rosine and Will's plane was just landing in Salt Lake City. Following her arrest and arraignment, Rosine had to cope with the resulting personal indignity of being arrested as a murderer and, worse yet, the bad Family publicity. Coping was not something she did well. She tried to set things right by releasing her own statements that it was an "accidental" shooting, and, in an interesting example of convoluted thinking, by blaming the victim—after all, it wouldn't have happened if Joe hadn't been there. Under that logic, John Wilkes Booth wasn't guilty—after all, it wouldn't have happened if Lincoln hadn't been at the theater.

Whether they really believed her or not, the usual McFaddin entourage offered their support, but, just like the Grand Jury, the general public wasn't buying it. Ever since they could remember, Rosine had been blunt, arrogant, and demanding. Just as describing the *Titanic* as having had a "leak" isn't the full story, Rosine's self-effacing admission that she had a "tart tongue" didn't go nearly far enough. In the past she had merely verbally skewered people, now she shot them. Rosine was just not a likeable person.

Talk of her affair with Joe gained momentum too. Rumor had it that the affair, coupled with the Humphries' Spindletop claims, was the motive for Joe's murder; she had used Joe and then, after they had a falling out, killed him when he threatened to go to the Humphries and reveal her Family's secrets showing how the McFaddins had cheated the Humphries out of their rights to Spindletop.

Her lawyer, Lum Hawthorn, had a number of strategies he wanted to try. Some looked promising, but Rosine could not leave the fate of a McFaddin charged with murder in the hands of a Jefferson County jury.

In the meantime, she still had the Humphries to worry about. While Joe himself could no longer be a source of information, she had to know how much Jim Petty knew. Petty could be real trouble. He had the credentials. People would listen to him. Had Joe talked to him? She found Jim's number as soon as they got to their room at the Marriott in Salt Lake City.

Jim was busy researching in the Family History Library downtown, so it was Mrs. Petty that answered the phone.

Rosine was her usual demanding self, intense and insistent: no matter that he was out working on another project; she had flown in especially to see Mr. Petty; it was very, very important; she just had to meet with him today; she had to return tomorrow; where was he?

After getting directions and Jim's description from the unsuspecting Mrs. Petty, Rosine and Will found Jim at work in the library that same afternoon. They introduced themselves, saying they wanted to engage him to do some genealogy research on the McFaddin Family.

Jim Petty is an intelligent and perceptive man. From the outset, Rosine's stated purpose for meeting with him didn't ring true. Flying from Beaumont to Salt Lake City particularly to hire Jim, without having contacted him ahead of time to, if nothing more, make sure he would even be there, was not normal or rational. But, to the genealogist, what was even more telling was that, for someone ostensibly wanting to start a genealogy project, Rosine brought no papers or family documents with her. That was truly an aberration.

As planned, the discussion turned to Jim's work for the Humphries. As Rosine identified McFaddin Family members, Jim recognized them as the same McFaddins that were in opposition to his clients, the Humphries' heirs. Faced with this ethical problem, Jim did the right thing. He told Rosine he could not undertake her project because of the conflict he would have since he was already representing the Humphries.

Her opening subterfuge had worked. The Humphries question was now open and the real purpose of Rosine's trip to Salt Lake, learning how much Jim Petty knew about the Humphries and McFaddins, began. Her interrogation started. What did he know about the Humphries? Could he prove their claims to Spindletop? What conclusions had he come to? Trying to be courteous and at the same time protect his clients' confidentiality, Jim replied that his work was not finished, and he had made no conclusions yet. Rosine learned nothing about the Humphries from Jim Petty, and she and Will returned to the Marriott.

Later that evening Jim had a few questions he thought Rosine could possibly help him with. He called their room at the Marriott. Will answered and Jim asked his questions. Rosine was in her usual form. Jim could hear her cursing in the background. "He knows so damn much, let him figure it out."

The very next day Jim got a call from one of his Humphries Association clients, "Have you heard? Rosine McFaddin Wilson was arrested. She killed her ranch hand. He was her lover, and they argued, and he threatened to go to the Humphries and tell how the McFaddins cheated the Humphries out of the Spindletop land, so she shot him."

While that story would explain Rosine's strange behavior, how could it be? After all, just yesterday, Rosine was in Salt Lake City, Utah. If she had been arrested for murder, how could she be out of Texas? The Pettys couldn't believe it.

Neither could the Jefferson County sheriff's office. In disbelief, Mrs. Petty broke her own rule and made a *daytime* long-distance call to the Jefferson County sheriff. It was true. Rosine had killed her ranch hand. She had been arrested and indicted for first degree murder. She was out on bond and should not have left Texas.

The realization that a McFaddin, who killed to prevent disclosure of family secrets about the Humphries and Spindletop, jumped bond and came to Salt Lake City just to find Jim Petty, the man hired to help the Humphries prove their claims against the McFaddins, greatly disturbed the Pettys. What would Rosine have done if Jim had told her he found out something she didn't want people to know?

Tribulations and the Trial

It wasn't that Rosine didn't want people to know about the Family, she just wanted to be the Family press agent and publicist. And she didn't need any help from Jim Petty on McFaddin Family genealogy either. The November 1980 issue of *The Texas Gulf Historical & Biographical Record* published "The McFaddin Family: Lands, Cattle, and Oil, on the Texas Gulf Coast, *by Rosine McFaddin Wilson.*" An appropriate title because in the Family, clearly, "Lands" are first.

In the article, Rosine describes W.P.H. McFaddin as an "empire builder" and says of him, "Acquiring land was his art, and he always said that all he wanted was what was his and what was next to it." She also described W.P.H. as "often becoming involved in arguments and lawsuits," a trait she shared with her grandfather. In addition to the murder

The Beaumont, Texas home of W.P.H. McFaddin. Built in 1906, after the gusher at Spindletop.

charge, Marie and Joe's children filed wrongful death lawsuits against her.

But Rosine's lawyer, Joseph C. "Lum" Hawthorn, was uniquely qualified for the task ahead of him. Lum's work as a former FBI agent, a Jefferson County assistant district attorney, and as an assistant United States attorney, served him well. While some may question how a person can move so effortlessly from one side of the jail door to the other—from locking them up to getting them out—it apparently didn't bother Lum. He was successful and well recognized, serving as president of the Jefferson County Bar Association and as a director of the Texas Criminal Defense Lawyers Association. In addition to Rosine's little problem, Lum was helping out Andrew Weller, a nice young man accused of killing his parents by shooting his 60-year-old mother Eleanor in the head, and his 74-year-old father George, a retired Beaumont lawyer, in the face, with a 12-gauge shotgun.

Lum's strategy for Rosine had three basic and intertwined components: influence public opinion, attack the legal technicalities of the State's case, and assert the "accidental" shooting theory. Born in Beaumont, Lum had the benefit of personal knowledge of the public's general perception of the McFaddin Family. Most were unequivocal; they either held the Family in esteem or in contempt. Not surprisingly, their opinions divided along the lines of those whom the Family considered worthy of admission to their social circles and those less worthy. Jefferson County jury members were most likely to be the latter. That was a critical concern. If he couldn't otherwise make the case go away, a change of venue was absolutely necessary.

On the personal side, and with plenty of news coverage, Lum attacked the actions of Justice of the Peace Cravey, the supposedly politically motivated misdeeds of the Jefferson County prosecutors, and, of course, the character of Joe and Marie Perkins. Through obtaining a postponement,

Lum effectively removed the lame duck district attorney from prosecuting the case, since his elective term would be over if and when the case went to trial. On the legal side he filed fourteen pretrial motions. While all the motions had a role in the defensive strategy, two were significant: a motion to dismiss the indictment and a motion for change of venue.

The motion to dismiss was critical. If it was successful, the first degree murder case against Rosine was over. She was counting on it. The matter came before Judge Gist on January 20, 1987. Unfortunately for Rosine, the judge was not impressed with the motion. He gave Lum an additional ten days to try to convince him otherwise.

That bad news may have been too much for Rosine. Seven days later, on January 28, 1987, at 6:00 a.m., Will found her unconscious in her bedroom. Taken by ambulance to Beaumont's St. Elizabeth Hospital, Rosine was treated for an overdose of pills and alcohol. Meanwhile, as might have been expected from his earlier review, despite the additional time, Lum was unable to change Judge Gist's mind. On February 5, 1987, the motion to dismiss was denied. However, having "taketh" away, it was time to "giveth."

On Wednesday, April 29, 1987, after a hearing spanning two weeks and testimony from over a hundred witnesses (only two called by the district attorney), Judge Gist granted Lum's motion for a change of venue. It was a tremendous victory for Rosine. Now, at least, Rosine would not be tried by a Jefferson County jury. After some skirmishing, Lum and the new district attorney agreed to hold the trial in the 174th Judicial District of Harris County, Texas. That meant the actual trial would be held in Houston, the county seat of Harris County.

Lum could not have done better for Rosine. Fast growing Houston is not only the largest city in all of Texas, it is the fourth largest city in the entire United States. As is regretfully true of all large American cities, murder is commonplace in Houston. Rosine's little misdeed would be routine, and, even though Houston is less than a hundred miles from Beaumont, a Houston juror was unlikely to have even driven on "McFaddin" Street in Beaumont, let alone be familiar with the Family.

Trial began on Tuesday, August 18, 1987, exactly one year after the killing. The sheriff's office and district attorney were ineffectual. Despite Mrs. Petty's call to the sheriff, no homicide investigator had contacted the Pettys. No one had followed up on Rosine's trip to Salt Lake City. Aside from merely characterizing Joe as "an annoyance" to Rosine, the district attorney offered no evidence of motive. Trial went quickly. Both sides rested before noon on Friday.

Judge Gist devoted Monday to other Jefferson County matters and the case was given to the jury on Tuesday, August 25, 1987. In murder cases, juries need a motive. When they didn't get one, the "accidental shooting" argument carried the day. Rosine was found guilty of mere involuntary manslaughter, given five years probation and a $5,000 fine, and ordered to pay $100 in court costs.

The wrongful death lawsuits against Rosine were settled out of court.

Money Matters

The judicious use of money can assure dramatic successes. It was the application of sufficient amounts of Family money that permitted Rosine to outmaneuver and thereby avoid the aggressive Jefferson County district attorney who obtained the first degree murder indictment; it was Family money that enabled Rosine to move the trial to Houston and avoid the dreaded Jefferson County jury; Family money settled the wrongful death lawsuits brought by Joe Perkin's family. The relationship between Family money and both the absence of a follow-up investigation on Rosine's meeting with Jim Petty in Salt Lake City as well as the new prosecutor's failure to offer a viable motive for Joe Perkins' murder remains a question too.

The *injudicious* use of money assures exciting results as well.

Wednesday evening, May 4, 1966, the White House, Washington, D.C.

Secretary of State Dean Rusk's limousine passed through White House security without pause. Ernest and Margaret Medders, riding with the Secretary and Mrs. Rusk, had already had a busy day. Ernest lunched with the Texas Delegation, as Congressman Percell's guest, while Margaret attended a tea given in her honor by Mrs. Percell. Later they attended an early reception at the Mexican Embassy. Now they were about to renew their acquaintance with the President and Lady Bird Johnson.

Ernest and Margaret flanking Congressman Percell (L) and Pat Jennings.
Photo by Shel Hershorn, Black Star

Actually, the past several days had been busy for the Medders. On Thursday, April 29, they attended the President's Club Ball in Houston. They dined with the President, Lady Bird, Lynda Bird, Luci and her fiance Pat Nugent, Governor Connally, Senator Yarborough, and many other notables—plus they were entertained by Danny Thomas.

The next day they returned to Colonial Acres, their Texas ranch, and hosted a barbecue in honor of Texas Attorney General Waggoner Carr and his wife. Their invitation to the White House to attend a reception in honor of the Chiefs of Diplomatic Missions and their wives, came that same day. After some rushing around, including a trip to Neiman-Marcus eighty miles away in Dallas, they left for Washington on Tuesday, May 3.

Ernest and Margaret with Texas Attorney General Waggoner Carr and his wife.

The Medders enjoyed themselves at the White House. Margaret was effusive about the White House decorations, the beautiful dresses, dancing in the East Room to the Marine Band, and the people she met: Vice President Humphrey, Secretary of Defense Robert McNamara, Senator Fulbright, Chicago's Mayor Richard Daley, and even Hollywood star Eddie Fisher. Ernest was particularly impressed with Vice President Humphrey and Secretary McNamara.

The Medders were among the privileged few invited to the President's private quarters later that evening. Joined by fellow Texans Mr. and Mrs. Stanley Marcus of Dallas (of Neiman-Marcus fame) and Mr. and Mrs. Roy Hofheinz (the builder of the Houston Astrodome), the President gave them a personal tour of the private quarters. Later they enjoyed a late supper with Lyndon and Lady Bird, followed by home movies of the Johnson Ranch. They stayed until about 2:00 a.m., Margaret was kissed by the President as they left, and the following day they flew back to Texas with the President on Air Force One.

This was heady stuff for Ernest and Margaret. Their modest background hadn't been designed to lead them to dinners with the President in the private quarters of the White House or flights on Air Force One. It was said of Ernest that when you asked him a question, Mrs. Medders would answer it. Ernest was a former mechanics' helper and produce peddler originally from Centerville, Alabama. In his entire working life he had never earned more than $60 a

Ernest, Margaret, and the kids—pre "Uncle Pel"

week. In school Ernest had only gone as far as the third grade. He could write only enough to sign his name, could only count up to "about" 100, and could not read. As for Mrs. Medders, the former Margaret Smiddy Riggs from Jellico, Tennessee, mother of eight (four by a prior marriage and four more with Ernest), it was a fairy tale. She had worked as a nurses aide, and it wasn't that long ago they were living in Memphis where Ernest was unemployed and she was working a double shift just to make ends meet. But thanks to Uncle Pel, it was all true. Spindletop changed their lives. The past six years had been exciting.

Party Time

In December 1961 the Medders moved from Tennessee to Texas—from Memphis to Muenster. After locating acceptable acreage outside Muenster, they began construction of their twenty-room home, "Colonial Acres." They allowed nothing but the finest woods and number one construction materials in their home. Margaret hired a decorator from Dallas to assure the interior was also perfection itself.

After the house was completed, they turned their attention to the business of ranching. Deciding they should be award winning horse and cattle breeders, Ernest and Margaret bought Appaloosa horses and the best black and red Angus they could find. That's when they added the "showbarn" to Colonial Acres.

The showbarn, often called the "party barn," occasionally the "Colonial Acres Coliseum" and even the "Astrodome of showbarns," had a portable floor to transform it from a barn for the showing of cattle and horses, to a party palace.

The first of many parties to be held in the barn was the black tie "barnwarming" on November 23, 1965. Dallas guests were brought to the ranch in luxury chartered buses complete with built-in bars. Those from other cities were

Colonial Acres with the party barn in the background.
Photo by Shel Hershorn, Black Star

flown to nearby Gainesville in chartered planes and then ferried to the ranch by helicopter. In keeping with the spirit of the gala event, even the helicopter pilot wore a tuxedo. After negotiating a receiving line made up of Ernest, Margaret, and the children, the nine hundred guests in tuxedos and gowns were entertained by Guy Lombardo's Royal Canadians.

The showbarn was alive with color. In addition to the red coats of the Royal Canadians, circular tables were draped with green, gold, and burnt orange satin, and each contained an elaborate flower arrangement with color coordinated chrysanthemums and candles.

Catered by the Sheraton-Dallas Hotel, the guests enjoyed dining on 250 pounds of roast beef, 320 pounds of Butterball turkey (it was, after all, nearly Thanksgiving), 160 pounds of baked Virginia ham, 3,000 biscuits, 1,500 canapes, 1,500 hot hors d'oeuvres; plus 2,000 shrimp (just over two shrimp per guest—a bit skimpy), caviar, ribs, and tenderloins. As if that wasn't enough, there was also a midnight supper of steak, scrambled eggs, chicken livers, and honey buns. Just getting the food, equipment, and necessary people from the Sheraton-Dallas to the ranch required two trucks and a Greyhound bus. The gala event was well covered in the Texas media, and although *LIFE* didn't actually carry the story, its photographers were there busily snapping pictures. The Medders had spared no expense.

Medders typical "gala event" at the party barn.
Photo by Ralph Crane, LIFE Magazine©TIME Inc.

The Medders family receiving line: Ernest, Margaret, and six of the children.
Photo by Wichita Falls Times and Record News

The frequent subsequent parties spared no expense either. They were lavishly decorated with dozens of ice sculptures, white doves, and even Colonial Acres Farm flags—held by wooden English soldiers. Indulging their own musical tastes, along with Guy Lombardo, the Medders' guests were treated to Jan Garber, Si Zentner, and members of the Lawrence Welk troupe, including Myron Florin on the accordion.

The guest lists were eclectic. In addition to Attorney General Carr, the Medders hosted horoscope columnist Jeanne Dixon, Maria von Trapp, nuns and priests, Governor Connally, the National Cutting Horse Finals, the Portuguese Ambassador to the United States and, from Italy, the entire cast of *Rigoletto*. In Muenster, for a time, being invited to the Medders' parties conferred social standing.

Muenster conferred on the Medders such of the honors and benefits it had available. Margaret was named vice-president of the Muenster Chamber of Commerce, she was appointed to the board of the new library and was active

35

Ernest showing Governor Connally one of his award winning horses.
Photo by Boyd and Breeding

in the Civic League and the Garden Club (which often met at Colonial Acres). Ernest was Muenster's representative to the West Texas Chamber of Commerce, and Margaret and Ernest were both sustaining members of the Muenster Junior Chamber of Commerce.

The Medders enjoyed their new life. They had governesses, maids, chauffeurs, and handymen. Margaret wore Paris originals, furs, and expensive jewelry. She had her own in-house beauty shop, a social secretary, and a public relations man. The Medders traveled extensively. They sent the girls to exclusive Hockaday, an expensive finishing school in Dallas. Rather than have the girls stay in a dormitory, Margaret bought a $40,000 house for them near the school.

The Medders also enlarged their Colonial Acres empire. They added acreage and oil wells by purchasing an oil field with thirty-seven wells, another ranch near Saint Jo, and a farm north of Muenster. By the time they were done there were 1,400 acres in Colonial Acres. In addition to the prize herds of red and black Angus and their show winning

Appaloosas, they had Cadillacs, trucks, stock trailers, farm machinery, irrigation systems, and $40,000 worth of Christmas decorations.

And it was fun to show off to the homefolks. In September 1966 the Medders made a triumphant return to Memphis. Ostensibly they were there to show Colonial Acres' prize winning cattle at the Tennessee State Fair—but what a great opportunity for another party!

They took over the entire second floor of the Holiday Inn-Rivermont Hotel for the pre-dinner cocktail party. The details of elegance have always been important to Margaret. She instructed her social secretary to have the invitations clearly require that the women guests be "gowned" rather than appear in mere cocktail frocks. The men, of course, were to wear tuxedos. To the woman who demanded that her helicopter pilot wear a tuxedo, staff details were important too. She required two dozen waiters, in white gloves, to look after the needs of their 250 guests.

After indulging in a sumptuous array of hors d'oeuvres, the delights of the bar, and the beauty of the decorative ice carvings, the elegantly gowned and tuxedoed guests moved to the Rivermont Club on the fourteenth floor for dinner. Margaret's attention to detail was apparent here too. Reminding everyone that they were now successful cattle breeders, she had each table supplied with a ceramic black Angus container filled with red and white flowers (representing Colonial Acres' "colors"). The guests sat down to Chateaubriand, served from carts at the individual tables, famous Memphis *crabmeat Justine*, and other treats, followed by flambeau cherries jubilee.

Ernest and Margaret's social triumph in Memphis was complete when Mayor William B. Ingram presented them the keys to the city. Ah money, what fun!

Get Thee to a Nunnery

The Medders' trek to Texas, their award winning cattle and show horses, their lavish entertaining at Colonial Acres and in the showbarn, their expanding social circles, their visits with the President, their flight on Air Force One, all began in 1959 with a small notice in the Tuscaloosa, Alabama, newspaper and a thirty-dollar investment.

The notice requested information leading to the location of the heirs of one Ruben Medders. Ruben Medders, the story went, was the brother-in-law of Pelham Humphries. And Pelham Humphries, it was said, was the true owner of a league of land that lay inside the famous Spindletop oil field in Texas. Thus, the heirs of Ruben Medders were also the heirs of Pelham Humphries and were entitled to recover *five billion dollars.*

Ernest's uncle John Medders saw the notice and began gathering the clan. Two hundred Medders, including Ernest and his brother Isom Medders, met in Centerville, Alabama, to plan the strategy to recover the estate. They each pitched in thirty dollars to press the case. Money was so scarce for Ernest and Margaret that Ernest had to pay his thirty dollars in installments.

After supplying birth certificates to demonstrate their kinship to Ruben Medders, Ernest, Isom, and their other brothers and sisters received an "official-looking letter" telling them they actually were the heirs of Ruben. Using borrowed money, and taking along an attorney, Ernest and Isom flew to Beaumont to investigate matters themselves. It was Ernest's first airplane trip.

The trip was an unqualified success. Margaret, describing the results of Ernest's first Beaumont trip some years later, said Ernest and Isom (and presumably the attorney they took along) found "corroborating evidence" that they were indeed Ruben's heirs and that the **"estate was there!"** Ernest's claim to a share of the fabulous riches from the Pelham

Humphries League were now being pressed in court by their attorney, W.T. Weir, along with approximately 3,000 other heirs seeking their share, against W.P.H. McFaddin and the oil companies.

For health and tax reasons, Ernest and Margaret decided to move to Texas while awaiting the settlement of the estate. There was a small problem. While they were to soon be rich beyond their wildest dreams, they needed a way to finance their immediate needs until the settlement of the estate. When one is about to inherit 500 million dollars (the amount Margaret calculated was Ernest's share of the estate), continuing to just "work" is not an option to even be considered. Margaret prayed for a happier solution.

Although raised a Southern Baptist in Jellico, Tennessee, Margaret was a converted Catholic. Her son Gene attended a Catholic school, the Subiaco Academy in Arkansas. Margaret worked for years as a nurses aide at St. Joseph's Hospital in Memphis. St. Joseph's Hospital is operated by the Poor Sisters of St. Seraph, an order of nuns located in Mishawaka, Indiana. "Poor Sisters" is a misnomer.

Margaret was blessed with the gift of persuasion. She related the story of the fabulous inheritance and their desire to move to Texas. The Subiaco Academy suggested the Medders consider moving to Muenster, Texas. Muenster, it seems, had a Catholic school with nineteen teaching sisters. Convincing Ernest and Margaret that the Catholic community at Muenster needed them (and perhaps their expected financial support) as much as the Medders needed Texas, the Subiaco Academy loaned Ernest and Margaret $20,000 for a house, and the Medders moved to Muenster.

While that was a good start, it wasn't enough. A simple house didn't fit the lifestyle they anticipated. They wanted something befitting their expected affluence, and they didn't want to wait.

The happy solution wasn't really all that complex. After all, they all had faith. Ernest made out his will with a provision that it was his intention to give ten million dollars to the Sisters of St. Francis, and if the money wasn't given during his lifetime, then it was to be given after his death. Despite the "Poor Sisters" name, over the next few years the nuns at St. Francis regularly sent checks to the Medders, totaling nearly two million dollars.

Credibility and Credit Ability

Margaret and Ernest did not disclose their arrangement with the Poor Sisters to their new Texas business associates, their friends, neighbors, or even other Medders' family members. The situation was somewhat like the popular early television show *The Millionaire*, where each week multimillionaire John Beresford Tipton sent Michael Anthony to deliver one million dollars to some lucky person—but with the restriction that they couldn't tell where the newfound money came from. Just as happened on the television show, the Medders' new friends and neighbors were curious. Ernest and Margaret liked to say the money flowed in when he drilled for water but struck oil. Without a straight answer, naturally there was speculation and rumor. Many thought the Medders had inherited a huge estate but were required to live in a Catholic community to keep it. Others thought they had inherited a huge estate but had to spend at least $50,000 a month to keep it. The Medders certainly seemed to be working hard at doing just that.

Regardless of its source, what was perfectly clear to all about them was that the Medders had money, and lots of it. And so they did. But the Medders quickly learned how to spend lots of money. Lavish parties, land, prize stock, large political donations (could that explain the White House visit?), all require large amounts of money. And besides, as everyone knows, two million dollars will only go so far.

The Poor Sisters will only go so far too. In April of 1966 the Poor Sisters got a new Mother Superior. She shut off the cash flow. Margaret called when the usual check didn't arrive. The Poor Sisters told her that they thought that two million was enough and that she and Ernest should now be able to get along on their own. Well, one might think so, but Ernest and Margaret had become addicted to spending money on a grand scale.

As everyone also knows, banks and businesses are only too happy to lend money or extend credit to those who already have money. And, as was obvious by even a cursory look, the Medders clearly fit that category. Accordingly the Muenster State Bank, the First National Bank in Dallas, the City National Bank of Wichita Falls, and the National Bank of Commerce of Memphis were all delighted to loan the Medders money, in all some $910,000. And, their credit was unquestioned at Neiman-Marcus, the Sheraton-Dallas Hotel, their feed company, Margaret's favorite photography studio, and with all the other tradesmen necessary to their somewhat unique lifestyle. But Ernest's sister-in-law Margery, his late brother Isom's wife, didn't understand what was happening.

From Party Barn to the Big House

In hindsight, it would have been better for Ernest and Margaret to tell Margery that it was all just borrowed money. Or at least they could have kept a lower profile. Perhaps throwing such an elaborate party at the Memphis Rivermont, almost in her backyard, was the final straw. In any event, Margery couldn't understand it. After all, Isom was a Medders too. In fact, it was Isom who first told Ernest about the inheritance and the meeting in Centerville. Isom and Ernest went to the meeting together. Isom paid his thirty dollars, just like Ernest did. He got the same "official-looking letter" Ernest had gotten. Isom had even gone to Texas with Ernest and the lawyer. So why didn't she, as Isom's widow, have all that inheritance money that Ernest and Margaret were spending so freely? Where was hers?

With the help of some nice men (who had been recruiting family members in anticipation of getting a piece of Pelham's estate themselves), Margery became convinced that Ernest and Margaret were getting all the Spindletop money—at the rate of $40,000 a month—and not giving her Isom's rightful share. She signed some papers the nice men had.

On October 21, 1966, less than a month after the big party at the Rivermont Hotel, attorney Ralph Elliot, acting on Margery's behalf, filed a lawsuit against Ernest in the Federal District Court in Sherman, Texas. The lawsuit sought an accounting of the funds Ernest was purportedly receiving from the Pelham Humphries' estate. It was the beginning of the end.

At first, despite Margery's lawsuit, Ernest and Margaret continued life as usual. In November they had a big party for Jeanne Dixon. Si Zentner brought his band for a dance they held on December 17, 1966. The Medders bought radio spots to wish their friends a Merry Christmas. Jan Garber brought his band for an after Christmas affair—he loved the Christmas lights, commenting "You could see their house lighted up for twenty miles around. It must have been a million lights." For New Years, the Medders chartered a special seven-coach train to bring 300 of their daughters' classmates from Dallas for a big party in the showbarn.

But the end didn't take long to arrive. Margery's lawyer, Ralph Elliot, took Ernest's deposition. Under oath Ernest stated he had received nothing from the Pelham Humphries lawsuit. Not only that, all of the money he had been spending came from loans! That caused a panic among all of the creditors and a flood of lawsuits.

Ernest Medders and Margaret Medders
Photo courtesy of UPI/CORBIS-BETTMANN

Out of that chaos came order when, on February 22, 1967, seven of the creditors brought involuntary bankruptcy proceedings against the Medders. Without counting the two million owed to the Poor Sisters, the Medders owed $1,119,213.88. By March 10, 1967, with 200 creditors now looking for their money, Ernest and Margaret recognized that bankruptcy was their best solution. As it turned out, having filed for bankruptcy in 1951, 1952, and 1955, they were aware of the benefits available to them. The Medders voluntarily agreed to the bankruptcy. They knew they would not be destitute. Declaring Colonial Acres their "homestead," under established Texas law they were permitted to keep the original 185-acre site, their palatial house, and even the famous showbarn. In addition, Texas law permitted them to keep their "buggy" and "wagon." Under the modern application of that law, it meant they were able to keep one of the Cadillacs and a pickup. Everything else was to be sold at auction to satisfy the creditors' claims. After that the Medders would be free of their debts. But their trials were not over yet.

First, Margaret had written some bad checks. Jan Garber and Si Zentner were among those whose checks bounced. In Texas, as elsewhere, passing a bad check is a criminal offense. Margaret was indicted on March 3, 1967, for a bad check to her photographer. The March 20, 1967 issue of *Newsweek* ran a story on the Medders titled "Son of Billie Sol," comparing Ernest to the notorious con man Billie Sol Estes who once captivated Texas. The article carried a nice picture of Ernest with Jeanne Dixon. On March 24 Margaret was indicted again, this time for a bad check to an entertainment agency. Then, in its April 7, 1967 issue, *LIFE* found an opportunity to use some of the photographs taken at the barnwarming. *LIFE* ran a six-page story titled "$3,000,000 Sham." They used thirteen photographs and were not kind. They did show a nice aerial view of the house with the party barn in the background. Four days later on April 11, 1967, Margaret and Ernest were both indicted for fraud. It seems they sold some red Angus cattle that had already been mortgaged to one of the banks. Margaret didn't cope well with this new kind of publicity. Suffering from "an acute depressive reaction," she was hospitalized in nearby Sherman, Texas.

But Margaret Medders was a survivor. She "recovered," and she and Ernest both got lucky again. First, on June 29, 1967, the jury on the fraud charges hopelessly deadlocked at 9-3 for conviction. With the hung jury, Margaret and Ernest escaped conviction and jail time. A few months later on December 4, 1967, Margaret went to trial on the bad check charges. Although she was convicted, she again dodged jail time, receiving only probation. Having now successfully avoided both their creditors and prison, while still managing to keep the ranch with its splendid home and furnishings, the party barn, and the other buildings, plus a Cadillac and a pickup, all bought with other people's money, the Medders should have counted their blessings and faded into obscurity. But Margaret wasn't quite done.

Margaret liked her monied lifestyle. With their income now reduced to Ernest's disability social security payments, she needed to find another source. They sold Colonial Acres and, for a time, lived elegantly again. Not in their former showbarn party style, but certainly far exceeding their pre-Pelham Humphries existence. In fact, in January of 1975, while Margaret's daughter Polly (her third child by her first husband) needed food stamps just to get by, Ernest and Margaret were living in East Memphis, just across town from Polly, in a four-bedroom house with two Cadillacs, two chauffeurs, a cook, and a maid. They moved to Brownsville, Texas, shortly thereafter, and Margaret's good luck seemed to have run its course.

Ernest died in November 1975 and was buried in Muenster. Earlier, Margaret had decided to write a book about their experiences. To get the book published, she and Ernest combined their names and formed Marest Publishing Company, Inc. There was some talk of a movie based on the book, mostly from Margaret herself. But, the movie didn't happen, and the book was not the solution to her problems. As it turned out, the book contributed to them.

On September 13, 1976, Margaret, along with Sol Fielding, was arrested at the Los Angeles International Airport trying to buy plane tickets with a stolen credit card. They were charged with credit card forgery, having used the stolen card to pay for their stay together at a posh Beverly Hills hotel. Mr. Fielding was identified as a Los Angeles "producer," purportedly interested in making a movie from the book. The hotel bill was paid and the charges were dropped. But Margaret wasn't through with the law.

In September 1976 Margaret was indicted by the Shelby County, Tennessee Grand Jury on five different counts. First, she represented that her company, Marest Publishing, was a "thriving and profitable business." On the strength of that misrepresentation she sold a one-third interest in Marest and obtained $24,800 from an elderly Memphis woman. Then she convinced the same woman she had an exclusive lease on coal rights and sold them to her for $3,000. She then sold the same coal rights to another elderly woman for $4,000. Following that, she told the first woman she had the rights to sell furniture and the contents of the home of the second woman and got a $1,000 deposit. Finally, she represented to yet a third woman that she had the right to sell some antiques and got another $2,500. As if that wasn't enough, the next month she was indicted by a Texas Grand Jury for failing to pay a Dallas hotel bill of $14,485.

The police found Margaret at a Beverly Hills, California hotel, arrested her on the Texas indictment, and returned her to Dallas for trial. Meanwhile, Tennessee placed a detainer on her because of the Shelby County indictment. She was convicted in Dallas on May 4, 1977, and was sentenced to five years in prison. She actually served seven months in the Huntsville prison. She was then taken to Memphis where she pled guilty to the five charges. The Tennessee court sentenced her to three years in prison, the judge refusing to consider probation because of her "manipulative tendencies." She got out in April 1980.

A final footnote on Margaret. During her stay in the Huntsville prison she was asked to write a skit for an Alcoholics Anonymous program. As a part of that process she began corresponding with a convict in another prison within the system. It seems her new friend, a Mr. Orr, although a former Baptist minister, had a drinking problem and had killed his wife. He was serving a term for manslaughter. When Margaret was released in 1980, she went to see Mr. Orr. They were married in his prison chapel. Orr was paroled in September and they honeymooned at Horseshoe Lake, Arkansas. A relative remarked that Margaret was the only woman she knew "who could go into prison and come out with a husband."

The Lawsuits

A Primer

Ever since the English concept of individual ownership of land, the transfer of property has always been a significant event. In those early days, the parties to the transaction met on the land itself and in the presence of witnesses. The man transferring the land picked up a clump of the earth, handed it to the person he was transferring it to, and announced orally to the witnesses that he was transferring ownership of his land. The witnesses were there to make the transfer public knowledge in the event it was challenged in the future. In some cases, it was customary to compel a group of small boys from the area to watch the transfer. Then, after the transfer was completed, each boy was given a sharp clout on the head to impress the event on his memory. Using young boys insured that the "public knowledge" lasted longer into the future. Today, we accomplish that same goal, public knowledge of land transfers, with less trauma to young boys, and it lasts even longer. We use written public records.

Maintaining official public records is the job of the clerk of the court of every county in the United States, including Jefferson County, Texas. Documents regarding land, most often mortgages and deeds, may be "recorded," which means a copy of the document is placed in the public records. Originally, the clerk hand-copied each document, word for word, right into the records book. Some clerks had beautifully legible handwriting, others did not. Today's clerks usually take a photograph of the deed or other document, assign it the next available page number in the current official records book, and return the original to its owner. Documents may be located by knowing the official records book and the page number where they were recorded. The clerks maintain indexing systems through which book and page numbers may be found by knowing the names of the parties to the document. The general public may view the records during normal business hours, and photocopies of every document are available for a nominal fee.

The ownership history of a particular piece of property can be determined by a routine examination of the public records. For example, an examination of the Jefferson County public records reveals that on December 18, 1900, the clerk of the court Lee Blanchette, in his own (very legible) handwriting, recorded the lease between Anthony Lucas and W.P.H. McFaddin, Wiess and Kyle—the lease for the oil and mineral rights on the Pelham Humphries league—in official records book 34 at page 488. Three weeks later the Spindletop gusher erupted on that same leased property and forever changed Texas.

The public records serve an important function. Much of the ordinary day-to-day business of the nation concerns the transfer of land. Property is leased, bought, sold, mortgaged, and inherited daily. Construction is a large segment of our economy. Mechanics lien laws protect unpaid suppliers and contractors through forced sale of the land itself to pay the debt. Unfortunately, lawsuits are also commonplace events. Lawsuit judgments are routinely recorded on the public record. They may become a lien against the property of the losing party. Unpaid taxes may also become a lien against property. Clearly, people considering purchasing property—or loaning money with the property serving as security for the loan—need a reliable and accurate method of determining the legal status of that property. That method is examination of the official public records where the land is situated.

As a general rule, those property interests which are recorded on the official public records take precedence over any *unrecorded* interests in land. Priority among recorded interests on the same land is determined by the date and time of recording. The first recorded has priority. For example, a second mortgage or a lien, recorded later in time to a first mortgage, is said to be junior or inferior to the prior recorded interest. (Some tax liens may have priority because of public policy.) Thus, to preserve priority, timely recording is an important consideration. When a claim against land is no longer valid, for instance when a judgment or a mortgage is paid off, it is said to be satisfied or released, and the prudent landowner will record the satisfaction or release. Accordingly, in addition to ownership history, including the most recent owner "of record," an examination of the public records reveals any claim not released or satisfied.

All court papers filed in a lawsuit become part of the public records. Because of our concern for the orderly disposition of land, lawsuits concerning land must follow what is commonly called the "local action rule." That is, they must be filed in the county where the land is located. Through the filing of a paper called a *lis pendens*, Latin for "a pending suit," those persons who may be interested in the particular piece of land are put on notice of the pending litigation. Thus, the existence of and the outcome of a lawsuit concerning land can be discovered by an examination of the public records of the county in which the land is located.

The United States is a "common law" country, having adopted the English common law upon achieving our own independence. Texas started following the common law of England when the fledgling Republic assumed sovereignty in March 1835. In deciding lawsuits, courts in the United States rely on the usages and customs of antiquity, especially the ancient unwritten law of England. Essentially that means that the various state and federal courts, including those in Texas, following the common law principle of *stare decisis*, Latin for "to abide by, or to adhere to decided cases," will abide by already established legal rules, called "precedents," in making their decisions. Under this concept we don't reinvent the legal wheel each time a new case is decided, and the public has at least some assurances that, if they follow the established legal rules in the conduct of their affairs, they will be protected by those established rules. While there are some variations on the rules from state to state (after all, our states are independent entities which may make their own laws), so long as they don't infringe on rights guaranteed by the United States Constitution, the law followed and its application by each state is reasonably uniform throughout the nation. The various state trial courts are bound by the precedents established in the decisions rendered by their own immediate appellate court and the supreme court of the particular state. While decisions from other jurisdictions may be persuasive in otherwise uncharted waters, they are not controlling on the trial court. When a federal court hears a nonfederal issue, like a land dispute in Jefferson County, Texas, it must apply the law of Texas.

The established precedents are found in the written decisions of the appellate courts of the individual states and the federal courts, including the highest court in the land, the United States Supreme Court. The recorded decisions of *all* of the various courts of appeal, state, and federal, are compiled in bound volumes, conveniently indexed, updated, and maintained in law libraries located throughout the country. Lawyers and the general public have access to these law libraries.

The doctrine of "adverse possession" is another long-standing legal concept important to the analysis of Spindletop claims. Because it seems to reward the wrongdoer, at first blush adverse possession appears contrary to our ordinary concept of the law. Adverse possession provides that the occupier of another's land, a squatter, can become the legal owner of the land if his occupation is actually *wrongful*. While specifics may vary from state to state, essentially, where a person has openly held the land, "exercised dominion" over it, for the specified number of years, he may acquire legal title over the claims of the "record" owner of the land.

Adverse possession is justified on several grounds. First is the observed human experience that one *true* owner of property will not permit another to wrongfully use and occupy his land. This is simply recognition of man's territorial instinct. There is also a fairness issue. An owner may not ignore his land and then reap the benefits brought about by the efforts and improvements of the adverse possessor. And those dealing with an adverse possessor and relying on his ownership of the land should be protected. It is also a reliable method of assuring certainty of title to land, so important in the ordinary business of the nation.

On June 30, 1923, sixty-seven-year-old W.P.H. McFaddin executed an affidavit and filed it on the public records in Jefferson County. The affidavit states that in 1883 he purchased the "whole of the Pelham Humphries survey sometimes known as the William Humphries survey, in Jefferson County, Texas." It goes on to say that in January 1884 he fenced all of the land except that part west of the railroad tracks (which he had sold); that the land had been continuously fenced and used for stock; that in 1894 his agent D.W. Lewis moved on the property and began cultivation in addition to looking after the stock; and that he and his successors have continuously used and claimed the whole of the land and paid taxes thereon. This affidavit preserves the factual circumstances of McFaddin's actual use and possession of the land against the event that some other person is successful in demonstrating a valid title to the property. This was a pre-emptive strike to establish adverse possession, just in case it was needed or useful in the future. It didn't hurt.

When advising a client or deciding to undertake a legal matter, an understanding of legal concepts like adverse possession; analysis of the legal effect of deeds, mortgages, liens, lawsuits and other documents appearing on the public record; and the application of the common-law rules required by *stare decisis* is the "business" of a lawyer. Oh yes, the legal "profession" is, after all, just another "business."

Lawyers' Relief: The Humphries' Lawsuits

Regarding Spindletop, it has been said that "Lawyers have made as much profit out of oil as the operators, with half the work, none of the gamble and twice the social prestige." *Twice* the social prestige? Well, one thing is certain, Spindletop provided employment to a crowd of lawyers. Before 1901 came to a close, there were purportedly more lawyers involved than drillers, operators, landowners, confidence men, or stock speculators. A considerable portion of their involvement was the ordinary, routine representation of business interests such as corporate matters, contracts, and leases. Then too, lawyers often headed up the various companies that grew out of Spindletop. For instance, lawyer and former governor of Texas, the Honorable James Stephen Hogg, was a player in the business venture that was to become the company we know today as Texaco. Also, there were the usual litigation matters to be expected as people in an emerging industry managed to break their contracts or otherwise failed to live up to their business obligations. For example, after he brought in that first gusher, Anthony Lucas was sued by his former partner in the drilling venture, Pattillio Higgins. It seems that in exchange for the talents (and financial assistance) of wildcatters Guffy and Galey, just before the well came in, Lucas cut Higgins out of the deal. But it is the massive litigation over ownership of the land and the mineral rights to which we direct our attention.

The Spindletop oil field covered all of Big Hill and its margins. While the first well came in on the Pelham Humphries survey, there were numerous ownership claims on the adjoining parts of the hill. Every acre was contested. The financial benefits of establishing a claim to a portion of the oil field were obvious and demonstrated early on in the Snow case. It seems that the oil speculators had failed to obtain the widow Snow's eighteenth life estate interest in the Veatch survey. (The Veatch and Humphries surveys share a common boundary.) Mrs. Snow's lawyers, working on a 50 percent contingency fee arrangement, convinced the court that her life estate entitled her to the mineral rights as well as the surface rights. That meant that Mrs. Snow was entitled to one-eighteenth of every barrel of oil produced on the Veatch survey. Even in the very early days of Spindletop, that amounted to almost a quarter of a million dollars! The lawyers got half of it. One-eighteenth of every barrel produced from the Humphries survey would be an enormous sum, and what was good for Mrs. Snow (remember *stare decisis*) was good for the Humphries heirs, if only they could establish their claim. Surely it was something worth fighting for.

Historically, examining the public records and the established law to be applied *before* starting a Humphries Spindletop lawsuit has not been the rule. Greed is such a powerful force. A host of "nice men" have aggressively asserted the claims of Humphries' heirs (and purported heirs), by suing relentlessly for ownership and the oil profits taken from the Pelham Humphries league. They have not been deterred by the pregusher recorded transfers of the Pelham Humphries league shown on the public record, nor by any of the decisions in previous lawsuits over the Humphries' claims. Attorney Ralph Elliot, suing Ernest on behalf of Margery Medders, was no different.

On October 11, 1965, the United States Supreme Court dismissed the appeal of the case of *Coral B. Jones, et al. v. W.P.H. McFaddin et al.* The "et al.," following Coral B. Jones, is an abbreviation for the Latin phrase *et alii* which means "and others." *Et al.* is used to save space where there are multiple parties in a lawsuit. After the first court paper naming all the plaintiffs and defendants, it may be added after the name of the first plaintiff or first defendant in subsequently filed papers. In this case the "and others" following Coral B. Jones was to include the claims of Ernest and some three thousand others claiming to be kin to Pelham Humphries. The *et al.* following W.P.H. McFaddin included the various oil companies on the land. The reader should also know that, despite his name appearing as the first defendant, W.P.H. himself, having passed away in 1935, was not a party to this suit. His heirs were. This was the lawsuit Ernest, Margaret, and the Poor Sisters were depending on for the vast wealth of the fabulous Pelham Humphries estate.

Ernest's lead attorney, W.T. Weir (there were three attorneys for plaintiffs and at least sixteen for the defendants), chose to begin litigation in the Texas state court system rather than the federal court system frequently used by other Humphries attorneys. Following the local action rule, he filed the case in the Jefferson County District Court (the same courthouse Rosine would first appear in some twenty-five years later). However, on January 18, 1963, Mr. Weir's case suffered a serious setback when the Honorable Jack Brookshire, Jefferson County's district court judge, granted defendant McFaddin's motion for summary judgment on the grounds of adverse possession.

Summary judgment is a shortcut method of ending lawsuits when the facts necessary to decide a case are *undisputed*. Summary judgment works because, where the facts are not in dispute, there is no need for a "fact finder," the traditional job of a jury. Thus, when the facts of a case are undisputed, the judge simply does his job of applying the recognized *law* (*stare decisis* at work again) to those undisputed facts, and the case is "summarily" decided without the necessity of a trial.

Judge Brookshire ended the case in favor of the McFaddins and the oil companies when he granted McFaddin's motion for summary judgment. That was a devastating blow. Having a jury, the "little people," decide their case is the goal of every trial lawyer with rich (often called "deep pockets") big business defendants like the oil companies and the McFaddins. Juries often identify with ordinary people and find against rich people and big business. While Mr. Weir, still practicing law at age eighty-seven, lost the case in Jefferson County without getting it to a jury, he was not done fighting yet. He did what lawyers do, he appealed!

Following the recognized appellate path, Mr. Weir duly filed an appeal with the Court of Civil Appeals in Texarkana, Texas. Unfortunately for the Medders and the rest, on September 1, 1964, the Court of Civil Appeals upheld Judge Brookshire. Margaret and Ernest attended at the Court of Civil Appeals and heard the arguments made by the lawyers to the appellate court. Margaret professes to have not understood anything that was going on but was proud of Mr. Wier's courtroom conduct on their behalf. When she contacted Mr. Wier to find out how things were going, the colorful and optimistic gentleman told her he was getting "all the pins in the dish" and "it won't be long." Visiting his office in Philadelphia, Mississippi, was even more encouraging. There, in his red stockings, the shoeless Mr. Wier shuffled amongst the high stacks of books and papers which cluttered up his office, from time to time reading passages from his law books to Margaret and Ernest, and otherwise exuding and inspiring superb confidence. Perhaps as an additional safeguard, as they left his office, Mr. Wier asked

Margaret and Ernest to pray for him and the success of the case. He also filed a motion for rehearing with the Court of Civil Appeals.

While Mr. Wier's courtroom and office performance inspired confidence in Ernest and Margaret, the Court of Civil Appeals was unmoved. The court denied his motion for rehearing, and Mr. Weir had lost again. But the indefatigable legal octogenarian was not finished yet. Putting his pins back in the dish, he filed an application for a writ of error (the next appropriate form of appeal) with the Texas Supreme Court. Apparently unmoved by red socks and legal passages, prayers, or pins, the Texas Supreme Court refused Mr. Wier's application. Not finished yet, Mr. Weir filed an appeal to the United States Supreme Court.

Federal law permits the United States Supreme Court to review state court decisions under certain limited circumstances: where the case concerns a treaty or statute of the United States, or where a state statute is repugnant to the Constitution, treaties, or laws of the United States. Mr. Wier argued that the case concerned the February 2, 1848 treaty between the United Mexican States and the United States of America signed at the City of Guadalupe Hidalgo (my but that sounded important), as well as international law. While that was creative, it didn't fly. The lawyers for the McFaddins and the oil companies filed a motion to dismiss on the grounds that the case did not raise a substantial federal question. The Supreme Court agreed.

And so it came to be that on October 11, 1965, while Ernest and Margaret were busily hiring tuxedoed helicopter pilots and arranging for truckloads of food for their expected nine hundred guests at the "barnwarming," just a month away, the U.S. Supreme Court disposed of the case in one, eighteen-word sentence:

> The motion to dismiss is granted and the appeal
> is dismissed for want of a substantial federal question.

That decision killed their chance for the Pelham Humphries Spindletop fortune. Oh well, at least the bad news didn't put a damper on the barnwarming festivities, their visit to the White House, or any of the other gala Medders' events in the coming year.

The Supreme Court's dismissal of the appeal meant that Ernest Medders' lawsuit in pursuit of the Pelham Humphries Spindletop fortune had now exhausted every appellate path available to it. The case had indeed been lost all the way to the Supreme Court of the United States. There was no further appeal.

The reader will of course realize that the Supreme Court's dismissal of *Jones v. McFaddin* on October 11, 1965, meant that a full year and ten days *before* the nice men sued Ernest to recover Margery Medders' share of the Pelham Humphries estate, it was already a matter of public record that Ernest's and all of the other Medders' claims to Spindletop were stone dead. The public records clearly showed that Ernest Medders had received no Pelham Humphries oil money and that he was not going to receive any Pelham Humphries oil money. Mr. Wier had dug deep, but it was a dry hole.

Thus, what attorney Ralph Elliot learned by taking Ernest's deposition—that Ernest had received nothing from the Pelham Humphries estate—he could have learned a full year earlier in about ten minutes at his local law library. But what would be the fun in that?

Generations of Humphries Claims

The Humphries claims to Spindletop divide nicely into two groups: those made just after the gusher, in 1901 and 1902, and those made in the 1940s, '60s, and '80s, the generation-skipping claims.

One of the early claims is noted for its longevity. The lawsuit naming W.P.H. McFaddin was started just after the Lucas gusher came in but before the birth of W.P.H.'s youngest child, James Lewis Caldwell McFaddin. During the pendency of this particular lawsuit, Caldwell McFaddin (who would later marry Rosine Blount and become the father of Rosine McFaddin Wilson) was born, grew up, and attended the public schools in Beaumont. He entered the university and eventually received a law degree. He was admitted to the practice of law in Jefferson County and, in 1926, now a lawyer acting on behalf of his father, moved for dismissal of the Humphries heir's case that had begun before he was born. Judge Campbell granted the motion.

We now advance in time, from Caldwell McFaddin's 1926 motion to dismiss an early Humphries case to November 1948 and another Humphries case, *Glover v. McFaddin* (and their *et als.*). In this case the Reverend L.B. Glover, a preacher at the East Tennessee Lick Creek Christian Church (and the uncle of Brown Peregoy, a gentleman we met earlier and one whom we will meet again), sought $500 million on behalf of himself and some twenty-five hundred other heirs of Pelham Humphries that had not actually joined as plaintiffs in the suit. Mr. E. Garland Brown was one of six attorneys representing Mr. Glover and his *et als.* The McFaddins and their *et als.* had eight attorneys.[1]

---

1   One of the eight attorneys representing McFaddins and the other defendants was George A. Weller. The reader may recall that Lum Hawthorne, at the same time he was looking after Rosine's little problem, was also representing Mr. Weller's son Andrew. Andrew, it will be remembered, was charged with killing his mother and father with a shotgun blast to the face.

    Prior to his retirement, George A. Weller had devoted a considerable portion of his legal career to successfully defending Spindletop cases. In addition to battling against E. Garland Brown in the *Glover* case, he also took on Ernest and Margaret's attorney W.T. Weir, Mr. Votaw, whom we meet shortly, as well as participating in the Humphries trilogy cases. If it hadn't been for

Perhaps Mr. Glover was deterred by the long history of Texas state courts denying Humphries heirs' claims. Perhaps he thought he would get a better judge. But, for whatever reason, he decided to bring his case in the federal court system. Following the local action rule, the Glover case was filed in the United States District Court for the Eastern District of Texas, sitting in Beaumont.

Glover's theory of the case, that is the purported legal reason why he and the 2,500 other Humphries heirs should recover possession of the land and money from the McFaddins and the oil companies, was that they were all "tenants in common" on the Humphries survey. In the text of his order, Chief Judge Kennerly summarized Glover's theory this way:

> Plaintiffs . . . allege they are some of the heirs at law of William Humphries, deceased, Betsy Jane Humphries Foust, deceased, and Elisha V. Humphries, Jr., deceased, who plaintiffs say were the sole heirs of Pelham Humphries, the original grantee of such tract of land. They also say that Defendants claim under one Jessee Humphries, a son of Elisha V. Humphries, Jr., and that, therefore, Plaintiffs and Defendants are Tenants in common of such tract of land.

Reasonable men, and even some lawyers (but obviously not E. Garland Brown), may not agree that, even if factually true, those facts would make Glover and the others tenants in common. But we need not dwell on that matter. That little mental exercise goes to the merits of Glover's position—which was never reached by a trial judge.

---

his son Andrew, Mr. Weller might have come out of retirement to participate against Max Wilson and Brown Peregoy in what would have to be one of the most satisfying cases for Spindletop defense attorneys.

The important thing for all Glover's kith and kin was the potential. As "tenants in common," the McFaddins and the oil companies could stay on the land, but they had to share the past profits—now measured at $500 million—with Glover and the heirs, plus, since as tenants in common Pelham's kin were also due title and possession of the land, they would also share in the future. What a delightful prospect for the Humphries. Not surprisingly, the McFaddins and the oil companies didn't share the Humphries' joy, and they certainly had no intention of sharing the land or their money. They moved to dismiss the case for lack of jurisdiction.

The authority for a federal court to hear any case and decide the issues, called subject matter jurisdiction, arises out of Article III, § 2, of the United States Constitution and Title 28 of the United States Code. It is not complex. Everyone understands that federal courts have the authority to hear those matters arising out of the U.S. Constitution and the laws of the United States, but they also have the authority to hear certain civil cases between the citizens of different states. This is called "diversity jurisdiction."

Diversity jurisdiction has essentially two requirements. The first one is easy. The matter in controversy in the lawsuit must exceed the minimum value or sum of money established by federal law. The federal courts are busy places, and they don't want to be burdened with cases over piddling amounts. In 1948 the amount necessary to maintain diversity jurisdiction was $3,000 (ten years later it was raised to $10,000 and again in 1988 to $50,000—that cut down the caseload). Let's see how that works out here. Mr. Glover sought five hundred million. (How many zeros again?) $500,000,000 divided by 2,500 heirs equals $200,000 each. Well, the amount in controversy was not the problem. "Diversity" itself was.

The second requirement of diversity jurisdiction, actual diversity of citizenship, is the tough issue because there must be "complete diversity" between all the plaintiffs and all the defendants. If one or some of them are citizens of the same state, diversity jurisdiction is not available and the plaintiff must seek his remedy in a state court. That was a potential problem in the Glover case because many of the oil companies were "citizens" of various states, as were the heirs, and where it was the same state, the "diversity" requirement was not met, and the court had no jurisdiction. With no jurisdiction, the court must dismiss.

Additionally, the law of Texas provided that Glover, as a tenant in common with the defendants, could not recover any benefits for the other (2,500) tenants in common who were not parties to the suit. Glover's lawyers argued that, under the federal rules of civil procedure, his was a class action suit under which, as representative of the others in the class, he could recover for them. Judge Kennerly disagreed.

As a general rule, when a federal court hears a civil case on a nonfederal issue, it follows the law of the particular state in which the court is sitting. Since the Glover case was to be heard in Beaumont, Texas, Judge Kennerly was to follow the law of Texas. But, even when hearing state issues, the federal court applies federal rules of civil procedure.

Judge Kennerly decided that permitting Glover to recover on behalf of the other heirs in a class action suit would not be in keeping with the established law of Texas regarding tenants in common and that the Texas law would trump the federal class action rule. But he didn't dismiss the suit; instead, he required that any of the other Humphries heirs who sought recovery had to join as plaintiffs. If they didn't join, they could not recover. We visit Glover again in 1951. By this time Judge Connally has inherited the case from Judge Kennerly, and there are now 1,000 plaintiffs and conditional intervenors (persons who the court permits to become parties to the suit because they profess a legal interest in the subject matter) and about twenty defendants.

Following Judge Kennerly's order, Glover had managed to join an additional 400 to 500 plaintiffs (even Judge Connally notes that there is no mention of what happened to the remaining 2,000). Twenty-two separate groups sought leave to intervene. Judge Connally divided all the conditional intervenors into four classes. The first two classes were additional Humphries heirs. The third class was made up of the heirs of William English, a purported 1836 grantee of William Humphries, and, in his own class, attorney E. Garland Brown.

It seems that some of the Humphries were now dissatisfied with the services of Mr. Brown. He was permitted to withdraw from representation of the dissatisfied plaintiffs; however, as they had conveyed to him a fractional portion of their claim as his fee, he was a proper intervenor too.

One of the two intervening classes of Humphries agreed with the theory of Glover and the other original plaintiffs. The second Humphries class had their own different theory of recovery. The English heirs naturally disagreed with all the Humphries. Mr. Brown's position was unique to all of the others.

Judge Connally recognized that there was not complete diversity among the parties, and accordingly he ordered that those plaintiffs and intervenors without complete diversity would be dismissed in thirty days unless they managed to find an alternative basis for the court's jurisdiction. One batch of conditional intervenors was dismissed because their interests would not be affected if they weren't included, but pursuing their claims would cause unnecessary delay and prejudice the rights of the original parties. That left only Mr. Brown to be considered. Judge Connally considered his case to be "ancillary" to the main action, another basis for jurisdiction in a federal court, and permitted him to remain even though he was also a citizen of Texas and not "diverse" from some of the defendants.

The factual situation Glover (and the other survivors of Judge Connally's order) asserted was that "Pelham" Humphries owned the land; that Pelham was killed on September 5, 1835; that at his death he was single, without children, and intestate (without a will); that his heirs were his brother William, sister Betsy, and half brother Elisha; and that William, Betsy, and Elisha were at all times residents of the state of Tennessee. Perhaps they should have thought that through a bit more. They neglected two important considerations.

First, on September 5, 1835, Texas was still part of Mexico. The Independent Republic of Texas did not assume sovereignty until November 7, 1835. Which of course meant that the controlling law as of September 5, 1835, was Mexican law. And second, that, under Mexican law, aliens to Mexico were ineligible to take real property by inheritance. If there were no heirs capable of taking the property, and under the facts asserted by Glover there were not, the property "escheated" (a fancy way of saying it reverted or went back) to the Republic of Mexico upon Pelham's death. As lifelong residents of Tennessee, William, Betsy, and Elisha were all aliens to Mexico. Gee, they missed it by just sixty-three days. The defendants moved for summary judgment on the facts alleged and the application of the Mexican law. Judge Connally granted the motion. Glover and the others were out at the trial level. Naturally they appealed.

In 1953 the Glover case was reviewed by the United States Court of Appeals for the Fifth Circuit, the appellate court for the federal district courts of Texas. The Fifth Circuit carefully analyzed the issues and upheld Judge Connally. Glover's last gasp ended when the United States Supreme Court denied his petition for a writ of certiorari (the method of appeal available to Glover).

After five years the Glover faction of Humphries heirs, having had their day in court, were finally through. Or were they? We will return to Mr. Glover's nephew, Brown Peregoy, and his romp through the legal systems in the 1980s and on into the '90s, but, first, we finish up the 1950s with a Humphries case that accomplished something none of the others did. It was actually heard by a jury.

McBride v. Gulf Oil Corporation (and their *et als.*) may have been one of the more economical of the Humphries cases. It was filed in the Texas state court system in Jefferson County's district court in Beaumont. While it too started with numerous Humphries heirs as plaintiffs, by the time it went to trial all but nine had dropped out. Probably the most telling sign of its economy is that there was only one lawyer for the plaintiffs, a Mr. Votaw, and just three Beaumont law firms and one Houston lawyer for the defendants.

The Humphries in *McBride* took the position that Pelham was originally from North Carolina, not Tennessee, and that he had no family. Both positions were contrary to the original, and legally accepted, headright petition and related certificate documents appearing on the public record. The problem for the heirs was that they could offer no admissable evidence to support their claims or to otherwise legally refute the documents already on the public record. Thus, it was clear that the Humphries who was granted the league of land in Jefferson County could not be the same Humphries through whom the *McBride* heirs claimed. When the heirs failed to present admissable evidence to support their position, the jury had nothing to decide.

Judge Melvin Combs granted the defendants' motion for a directed verdict. A directed verdict is somewhat analogous to what happens in a summary judgment. At trial, where the plaintiff fails to put on legally sufficient evidence from which a jury could decide a critical point, the judge will not allow the matter to be decided by them. Without acceptable evidence, there is nothing to "decide." In that case the judge "directs" the jury to find in favor of the defendants. That's what happened in *McBride*. Thus, while *McBride* has the distinction of actually getting to a jury, the matter was taken away from them by the directed verdict for the defendants. For the Humphries, it had the same effect as the summary judgments and dismissals granted in the other cases—they were out.

Mr. Votaw appealed. On December 1, 1955, the appellate court upheld Judge Combs' decision. On March 14, 1956, they overruled a motion for rehearing but later clarified their opinion on minor points. Two more motions for rehearing were denied, the last one on June 27, 1956. The application for a writ of error to the Texas Supreme Court was refused, as Mr. Weir's would be refused nine years later, and the *McBride* case was over.

We now return to the 1960s. In addition to the Medders' ill-fated case, there were three other landmark Humphries cases decided in the '60s. The courts began to tire of the Humphries' favorite pastime.

The Humphries Trilogy

On April 9, 1968, the Fifth Circuit issued decisions on three cases attempting to recover the Pelham Humphries fortune, all with different theories to justify their claims. The three were considered together and called the Humphries trilogy. They were intended to end future Humphries litigation.

In the first one, *Humphries v. Texas Gulf Sulphur*, the Humphries said the land was originally granted to *Pelham* Humphries, not *William* Humphries, and, therefore, the power of attorney to Inglish to alter "Pelham" to "William," and all subsequent transfers of the land, were fraudulent. In *Beasley v. W.P.H. McFaddin*, the heirs said that the William Humphries who conveyed to William Inglish was not the heir of Pelham and therefore had nothing to convey. The third case was a little different.

The case of *Green v. Texas Gulf Sulphur* was unique in that the heirs argued that an 1850 tax deed[2] vested title to the land in the State of Texas; and that, if they could set aside the tax deed, then they would be entitled to the mineral rights. To get the tax deed set aside they also had to sue the Texas commissioner of the general land office.

At the trial level the three cases were all decided in Beaumont by United States District Court Judge Joe J. Fisher. Judge Fisher granted defendants' motions for summary judgment in each case. He held that, as in *McBride*, the heirs having presented no admissable evidence otherwise, the deeds in question were valid and their legal effect was to divest Humphries of title; plus, in any event, the defendants had gained title by adverse possession. In *Green*, he dismissed the commissioner on the ground of sovereign immunity and then granted summary judgment for the remaining defendants without commenting on the validity of the tax deed.

Circuit Court of Appeals Judge Thornberry began his opinion in *Humphries v. Texas Gulf Sulphur* this way:

> This diversity action proves that unlike old soldiers, expectant heirs never even fade away. It is one of a trilogy that hopefully will terminate the continuing battle between the heirs and active users of the Humphries survey.

Judge Thornberry went on to confirm Judge Fisher on all three cases and to hold that the absolute nonuse and nonclaim to the land by the plaintiffs and their predecessors for more than 125 years, when measured against the defen-

---

2   As is demonstrated by the result in the *Green* case, the tax deed is a non-issue. Another case, *Foster v. Gulf Oil Corporation*, 345 S.W.Sd 845 (Tex. Civ. App. 1960), similarly dealt with the tax deed. Plaintiffs could not make a case that the State had regained title to the land by a tax deed.

dants' active use and claim, justify a "conclusive presumption" that *all the Humphries heirs have lost their title.* He concluded this way:

> The Pelham Humphries litigation is over and the Humphries heirs have no title in the league of land.

A reasonable person, certainly a reasonable lawyer, should clearly recognize that it would be unwise to bring another Humphries heirs case. And for a decade the Humphries let the matter lay. But at 3:00 a.m. one morning in 1979, Brown Peregoy, whom we may not describe as "reasonable," awoke with a revelation: "I can win it!"

Brown Peregoy

Brown Peregoy's early morning inspiration had absolutely nothing to do with the merits of the case. He hadn't even thought about the lawsuit in years. He had found no smoking gun. No "deepthroat" had come forward to reveal a chink in the McFaddin armor. Peregoy's revelation was a simple marketing issue. For all these years they had targeted the wrong demographic!

The Humphries had never been able to sell their convoluted Uncle Pel story of fraud, conspiracy, and murder to the McFaddins, or to the oil companies, and certainly not to the many judges they pitched over the years. Peregoy realized that for almost eighty years now the one place the Uncle Pel story sold well, in fact, very well, was with the other Humphries heirs. And the one thing there was plenty of were other heirs or wannabe heirs of Pelham Humphries. (Some wannabes wanted in so bad they offered to pay to be adopted by a Humphries.) Peregoy's idea was to organize the heirs into a group and get them to pool their resources.

A jointly funded effort was not exactly a novel idea among Pelham Humphries litigants. In the '40s and early '50s, even

Peregoy's uncle, the Reverend L.B. Glover, had organized to some extent, and they "passed the hat" at every opportunity. The reader might also recall that in the early '60s, Ernest and the other Medders had all "pitched in" to help pay for their lawsuit. But Peregoy's idea to organize and raise money was on a much grander scale.

Brown Peregoy

Photo courtesy of the *Beaumont Enterprise*

In addition to the longtime believers, Peregoy intended to proselytize among the new, far flung, and untapped generations of Humphries kin. He envisioned both an initial contribution and a continuing annual contribution. Plus, he had some ideas for additional revenue sources. Most important, Brown Peregoy was to be the keeper of the key. Of course his "expenses" would have to come out of the fund.

He was successful. Peregoy may have inherited some of his religious fervor from Uncle L.B., but, with the ever present "greed" factor, no in-depth analysis or long explanation is necessary for why his effort worked so well. Peregoy sold them the gospel of Pelham with a simple pitch, by reminding them of the past failures against Big Oil money: "How could you win? They can fight you with your own money. Uncle Pel's money." He easily convinced the heirs that to successfully fight against the Big Oil money, they needed a huge war chest too. They had to get on an equal footing with Big Oil. To win, they needed to hire the best lawyers and genealogists money could buy. The heirs bought it. Peregoy's organization was called "Pelham Humphries Heirs Association." It was his additional revenue sources that first got him into trouble.

Brown Peregoy with "Uncle Pel" T-shirt.
Phto courtesy of the *Houston Chronicle*

Formerly in the construction, flea market, and fruit stand business in Gray, Tennessee, Brown had some new ideas on how to increase revenues. He expanded his flea market and fruit stand operation by offering records and cassettes of "the Ballad of Pelham Humphries" and Pelham T-shirts, with a picture of "Uncle Pel," both brisk sellers. It was the kickback he expected from genealogist Jim Petty that caused the problem.

Each association member that wanted to participate in the fabulous Pelham Humphries fortune needed to be able to prove up his *own* kinship to Pelham. When Brown contacted Jim Petty regarding the genealogy work for "thousands" of association members, he wanted Jim to refund twenty percent of his fees to the association fund. With the potential for so many individual clients, that was not an unusual or unreasonable request and Jim agreed. However, when Petty was about to send them the first refund check of $3,200, Brown demanded it be made payable to himself. That sounded too much like a kickback to Brown Peregoy instead of a refund to the association. Jim Petty refused. Instead, to honor his commitment to the association, Jim made the refund check payable to the board of directors of the Pelham Humphries Heirs Association. Unfortunately, when the cancelled check came back Jim realized he hadn't solved the problem. The check had simply been endorsed by Brown, his wife, and another insider. Jim contacted other association members and learned they knew nothing of the refund. He sent them a copy of his cancelled check. The association members confronted Peregoy, and that lead to a parting of the ways between the organization and Peregoy. He says he quit because his feelings were hurt by the accusation—the association says they fired him. Peregoy was not happy with Jim Petty.

That rift caused Peregoy to form another, separate and competing association, the Humphries Heirs Trust Association, and to cut a new deal with Harold Brooks-Baker, a genealogist from London's *Burke's Peerage*. The interesting thing is that, despite the mistrust generated by the kickback scheme, Peregoy was still able to raise almost a quarter of a million dollars in only forty-five days. Never underestimate the power of greed.

Peregoy knew his market so well and was so successful in winning new converts to the Pelham Humphries game that he reportedly had as many as 7,500 members in his association, from the fifty states and seven countries. He also amassed nearly a million dollars in cash, ostensibly to pay for the best lawyers. But Brown wasn't particularly anxious to get the matter to trial. He waited ten years from his 3:00 a.m. revelation in 1979 until the symbolic filing date of his lawsuit, February 14, 1989, exactly 154 years to the day from when Pelham received the grant of the league that was to become Spindletop. Despite his bravado, he and his lawyers knew that actually filing the suit would be the beginning of the end. And, of course, in light of the legal precedent established in the Humphries trilogy two decades earlier, it was.

Rule 11

A skeptic might wonder if Peregoy's choice of the local law firm of Wilson, Wilson & Crupp, from nearby Mountain City, Tennessee, was really the best available legal talent necessary to go head to head with Big Oil's expensive attorneys. While lead attorney Max Wilson had a high rating among his peers, the rating is based upon the standard of ability for the area where the lawyer practices. Mountain City has a population of 2,125. It is located in extreme upper and eastern Tennessee, just inside Tennessee where the common borders of Tennessee, North Carolina, and Virginia converge. It is true that Mountain City is the county seat of Johnson County, but the entire population of Johnson County is less than 14,000 people. The largest nearby city is Johnson City, Tennessee. Well, in the light of their past record of accomplishments, one thing was certain: he couldn't actually do any worse than the colorful Mr. Weir, Ralph Elliot, E. Garland Brown, Mr. Votaw, or any of the others. Or could he?

Max Wilson began by filing the February 14, 1989, action, *B.L. Peregoy et al., v. Amoco Production Company, et al.,* seeking 200 billion dollars in unpaid royalties, not in Jefferson County, Texas, but in the Federal District Court for the Eastern District of Tennessee. Perhaps Mr. Wilson wanted the "home court" advantage. Perhaps he really just wanted to avoid those unpleasant Beaumont judges. It really made no difference because District Court Judge Thomas Hull predictably applied the local action rule and ordered the case transferred to the Eastern District of Texas—back to Beaumont.

Mr. Wilson had argued that the lawsuit only sought "royalties," which were personal property, not land, and accordingly they shouldn't have to go to Jefferson County. Judge Hull thought that was nonsense, since establishing their claims required proving they were the rightful "owners" of the Pelham Humphries league, and was not dissuaded. Neither was Circuit Court of Appeals Judge Ralph Guy. Judge Guy denied Max Wilson's petition for a writ of mandamus, a legal maneuver designed to compel Judge Hull to hear the case in Tennessee. Actually, Judge Guy thought Judge Hull had been extremely conservative in not dismissing the lawsuit out of hand, considering the litany of prior cases and especially the Humphries trilogy. Be that as it may, the case was transferred to the district court sitting in Beaumont.

In Beaumont the case was assigned to District Court Judge Cobb. On December 6, 1989, Judge Cobb denied Max Wilson's motion to transfer the case back to Tennessee. The next day, for two and a half hours, Judge Cobb heard arguments on the oil companies' motions for summary judgment. To help influence the court's decision through a show of force, Peregoy brought in more than five hundred association members. They filled Judge Cobb's courtroom and overflowed into the adjoining hallways and the courthouse steps. Some carried signs saying, "Give us what is ours" or "Justice over the big oil companies." Inside, Judge Cobb was unmoved by the show of support by the association members or Max Wilson's oral argument. The judge said he would consider further argument until the end of January and promised a decision soon. When they left the courtroom, the crowd cheered Wilson and Peregoy.

In his follow-up written order, Judge Cobb denied Peregoy's pending motion for certification as a class action and granted defendants' motions for summary judgment, applying our old friend, the doctrine of *stare decisis* (and, for good measure, a few other doctrines that have similar effects: collateral estoppel and *res judicata*, different legal ways of saying, "we already decided this matter once and we're not going to do it all over again"). Judge Cobb threw the case out with these words:

This case is meritless. A simple and cursory examination of the table of cases in the Federal Digest System would have revealed the result which this court has reached so predictably. It is indeed regrettable that the heirs of Pelham Humphries have needlessly caused to be expended the judicial resources of the United States Courts of Tennessee, Texas, the Court of Appeals for the Sixth Circuit and the actual resources of the defendants.

Max Wilson and Brown Peregoy meet with the crowd of association members on the courthouse steps. Photo courtesy of the *Beaumont Enterprise*.

Judge Cobb was particularly unhappy with Messrs. Peregoy and Wilson, and he had a way to deal with them:

The eagerness of the plaintiffs and their lawyer to pursue this case in the light of numerous existing final decisions on the same issue may violate the provisions

which require the lawyer to make reasonable inquiry as
to the basis of his cause of action prior to filing an action in a United States District Court.

Judge Cobb was referring to the requirements of Rule 11
of the federal rules of civil procedure. As the judge correctly
pointed out, a lawyer has an obligation to make a reasonable
inquiry prior to filing a lawsuit. Had Max Wilson done the
"simple and cursory examination" Judge Cobb mentioned,
it would have revealed the long list of Humphries cases,
including the trilogy with its explicit language.

While Mountain City does not have its own law library,
a mere forty or so miles away in Johnson City Eastern
Tennessee State University maintains a law library with all
of the past Humphries cases readily available for the reading.
Additionally, at the federal courthouse in Greeneville, Tennessee, where Max originally filed the lawsuit on February
14, 1989, there is another law library that he could have
used. It is inconceivable that Mr. Wilson did not actually
read and analyze those cases. Surely he at least did that.
Taking that as a given, Mr. Wilson then consciously chose
to ignore his legal training and the common-law concept of
stare decisis (plus collateral estoppel and *res judicata*). That
was a dangerous thing to do. Max Wilson was about to
demonstrate that he actually could do worse than Messrs.
Weir, Elliot, Brown, Votaw, and all the others.

On November 2, 1990, Judge Cobb granted the oil companies' motions for sanctions under Rule 11, and, as a
penalty for filing this frivolous lawsuit, ordered that Brown
Peregoy, two other members of his association, *and Max
Wilson* pay the oil companies' attorney's fees for having had
to defend this meritless suit, some $115,746. Judge Cobb
also ordered that the money necessary to pay the fine could
not come from association funds. Finally, Judge Cobb specifically required that Max Wilson, individually, had to pay
one half of the money because:

> This court finds the plaintiffs' counsel in this case ut-
> terly failed to make a reasonable inquiry into either the
> facts of the case or the law applicable to this case.

Undaunted, Wilson said: "I feel like we got a good chance at an appeal." Wrong again. On April 23, 1991, after a full ninety years of Humphries' litigation over Spindletop, the appellate court upheld Judge Cobb's decisions on every issue, including the imposition of sanctions.

As a final insult, back home in Tennessee a restraining order was entered against Peregoy and the other officers of the association forbidding them from using any of the group's funds, after association members filed a lawsuit saying they were duped out of their money by Peregoy.

Peregoy managed to either pay his portion of the fine or, at least, pay a compromised amount. Max Wilson was another story. Due to some differences of opinion with the Internal Revenue Service, any surplus property or income Mr. Wilson may have had, from which he could have satisfied a judgment, was taken up by the IRS. The oil companies had to get in line.

A final note on Peregoy. It seems he was last sighted working as a consultant for a nice lady who wanted to contest an 1859 Texas land title (not to Spindletop) and needed some assistance in organizing and fund raising among the potential heirs to another fortune.

Thus, every single Humphries heir's lawsuit seeking the millions and billions of dollars in oil revenues from Uncle Pel's league at Spindletop has crashed and burned. But as we now leave those charred remains, it's important to remember that, like the phoenix, Pelham Humphries' lawsuits often rise from the ashes, just as Peregoy's did from the ashes of *Glover* and the trilogy. To try to prevent a repeat of that, Judge Cobb wanted to make himself very clear for anyone even thinking about a future Pelham Humphries' lawsuit:

[T]ake heed: there is no claim available to any heir of Pelham Humphries as to any part, parcel, or portion of the league of land commonly known as the Humphries Survey, nor the minerals extracted therefrom; nor is there any such claim by any heir of Pelham Humphries available to be asserted to that property or minerals extracted from the league since 1901. 'Any heir' of Pelham Humphries means *every heir*, past, present, or future.

To rational people, that statement is clear. But to hard-core Pelham Humphries heirs it's just another example of the cover-up that started way back in 1835 when Pelham was killed at the Hawthorne house in Nacogdoches. It's all part of the conspiracy designed to deprive the heirs of their rightful claims to Uncle Pel's land and the oil money. The heirs know they're right, because, well, after all, "that was our people . . . Daddy's always told us that."

Other Irrational Claims and Claimants

Just because the Humphries heirs' leaders are so colorful and the Humphries are so numerous, the reader should not get the impression that only the Humphries' heirs can make generation-skipping and equally outrageous and irrational claims to and about Spindletop. Far from it. There are other groups.

For example there is the King Heirs Association. In 1989 they had 400 members. They are the purported descendants of one William King who supposedly owned some Spindletop land at one time. Their 1989 leader, Delphine Arvin, said her husband's grandfather used to tell everyone the family had money down in Texas. For years no one paid any attention to grandfather "because he drank."

Then there is the "Meadors, Meaders, or Meadows" groups. These are not to be confused with the Ernest "Medders" family members. The Ernest Medders family's claims were based on Rubin Medders being the brother-in-law of Pelham Humphries. The Meadors, Meaders, or Meadows groups claim through one Ephraim Garonzik who purportedly had a 1907 deed from Anthony Lucas to some of Spindletop. Garonzik sold to James Meaders in 1911. The purportedly largest organized group of these Spindletop heirs was run by John Howard Meadows, who, in 1989, claimed to have an association of 20,000 members.

Along about 1982 James Clark and his cousin Dan Profitt, heirs of James Meaders (or Meadors or Meadows), thought it was time to recover their inheritance. Without tracing their legal footsteps through the appellate courts and the filing of new cases, suffice it to say that they kept the litigation alive until 1990. Their demand for money was far more reasonable than Brown Peregoy's 200 billion—Profitt and Clark wanted a mere 20 billion.

Dan Profitt is from Elsmere, Kentucky, and his cousin James Clark is from just across the Ohio River in nearby Cincinnati. In 1982 Profitt was an illustrator for a commercial advertising agency, Clark a roofing contractor. They acted as their own attorneys, handling their first go at litigation themselves. When their case was dismissed, Dan Profit was asked if he was going to give up. Mr. Profitt replied: "Its not a giving-up thing... I'm intending to get what is mine."

In 1994 Profitt still felt that way. He was then operating the "Puttin on the Ritz" limousine service. In a telephone interview, Mr. Profitt related the story that, during the pendency of their lawsuit, the oil companies offered them three billion dollars to settle. Profitt refused because, as he said, he wasn't going to be "bought off cheap." You got to like a man who believes in his case. I suppose we should pity a delusional man.

Clark and Profitt were faced with Judge Joe Fisher, just as Brown Peregoy was. They fared slightly better. At least they didn't have to pay the legal fees of the oil companies. Just like the Humphries heirs, Profitt was convinced they lost their cases because of a conspiracy. They just know they're right and their cause is just. After all, their daddy always told them so, too.

Daddy's Always
Told Us That

East Texas Idiosyncrasies

Having now determined, finally, that today's Humphries heirs have no legally enforceable claim to Spindletop and that they will never have a legally enforceable claim to Spindletop, no matter what they claim, we now turn our attention to the facts the heirs relied upon as the basis for their ninety years of litigation. Did they actually get cheated out of their rightful inheritance to Uncle Pel's land? If it hadn't been for those high-priced fancy Big Oil and McFaddin Family lawyers, and those bothersome little legal impediments like adverse possession, would the heirs of the '40s, '60s, and '80s *ever* have had a viable claim to Spindletop? To answer that question, we can't rely on what "Daddy's always told us." Daddy was wrong.

To actually learn about the true Humphries family in Texas, avoid Brown Peregoy's convoluted story and pathway. Instead, follow the trail first blazed by genealogist Jim Petty. Go not to Jefferson County or Beaumont, or even the Hawthorne house in Nacogdoches, but rather go just north to that area of East Texas which, until 1846, was part of Shelby and Marshall Counties: today's Panola County. One has but to look to understand. The answers are found in the public records still on file in the courthouses located in the county seat towns of Center, Marshall, and Carthage. Early census records contain a wealth of information, and even the ghost town of Pulaski plays an important role in sorting out and understanding the true Humphries family.

By the phrase "the true Humphries family" (notice the "f" in "family" is not capitalized), we mean those immediate family members actually related to the original owner of the Pelham Humphries league located in today's Jefferson County, Texas. This was the league acquired by virtue of the September 27, 1834, first class headright petition number 118, from the State of Coahuila and Texas, Mexico.

Before we begin sorting out the heirs' claims and identifying the true Humphries family, it may be useful to review again the various claims made by the Humphries heirs. The reader will recall Brown Peregoy's position: Pelham Humphries was a bounty hunter for the Mexican government; on September 5, 1835, Pelham was killed in a gunfight at the Hawthorne boardinghouse in Nacogdoches; he was killed on the orders of William McFaddin just when Pelham was about to arrest McFaddin for cattle rustling; McFaddin escaped arrest and laid claim to Pelham's league of land for his cattle operation; being unmarried and having no children of his own, Pelham's only heirs were his brother "William" Humphries, his sister Betsie Janie Humphries, and a half brother, Elisha V. Humphries Jr.; Peregoy and his group of heirs are the descendants of brother William Humphries; William's name was added to the original Spanish title as part of a fraud to take the land away from Pelham; William Humphries' true heirs never sold their interest in the Spindletop league and all deeds, including one to "W.P.H. McFaddin," are fraudulent; and in furtherance of the conspiracy to defraud the true Humphries heirs, the initials "W.P.H." in front of the McFaddin name stand for the adopted name "William Pelham Humphries" that McFaddin took to make people think he had a connection to Pelham Humphries.

While Peregoy's is the dominate story, probably because he has repeated it so often, there are variations on the theme. For example: Rubin Medders was Pelham's brother-in-law; Pelham was either married to Sudie Belle of South Carolina, or he was unmarried with no children, take your choice; in addition to Tennessee, some accounts have Pelham as originally from either Virginia, North or South Carolina, or Georgia; some say he was killed at the Hawthorne house by William English, instead of McFaddin, and on September 2, 1835, instead of September 5, 1835; others have his death in the 1860s or 1880s; and some say he was a horse thief and/or a killer himself, having killed men in either Hawkins or Carter County, Tennessee (or perhaps both). We'll begin there. Could Uncle Pel have been a killer?

Recognizing that it is almost impossible to prove a negative, that is, that Humphries *wasn't* a killer, especially 160 years later, we must accept the premise that he could have been. One hundred and eighty years before Rosine McFaddin Wilson killed Joe Perkins and made her own contribution to the Texas murder statistics, East Texas had plenty of bad hombres. After all, for years Texas, and especially East Texas, was a haven for men on the run for committing a crime elsewhere. At least part of the reason it was a haven was that, when the U.S. made the Louisiana Purchase in 1803, it also got a common border with Spain between what is now Texas and the state of Louisiana (and northward). But Spain and the U.S. couldn't agree on just where the actual border was, and in 1806 they sent their armies to fight about it.

To avoid bloodshed over a mere boundary, when only a narrow strip of land was in question, General James Wilkinson, the American military commander, said to his Mexican counterpart that, except for the point of honor, "the subject of our test is scarcely worth the blood of one brave man." General Wilkinson proposed a compromise. The idea was that they each pull their respective forces back behind the boundary line claimed by the other. The Spanish general, Symon de Herrera, agreed.

Thus, until the two governments reached a negotiated agreement thirteen years later, the two generals created an approximately fifty-mile-wide "neutral ground" between two waterways, the Sabine in today's Texas (claimed by the United States as the correct boundary) and the Arroyo Hondo in Louisiana (the line claimed by Spain). Since there was no law in the neutral ground, it became a natural haven for outlaws. That condition persisted for some time, even after the "official" end to the neutral ground in 1819, not unlike certain lawless neighborhoods in some of today's large cities.

In its southward flow through Texas, the Sabine River runs diagonally across Panola County from the northwest corner of the county to the southeast corner. Accordingly, nearly half of what became Panola County was included in the neutral ground and, presumably, was occupied by horse thieves, killers, cheats, and assorted other bad guys. Twenty years after the official end of the neutral ground, the area still played a role in the Regulators and Moderators war that ravaged East Texas for four years. And, as late as 1850, the inhabitants of Panola County were still wary of government people. Now part of the United States, the residents of Panola County apparently weren't too happy to have the U.S. census taker coming on their property and asking personal questions. Henry Swearingen, the assistant marshal census taker for that area of Panola County, had also been a Panola County deputy sheriff and the postmaster at Pulaski before taking on the assistant marshall census tasks. Apparently he was not well received by the residents. Mr. Swearingen felt compelled to note, in his certification of the 1850 Census that he had just taken, that it had been done "as near in acordance with my oath as I could do it, the people was hard to get along with."

Panola County was where the Humphries family lived. Since the Panola County area was his home, Humphries *could* have been one of them—both a killer and a horse thief. But, considering the available evidence, it's doubtful. That same evidence clears up the "Pelham" and "William" mystery. Pelham was not the brother of William.

Pelham or William

Pelham and William are one and the same person. The name "Pelham" appearing in the original petition was an aberration, a mistake. The controversy over whether there was a separate "Pelham" and "William" is easily resolved, even after 160 years, by examining four documents found filed on the public record: both a certificate of character and a bond for title[1] executed in San Augustine on September

---

1 This document is actually untitled. The term "bond for title" simply means an agreement to make title in the future on an executory or incomplete sale. It is used here since that clearly is the nature of the agreement and because that is how the agreement was described by the court in the case of *Humphries v. Texas Gulf Sulphur Company*, 393 F.2nd 69 (1968).

Bonds for title were commonly used in East Texas in connection with transfers of land in which the transferee had an interest, usually demonstrated by a headright certificate in their name, as did William

27, 1834; an affidavit and power of attorney executed in San Augustine on October 6, 1835; and the authorization for survey of a labor of land granted to William Humphries on February 16, 1838, by the Shelby County Board of Land Commissioners. These four documents are convincing evidence putting to rest the "Pelham" or "William" question.

The Documents of Saturday, September 27, 1834

Three documents relating to the land which ultimately became Spindletop were prepared on Saturday, September 27, 1834. The first one, written in Spanish, was actually done in three parts that Saturday: Humphries' petition; Commissioner Nixon's decree, permitting Humphries to proceed to the empresario for a report on the petition; and the report, or certification, that Humphries was indeed one of the colonists that Empresario Zavala introduced in fulfillment of his contract with the Supreme Government of the State. The report or certification section was completed by Anthony Hotchkiss, as "Atty of His Excellency, Lorenzo de Zavala."

The other two documents executed that September Saturday are a "certificate of character" for a *William Umphries*, and a bond for title between John Crippen and *Wm Umfries*, on the one hand, and Wm Inglish and Wyatt Hanks, on the other. These two documents are in English and are critical to resolving the Pelham or William question.

Humphries in this instance, but the land had not yet been patented or titled by the grovernment to the transferee.

Bond documents developed a more common format as time went on. For example, on March 1, 1841, Joseph Humphries executed a document entitled "Joseph Humphries Bond to Jas. T. Kelley" in which Joseph obligated himself, gave his bond, to repay James T. Kelley $5,000 (the purchase price) if he didn't make or cause to be made "a good Warranty Title" to a particular lot in the town of Pulaski, Texas. The administrators of Joseph's estate ended up making the good warranty title to Mr. Kelley.

To help understand the impact of the certificate and the bond, it is useful to compare them with Humphries' petition document prepared that same day. The petition is the document where the name "Pelham" first appears. Note the different spellings of the last name: "Umphres," "Humpries," and "Umfries," seen on the certificate of character and the bond agreement and "Humphries" on the petition. Clearly, in all three documents, the person actually writing down the last name was relying on a phonetic spelling of Humphries last name, as pronounced by Humphries himself, no doubt made more difficult by Humphries' accent or drawl. Just as clearly, and especially because of the commonly used and recognized letters "Wm" as an abbreviation for the name "William" and the correct spelling of the full name "William" in the certificate and the bond, the writer of the certificate of character and the bond *knew* that Humphries' first name was *William*.

The certificate of character and the bond were both prepared by Benjamin Lindsey. Mr. Lindsey was the alcalde or chief magistrate for the municipality of San Augustine. The municipality of San Augustine had just been created in March of 1834. It included some small portions of Newton and Jasper Counties, all of today's San Augustine, Sabine, and Shelby Counties, and all of that portion of today's Panola County that lay west of the Sabine River. This is the area where William Humphries and the rest of his family lived.

Although Lindsey does not expressly say it in the certificate, it is of course "implied" by the document itself that the person giving a "certificate of character" actually *knows* the individual he is commenting about. But Alcalde Lindsey eliminates all doubt on that subject when, in the text of the bond for title document, he says: "personally came and appeared John Crippen and Wm Humpries residents of said Municipality *whom I certify that I know.*" A statement which, of course, is perfectly consistent with the fact that William was a resident of Alcalde Lindsey's municipality. The bond for title of September 27, 1834, is convincing evidence of the true name as "William" for another compelling reason. It involved both a large amount of land and a large amount of money.

The bond recites that John Crippen and William Umphries were received as settlers and colonists in the colony of Zavala and that they each received an order of survey for a league of land. (Actually, although the order for survey became a part of the same petition document, and there was nothing further for Humphries to do, the order for survey of the Humphries league wasn't issued until Tuesday, September 30, in Nacogdoches.) Under the terms of the bond, Messrs. Hanks and Inglish paid Crippen and Humphries the immense sum (for 1834) of $1,999, each. In addition, Hanks and Inglish were also obligated to pay the costs of the survey and any other expenses.

The payment to Crippen and Humphries (and the expenses to be paid) were characterized as a loan payable upon the immediate *failure* of Crippen and Humphries to perform their own obligations under the bond for title. Here's how it worked. Along with the expense of getting the leagues surveyed, and the payments to Crippen and Humphries, Hanks and Inglish were to have the privilege of choosing where in Zavala's Colony the two leagues would be located. Crippen and Humphries were obligated to

> make or cause to be made a good title to the whole of
> said two Leagues of land excepting one thousand acres
> to the aforesaid William Inglish and Wiatt Hanks ... to
> be divided according to quantity and quality and value,
> as soon as the laws of the State will permit the
> same ... and to make the said title, in due form of
> law ... then and in that case the above first mentioned
> obligation of the payment of nineteen hundred and
> ninety nine dollars, to be void ....

Thus, in exchange for Crippen and Humphries "mak[ing] the said title," Hanks and Inglish paid nearly $4,000, plus the costs of two surveys. But, because the bureaucratic machinery necessary to obtain the "title" to the land involved acts still to be done by Crippen and Humphries in the future: "making... a good title," to protect their investment, Hanks and Inglish characterized the payments as a "loan," but with an important feature. The loan was to be discharged or satisfied, "the payment... to be void," when Crippen and Humphries followed through and did their part by making the title as required by the agreement.

It is readily apparent that the bond for title agreement is not a model of clarity. It was "inartfully drawn," as lawyers and judges are fond of saying when they are discussing confusing documents. Today, the agreement's lack of punctuation in critical parts would lead to lots of arguments over who was to get how many acres and how much was paid. Even though the document appears to say Crippen and Humphries got 1,999 "each," it may have been merely an expression that the two men were jointly liable for the full amount. And it could also be argued that Hanks and Inglish were to get title to all of both leagues, except 1,000 acres left for Crippen and 1,000 for Humphries (which would mean Hanks and Inglish were getting 6,856 acres for about 29 cents an acre, or 60 cents an acre if they paid both Crippen and Humphries). In any event, lots to argue about today. More lawyers' relief. But it really makes absolutely no difference to this discussion. Three things are perfectly clear from the bond for title agreement: it involved a lot of money; it involved the league of land that Humphries had just petitioned for that very same day; and Humphries was "William," not "Pelham."

It is well recognized in the human experience that when men enter a business transaction involving land and serious amounts of money, and especially where there is the possibility of some risk, they take great pains to *know* the party with whom they are dealing. Today we call that process "due diligence." It is most likely that, since they were all neighbors in the municipality of San Augustine, Hanks and Inglish already knew William Humphries and John Crippen. On the off chance that they didn't know them prior to this transaction, their "due diligence" requirement was met by acting through and under the auspices of Alcalde Benjamin Lindsey—who *did* know both Crippen and Wm Humphries.

Finally, Humphries' petition was prepared by a newly appointed land commissioner, George Antonio Nixon. Commissioner Nixon was one of three commissioners appointed in March of 1834 by the State of Coahuila and Texas to issue land titles to those qualifying colonists residing east of Austin's colonies. Nixon established his headquarters in Nacogdoches, outside the municipality of San Augustine. One of the other newly appointed land commissioners, Charles Taylor, had been a former alcalde of San Augustine and kept his headquarters in San Augustine. For reasons now unknown, Commissioner Taylor, who likely would have also *known* William Humphries, was not the commissioner in attendance at San Augustine on September 27, 1834. Commissioner Nixon, coming from Nacogdoches, who obviously did *not* know William Humphries, handled the land commissioner's business in San Augustine that Saturday. Thus the name "Pelham" was erroneously put on the petition by Nixon. Thereafter the name "Pelham" was carried forward on the Spanish follow-up documents, the survey field notes, the survey drawing itself, and, finally, the title of possession. It was this error in Humphries' title of possession that brought about the third document demonstrating that "Pelham" and "William" are one and the same man, the affidavit and power of attorney.

The Affidavit and Power of Attorney, October 6, 1835

As we now know, Wyatt Hanks and William Inglish had a legitimate financial interest in Humphries' league of land. When the title of possession was issued, someone (who could read) recognized that it inadvertently contained the name "Pelham" rather than the true name, "William." That was a problem.

To correct the error, four men appeared before Primary Judge Anthony Hotchkiss to give their affidavit on the subject. The reader will recall that Anthony Hotchkiss *knew* William Humphries. Hotchkiss, as the agent or "Atty of His Excellency, Lorenzo de Zavala," signed the section of Humphries' original petition that certified that Humphries was one of the colonists of Empressario Zavala, and thus entitled to the headright grant.

In their affidavit, the four men, E. Rains, Wm. Inglish, Johnathan Anderson, and Samuel McFadden, all swore "that they know Wm Umphries and that he obtained a title order of survey from George A. Nixon when in San Agustin [sic] in which his name was inserted Pilham Umphries in place of William...." Who were those men to swear that they "know Wm Humphries" and his petition to Commissioner Nixon? Well, we have already met William Inglish. Inglish certainly knew William Humphries from the agreement they entered into the day William did his petition. It is also safe to say that Samuel McFadden knew William Humphries. William was his brother-in-law (more on that soon). As to Johnathan Anderson and Emery Rains (for whom Rains County, Texas, was subsequently named), suffice it to say that all the available history records them as active, prominent, and respected members of the community.

The affidavit is followed by the power of attorney we saw earlier:

> I do hereby constitute and appoint Wm. Inglish my
> agent to take a title out of the Commissioners office in

Nacogdoches and to alter from Pilham to William my
true and propper name San Agustin Oct 6. 1835

his

William x Umphreys

mark

As we also learned earlier, for whatever reason, the *title of
possession* was not changed to William, his "true and propper
name." Instead, it was Humphries' original *petition* for the
league that was altered to read "William" instead of "Pelham." Considering the aggressively litigious nature of the
Humphries heirs and their lawyers, the " . . . eagerness of the
plaintiffs and their lawyer to pursue this case" as Judge Cobb
described it when he fined Peregoy and Max Wilson almost
$116,000, it most likely would have made no difference in
the number of lawsuits they brought.

Authorization for Survey Dated February 16, 1838

The final document showing that "Pelham" and "William" are the same person, is the Board of Land
Commissioners' authorization for survey of one labor of
land for William Humphries on February 16, 1838, certificate number 256, first class file number 117. To understand
the significance of this document, we must recall that under
the Mexican colonization laws, qualified colonists that were
heads of families were entitled to a *first class headright*, consisting of both a league and a labor of land. As we have just
seen, William Humphries was granted the *league* portion of
his first class headright entitlement by Commissioner Nixon
through Humphries' September 27, 1834 petition. That left
him still entitled to the grant of a *labor* of land. But important Texas historical events intervened for a time.

As we saw earlier in the *Glover* case, in November of 1835
the Independent Republic of Texas assumed sovereignty.
That same month the Mexican land office (along with all

the other Mexican government offices) was closed. But the new constitution of the Republic of Texas provided for recognition of those land grants made under the earlier Mexican law. In fact, the constitution provided that heads of families who arrived in Texas prior to March 2, 1836, the date of the declaration of independence of the Republic of Texas, were entitled to the same first class headright league and labor previously provided under the empressario system. On February 1, 1838, the General Land Office of the Independent Republic of Texas opened. William Humphries petitioned for his remaining labor of land two weeks later.

The Board of Land Commissioners' authorization for survey (and the subsequent grant of the labor) is the official government recognition that the Humphries who received the league of land under petition 118 is the same Humphries —William—who now completed his first class headright grant by the authorization for survey of the labor of land. William located his labor of land in what became today's southeastern section of Panola County, close to the Sabine, right next to his in-laws and close to the rest of his family.

Having established that William and Pelham are one and the same person, it's time to meet the rest of his family. We'll begin with his father, Joseph Humphries.

Joseph Humphries

Joseph Humphries was an entrepreneur. In addition to farming, Joseph operated a ferry on the Sabine River at a place called Humphries Bluff. Humphries Bluff (formerly known as Walnut Bluff because of its towering black walnut trees) was so named because of Joseph Humphries' ferry operation and the high, bluff-like riverbanks found there. Humphries Bluff is located about three miles south of where today's Highway 79 crosses the Sabine just outside of Carthage, Texas. In those early days the Sabine River was navigable from its Gulf of Mexico entrance at Sabine Pass, through Sabine Lake, and northward to at least Humphries Bluff.

In 1838 the Humphries Bluff area along the Sabine was geographically and politically located in the remote northern portion of the then vast Shelby County. Because of their remoteness from the seat of government, the people living in that area wanted their own county. On April 7, 1838, they petitioned the Senate and House of Representatives of the Republic of Texas, "in Congress assembled," as follows:

> Your petitioners would respectfully represent to your honorable body that we reside in a part of the county so remote from the county site [seat] that it is inconvenient for us, very frequently impossible, to attend to the calls of our country without leaving our farms uncultivated or our families at the mercy of reckless and hostile savages, who are continuously committing depredations on our frontier and consequently render it unsafe for us to leave our homes for any length of time. Moreover we are unorganized either in a civil or military capacity and for the purpose of obviating all these difficulties we have thought proper to respectfully demand at your hands a new county as our constitutional right . . . .

The petition then went on to describe the section of Shelby County that they desired to be included in the new county.

Essentially, they described the area from the 32nd parallel on the Sabine, north to Caddo Lake, west along the Big Cyprus to the "Cherokee or military crossing," then south to the Sabine, and back down the river to the beginning. Thus the new county was to include only land east of the Sabine. The petition was signed by 151 men, all certified as residing in the area the new county would comprise. Joseph Humphries was one of the signers of the petition. Although William's labor was only about twelve miles from Humphries Bluff, William was on the west side of the Sabine, not the east, and thus not in the "new" county area. That fact probably accounts for William not joining his

97

father in signing the petition. But William could still help in his father Joseph's new venture: Joseph was about to become a real estate developer.

Joseph was convinced that Humphries Bluff could be the site of the county seat of the new county, and he took positive steps to acquire ownership of the land. In February of 1838 the Board of Land Commissioners for Shelby County had issued a headright certificate for the third part of a league of land to Amos Strickland as the administrator of the estate of Benjamin Strickland. The petition for a new county was signed April 7, 1838. On May 11 Amos Strickland assigned the headright certificate to William Humphries, and thereafter William assigned it to his father, Joseph. The assignment from William to Joseph was attested to by C.H. McClure.

Joseph Humphries had struck a deal with Mr. McClure. Joseph needed substantial surveying work done in his new venture. Chuancy McClure was an authorized surveyor for Shelby County. In return for one-half of the Benjamin Strickland survey, McClure paid Joseph Humphries $10,000 (some portion of which may have been sweat equity for his survey work) and undertook the surveying work on the project.

On June 11, Joseph acquired another 1,280 acres through obtaining a Class 2 certificate on a portion of his own headright entitlement.[2] On August 20, Joseph put McClure

---

2   Joseph only obtained a Class 2 certificate for 1280 acres because when he appeared before the Board of Land Commissioners for the County of Shelby on June 11, 1838, he was unable to prove up his residency in Texas prior to March 2, 1836, the date of of Texas' Declaration of Independence. On June 26, 1841, now in Harrison County, Joseph filed a petition with Judge Hansford (who in less than a month will have his hands full with the Regulators and the trial of Charles Jackson). Joseph's petition says he is entitled to a full league and labor, and he can now present his proof. He asks for the additional 3,341 acres he deems himself entitled to under the law. After dealing with the Charles Jackson matter in July, Judge

to work and had this land surveyed and located on the west side of the Sabine, across from Humphries Bluff.[3] Then, on September 12, McClure located the Benjamin Strickland survey on the east bank of the Sabine at Humphries' Bluff—in the names of C.H. McClure and Joseph Humphries. Thus, before 1838 ended, Joseph had acquired ownership of all the land at Humphries Bluff, on both sides of the river. There, on a triangle of land formed by the river bends and a creek, he founded the town of Pulaski.

Surveyor McClure laid out the town in a grid, with Main Street running east and west, while Water and River Streets ran north and south, parallel with each other. Joseph built a log courthouse and sold town lots. The petition for the new county was successful, and, on January 29, 1839, the new county of Harrison was created. Pulaski became the county seat.

In 1840 Joseph acquired an interest in even more property adjoining Pulaski. The land immediately to the south of Joseph's and McClure's third of a league was occupied and claimed by Joseph's friend David McHeard. Joseph was the chief beneficiary and named executor of David McHeard's last will and testament. In February of 1840, following McHeard's death, Joseph petitioned for letters of admini-

---

Hansford held a jury trial on Joseph's claim during the September term. The jury found Joseph entitled to the additional land on September 10, 1841.

3   As is clear from a glance at the General Land Office map of Panola County, this land was not patented in Joseph Humphries name. Joseph sold fifty acres of it to James Kelley, giving his bond to make a title on March 15, 1841. On June 30, 1846, Joseph's widow, Sarah, along with S.P. January serving as administratrix and administrator of Joseph's estate, with the approval of the probate court, fulfilled Joseph's obligation under his bond and made a title to Kelley. Apparently the original survey was lost, and Kelley had it surveyed again. Exactly what happened after that is somewhat confusing. In 1910 this land on the west side of the Sabine, across from Humphries Bluff, now covered with conflicting patents, was being contested by Mrs. Pauline Baugh, who claimed title by inheritance through Kelley.

stration. In July 1840, after posting the required bond, Joseph's petition was granted, and he had more property to work with at Pulaski.

Panola County survey map: McFadden/Wm. Humphries surveys.

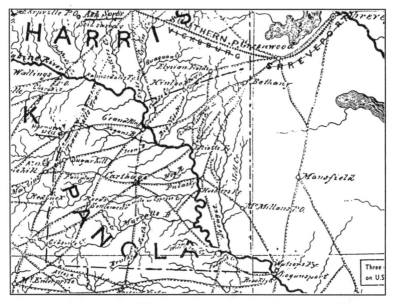

Panola County map, 1850 (town of Pulaski on east bank of Sabine River).
Map courtesy *Panola County History*.

Sabine River out of its banks. Photo courtesy *Panola County History*.

Pulaski is unique because it served, temporarily, as the county seats for both Harrison and Panola Counties—temporarily because Texas law requires a county seat to be centrally located within the county. Pulaski was obviously not centrally located in Harrison County, and, in 1842, Marshall became the county seat. After the creation of Panola County from parts of Shelby and Harrison in 1846, Pulaski served as Panola's county seat for two years until it lost out to centrally located Carthage.

On July 16, 1841, Pulaski, then serving as the county seat for Harrison County, was the site of a notorious murder trial fiasco in the early stages of the Regulators and Moderators war (more on that soon).

After Pulaski lost its county seat connections, it continued to thrive for a time. With useable roads so scarce, commerce on the river was still important. Joseph's Ferry continued to do business, although the county set the ferriage rates:

> Man and horse (when river was within banks) 10 cents, (when out of banks 20 cents); Wagon crossing (when river in banks) 50 cents, (when out of banks $1.00); Carriage crossing, 25 cents; Footman crossing, 5 cents; Loose Horses or Cattle, 5 for 3 cents.

Texas became part of the United States on December 29, 1845. A year later, a U.S. post office was opened at Pulaski. Henry Swearingen, the gentleman we saw serving as the assistant marshal for the 1850 Census, was the first postmaster.

Eventually, though, sometime after the Civil War, Pulaski faded from existence and even from sight. Although a historical marker was erected in 1936, even the marker is hard to find after years of disuse, new growth, and river meanderings. At first blush, Joseph would seem to have done all right with his Pulaski development project. He had land sales of $21,000 over about a two-year period. But, despite those sales, like many of today's land developers, when Joseph died in the spring of 1842, he was in debt. Joseph Humphries was survived by a large family, and this is a good time to meet the wife and kids.

Meet the Family

Joseph Humphries had two wives. By the first he was the father of sons William and George and daughter Tenia, sometimes seen spelled as "Tenny." While we do not know the name of his first wife, his second wife was the former Sarah Wilkerson. Sarah bore him four children; Thomas, Riley, Mary, and Philip. The 1850 Census shows Mary, at 18, Riley 17, and Philip 14 all living at home with Sarah. Thomas, at that time about 24 years old, was apparently living elsewhere.

Joseph's oldest son William married Mary McFadden. Like many girls named Mary in those days, she was nick-named "Polly." This is a good time to point out that Polly's family, the Panola County McFaddens,[4] are completely un-related to the Jefferson County "W.P.H." and Rosine McFaddins. There is no relationship whatsoever. (For one thing, the Panola County McFaddens don't capitalize the "F" in family.) The initials "W.P.H." stand for "William Perry Herring." "William" is his father's given name, and "Perry" and "Herring" are other family names. In fact, W.P.H. McFaddin was born February 5, 1856, twenty years after Brown Peregoy says he shot "Pelham" at the Hawthorne house in Nacogdoches. Peregoy's claim on that issue is patently absurd.

William and Polly had seven children together. In the 1850 Census, since Polly is listed as a widow, we know that

---

4   The Panola County McFadden name is seen spelled both "McFaddin" and "McFadden." The "en" spelling will be used to try to avoid confusion with the Jefferson County "in" McFaddin's.

William has died. We also learn the names and ages of William and Polly's children: Jane 15, Tina 13, Amanda (sometimes called "Mandy") 12, Jonathan 10, Andrew (also called "Holland") 9, Polly 8, and Mahaley (sometimes seen spelled as Mahley or Mahala) 4 years old.

Joseph's son George died unmarried, at least in the eyes of the Board of Land Commissioners. His headright certificate for a third of a league, the entitlement of an otherwise qualified but single man, was issued to the administratrix of his estate, Elizabeth Nail, on February 22, 1838. It too is located in today's Panola County, a few miles north and slightly west of William's labor. While there were no known children as a result, George clearly had a relationship with Elizabeth that the rest of the family treated as marriage. Elizabeth received grants of property equal to the other children of Joseph. Elizabeth is also seen as a creditor in Joseph Humphries' estate, but no amount owed is listed.

William and George's full sister Tenny Humphries married Joe Story. They had a large family. The 1850 and 1860 census records identify nine children: Joseph, Matilda, William, Robert, Felena, Alexander, Ellen, Thomas, and Layla.

Thomas Humphries, Joseph's son by his second wife, married Mary Witherspoon on December 26, 1853. From the Panola County public records we learn that a few years before he married Mary, Thomas had sold all of his interest in his father's estate, "if any," to a neighbor, George Nippert for $100. If Nippert didn't have to bring a lawsuit to perfect his interest, Thomas was to get an additional $35.

The 1870 Census records show Thomas and Mary with three children: 14-year-old Elizabeth, 7-year-old Thomas, and 6-year-old Margaret. The 1880 Census shows him at age 54 and now married to 31-year-old "Jane." Their children are listed as William T, age 16 (who was not accounted for in the 1870 Census when he would have been 5 or 6 years old); Margaret, now 15, and Bula, age one year.

Thomas Humphries' obituary shows he died on October 22, 1889, still living in Panola County near McDaniel's ferry. Thomas' brothers Philip and Riley, and for that matter his sister Mary, all died without issue or surviving spouse.

Census records for 1850 showing Polly Humphries and Sarah Humphries.

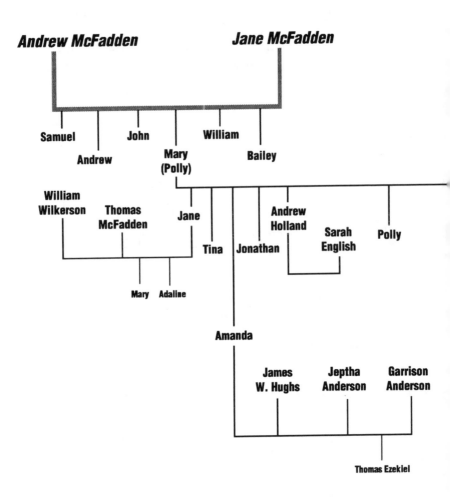

Humphries family tree

Note: The spelling of many of the names often varies from document to document, and from what we may consider the common spelling of otherwise familiar names. These inconsistences appear because the choice of spelling was often left to the whim of the scrivener when the person giving his name was illiterate and could neither spell it for the scrivener, nor verify that it was recorded correctly. The accent or drawl of the person giving his name probably didn't help matters.

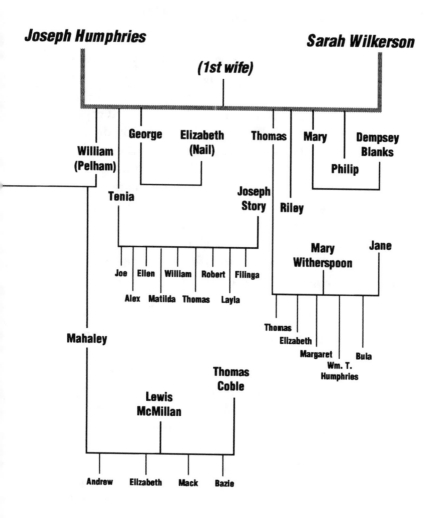

Brown Peregoy: Wrong Again

Looking now at the immediate family we just identified, we see that Brown Peregoy was wrong again. First there was no separate Pelham; there was no sister named "Betsie Janie;" and there was no half brother named "Elisha V. Humphries Jr." There wasn't even an "Elisha V. Humphries Sr." Moreover, since there was no Pelham, he couldn't have been killed at the Hawthorne house, or any other house in 1835. And it couldn't have been William who was killed in 1835 because, not only did he assign the Benjamin Strickland headright certificate over to his father in 1838, in 1842 he succeeded his father as administrator of the David McHeard estate probated in Harrison County, and he was alive at least until 1845 or '46, to father his youngest daughter Mahaly. Brown didn't get anything right. But he wasn't the only wrong one.

The claim that "Rubin Medders" was the brother-in-law of Pelham Humphries is bogus too. Once again, there was no Pelham. The only possible brother-in-law that theoretically could have been an heir to William was Joseph Story, Tenny's husband, not Rubin Medders. Ernest and Margaret never, ever, in their wildest dreams, had a chance at the Spindletop fortune. That's a critical pin that Mr. Weir would never have gotten in the dish. So much for all the Medders claims.

Nor was there any "Sudie Belle," and, although it really makes no difference what state Humphries came from, just for the record, Tennessee is where the real ones said they were from. All of those outrageous lineage claims are bogus. But William did have some interesting in-laws.

Polly Humphries' family were McFaddens. They all lived in the same neighborhood in today's southern Panola County. The McFaddens even show up on the first census of Texas, 1829-1836. As is shown on the General Land Office maps, William and Polly located William's labor of land in southern Panola County just west of the Sabine and adjoining Polly's parents Andrew and Jane McFadden's headright. McFadden Creek runs through Andrew McFadden's headright. During the Regulator and Moderator war, this was Moderator country.

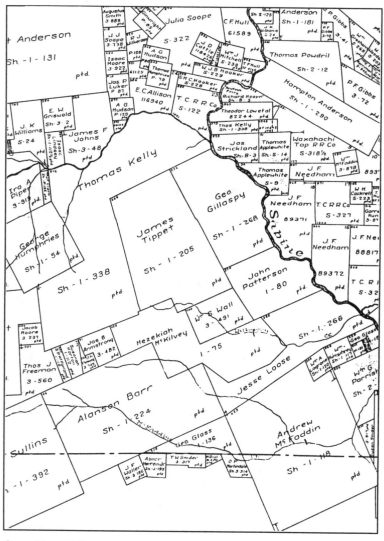

General Land Office map of Panola County

Regulators, Moderators, and McFaddens

Most accounts of the Regulator and Moderator war cite a 1839 dispute between Alfred George and Joseph Goodbread as its catalyst. It seems George sold a slave to Goodbread and was paid with headright certificates to thousands of acres. When the certificates were declared fraudulent by the Board of Land Commissioners, George wanted his slave back. Goodbread refused, and George stole the slave and hid him in the woods. Goodbread retaliated.

George was running for sheriff of Shelby County at that time, and Goodbread made the stolen slave matter public hoping to cause George to lose the election. That annoyed George. Knowing that in the past Goodbread and a certain Charles W. Jackson had had a bitter dispute between them, though now supposedly settled, George went to Jackson and told him that Goodbread intended to kill Jackson the next time he saw him.

Texans don't take threats well, and from all accounts Jackson was one bad character. Jackson went to Shelbyville, found Goodbread, unarmed, and shot him dead. He then went to the justice of the peace.

In those early days, especially in sparsely populated rural areas, courts were not in session daily. The "circuit" courts were so named because the judges regularly traveled from place to place, attending to the local legal business by holding scheduled sessions of court within the "circuit." The regularly scheduled sessions of court were called "terms." For special cases, "a special term" could be scheduled.

The day Jackson killed Goodbread, court was not in session in Shelby County. Jackson posted a $200 bond with the justice of the peace, conditioned on his appearance at the next term of court. George won the election for sheriff and enjoyed the value of the slave without further hindrance from the now dead Goodbread.

Jackson later learned that he had been indicted for first degree murder, just as Rosine McFaddin was indicted 145 years later in Jefferson County. And, just like Lum Hawthorn's strategy for Rosine, Jackson wanted a change of venue. He knew that Goodbread had many friends in Shelby County that would serve on a jury or testify against him. He managed to get the trial moved to Pulaski, the county seat of newly formed Harrison County. However, when he granted the change of venue, the judge instructed the sheriff to hold Jackson in jail, without bond, for a special court term at Pulaski. When Sheriff George complained that the jail was so run-down it couldn't hold prisoners, the judge instructed him to keep the prisoner under guard. When the judge left to continue on his circuit, George let Jackson out.

Jackson still had the problem of men testifying against him. He knew that Goodbread also had lots of friends in what had recently been northern Shelby County, now Harrison County, the location of the trial. Among Goodbread's friends were James "Tiger Jim" Strickland and two of Polly Humphries' brothers, William and Bailey McFadden. (Some accounts list the two brothers as William and John McFadden.)

To counteract the influence of the friends of Goodbread, Jackson organized a band of bad characters, some still occupying the "piney woods" in the former neutral ground. They called themselves "Regulators." The Regulators were ostensibly formed to bring law and order to the area, and some naive but otherwise upright men may have joined, too. In the beginning, what the Regulators actually did was take action to prevent the friends of Goodbread from testifying against Jackson. For example, seeking to intimidate them, the Regulators rode to the area of McFadden Creek on Andrew McFadden's survey, looking for Goodbread's friends Tiger Jim Strickland and the McFadden brothers.

Along the way they found and horsewhipped Squire Humphries (no relation to the Joseph and William Humphries family).[5] When they didn't find Strickland and the McFaddens at home, Jackson and his band of Regulators turned their families out into the cold and burned their homes and all their possessions. That was a foolhardy act.

McFadden Creek

---

5   Squire Humphries was the son of another William Humphries. Squires' father died in 1830. Samuel Strickland was the administrator of his estate and later married his widow. Squire had two sisters: Susan Humphries who married Wade Hampton West, and Nancy Humphries who, although they hadn't married, lived with a man named Robinson who was later killed by the Moderators. Although Nancy and Robinson purportedly had some children together, she died without an heir. Susan and Hampton West had ten children. There is no connection between this Humphries family and the family of Joseph Humphries.

Road through McFadden survey near McFadden Creek.

Family, hearth, and home are sacrosanct. There is a predictable response to such an outrage to a man's home and family. Just as even a small dog will attack people and larger animals to protect his master's home and property, a man will act to protect his home and family, even against overwhelming odds. While the social scientists have given this basic phenomenon the fancy label "territorial behavior," it has been commonly observed in the ordinary behavior of both man and animals. One might suspect that Jackson had somehow missed that little life experience lesson or thought himself so powerful that he could ignore it. Strickland and the McFaddens swore vengeance, and they got it.

This was something they needed to do with their own hands. Especially in areas where there is no effective law enforcement presence, but often even when there is, Texans are prone to take things into their own hands anyway. On "territorial" issues such as were motivating Tiger Jim and the McFaddens, *all* men tend to respond personally. But they would have to bide their time and carefully choose when and where to exact their vengeance. Jackson kept himself surrounded with a large force of heavily armed men. Their time would come. Meanwhile, in opposition to the Regulators, a force calling themselves "Moderators" began to assemble.

Jackson's trial was set for a special term of court in July 1841, in the courthouse Joseph Humphries helped build in Pulaski. To assure his success, the supposed prisoner Jackson came to court armed with a rifle and a pistol. He was escorted by an armed guard of about twenty men—but they were his own Regulators. At the courthouse they were joined by another large group of Regulators. All together, Jackson had about one hundred armed supporters present.

After fining the sheriff for allowing his prisoner to come to court armed, Judge Hansford spent the remainder of the day picking a jury with the trial to begin the next morning. But the Regulators' strong show of force had the desired effect on the judge. That night he wrote an order to the sheriff:

> Being unwilling to risk my person in the courthouse any longer when I see myself surrounded by bravos and hired assassins and no longer left free to preside as an impartial judge, at the special term of the court, called for the trial of Charles W. Jackson, I order you to adjourn court tomorrow at 8 o'clock by proclamation with day. From your hand at the regular term I shall expect the prisoner. You will keep the prisoner causing him to be securely ironed, and keeping a strong guard until delivered by the course of laws.

The strong show of force had the desired effect on Sheriff George and the prosecutor too. Jackson and his Regulators refused to be "adjourned" and held a farce of a trial themselves. Jackson's lawyer lectured the jury on the rights of an accused person, the prosecutor refused to present his case, the jury voted for acquittal, and Jackson and his Regulators went home in triumph.

Jackson grew too confident in his newfound power with the Regulators. Tiger Jim and the McFadden brothers found their chance for retribution. Jackson and just one other man, Lofer, were returning from Logansport to Shelbyville. Tiger Jim, the McFaddens, Squire Humphries, and others ambushed Jackson at the fork in the old Shelbyville and Nacogdoches road. Strickland and the McFadden brothers got their vengeance when Jackson and Lofer died in a hail of their gunfire. In the long run, though, this one went to the Regulators.

The Regulator forces were quite strong at this point, and the main body of Moderators were effectively confined to the northern sections of Shelby and on into new adjoining Harrison County. After killing Jackson and Lofer, the McFadden brothers first went to the home of John McFadden. The Moderators rallied to protect them, but it was still too dangerous for their families. The McFaddens hoped to avoid capture by going south and west.

Furious that Jackson had been killed, the Regulators chose Charles W. Moorman as their new leader and determined to capture Jackson's killers. Sheriff George had absented himself from Shelby—fled to Nacogdoches in fear of his life, is how some historians describe it—and his deputy, John Middleton, was in charge. When they learned that the McFadden brothers were moving away from their northern strongholds, Middleton "deputized" eight Regulators, including Moorman, and they started after the McFaddens.

After an arduous journey, three McFadden brothers, William, Bailey, and younger brother Andrew, were caught near the town of Montgomery in early October of 1841. The Regulators took them back to Shelbyville where the citizens, all 174 of them, voted for hanging. Henry Reynolds felt they shouldn't hang Andrew, a boy of about fourteen, and convinced the crowd to spare him, but Andrew had to watch his two older brothers die. One account reports the younger McFadden brother also suffered twenty strikes with a blackjack.[6]

The hangings took place in the public square at Shelbyville immediately following the vote and Reynolds' plea to spare the younger McFadden. The Regulators also hung Squire Humphries. Other than the killing of Jackson and Lofer, no Regulator was ever held accountable for the burning of the Strickland and McFadden homes.

Historians are careful to point out that not all of the citizens in the affected areas either willingly participated in or countenanced the Regulators' and Moderators' actions. But it was hard not to take sides. Often citizens were forced by one group of armed men or another to declare whom they were for—the Moderators or the Regulators. Woe be it to the man who gave the wrong answer. Horsewhipping them was popular. There were also vicious battles between the two warring groups.

The Regulators evolved to be the dominate force, with the Moderators still trying to end the Regulators' siege of the country. Moorman's power grew and with it, his political aspirations. And, as we all know, power corrupts. When Moorman drew up a list of twenty-five citizens that he demanded leave the area or be executed, it was finally too much. Outraged citizens, who had otherwise managed to stay neutral, joined the Moderators, and the stage was set for large-scale carnage. The government finally had to act.

President Houston called in 600 militia men. Holding that big stick, Houston got their attention and was able to

---

6   Accounts of which McFaddens were hung and which McFadden was spared differ. According to the 1836 Census, by the time of the 1841 hangings, William McFadden would have been approximately 34 or 35, Bailey 22 or 23, and John 17 or 18, surely all old enough to hang. Andrew, who should have been either 14 or 15, is the one McFadden brother young enough to be spared with a mere twenty blackjack strikes.

personally mediate the differences between the two factions. Thus, in 1844, Sam Houston himself ended a reign of terror which lasted four years and took the lives of fifty men, including two of Polly Humphries' brothers.

The Heirs of William Humphries

William Humphries died without a will, "intestate" as the lawyers like to say. Even when there is no will, a person's "estate," his property, is still distributed to his heirs. But in such a case, the distribution—who gets what—is governed by the laws of descent and distribution, instead of the plan for distribution of his property a deceased person may have wanted. If he didn't make out a will, it goes to his "heirs at law."

The Texas laws of descent and distribution have another important feature. Whenever a person dies intestate, all of his property vests immediately in his heirs at law. However, the property of the estate, even though it is now in the hands of the heirs at law, is still liable to be sold for payment of any debts of the estate.

There was no probate estate opened for William. That's because there was no work for an administrator to do. This tells us that, unlike his father, William either wasn't in debt or at least wasn't significantly in debt. We know that because a creditor could have had an estate opened to have the court compel the sale of William's property to satisfy a legitimate debt. And we know that William had property. So, the heirs at law got it all.

Who were William's "heirs at law?" That is a critical question to the followers of Brown Peregoy and the rest of the throng of people claiming to be "Humphries heirs." To answer it we again look to the factual circumstances and the law. When William died without a will, since he was survived by both a spouse and lineal descendants and since

117

the property of the estate was acquired during the marriage to the surviving spouse, the law of descent and distribution provided that by law Polly was to get one-half of the estate property and the lineal descendants the other half. Of course "lineal descendants" simply means the children and grandchildren of William Humphries. As we learned from the 1850 Census, when William died he and Polly had seven little lineal descendants: Jane, Tina, Amanda, Jonathan, Andrew, Polly, and Mahaley. Thus, under the law, since William had both a surviving spouse and children, *all* of his estate transferred to Polly and the kids, and to them alone. That is an important concept.

There are circumstances in which an intestate's collateral kin, that is, William's parents, his brothers and sisters, even his uncles and aunts, his grandparents on both sides, and their children and grandchildren, *could* have been William's heirs at law, but only if he died with no spouse or children. Factually, we know that was not the case. William died with Polly and the kids surviving him. Thus all of William's property belonged to Polly and the kids. It vested in them instantly upon his death.

Polly

In 1853 Polly petitioned for guardianship of the "heirs of William Humphries," stating that his headright in Panola County, the 177-acre labor, needed to be sold for their support. The court granted Polly's petition for letters of guardianship and appointed James T. Kelley, Andrew Robe, and Stephen L. Davis appraisers of the minors' estate. On December 14, 1854, Texas Governor E.M. Pease granted title to William's Panola County headright labor to "William Humphries, his heirs and assigns." The next day the title was delivered to James Rowe.

Polly Humphries died intestate in about 1855. From a petition for "letters of guardianship for the minor children as the heirs of William Humphries and Polly Humphries," filed by Polly's son-in-law, Thomas J. McFadden (who was both Jane's husband and her cousin), we learn that of Polly's seven children recorded in the 1850 Census, only four, Jane now 20, 17-year-old Amanda, 14-year-old Andrew, and 9-year-old Mahaley, had survived.

When Polly died, her estate, including all remaining property that she had inherited upon the death of her husband William, immediately vested in her heirs at law, Jane, Amanda, Andrew, and Mahaley, the surviving children.

Upon the deaths of his daughters Tina and Polly and his son Jonathan, that fraction of William's property which had vested in them on William's death either partially vested in their mother, if she survived them, and/or in their surviving brother and sisters. In any event, by 1855 all of the remaining property of the William Humphries estate was now vested in Jane, Amanda, Andrew, and Mahaley. No one else. No other person was entitled to a blessed thing from the property of William Humphries.

Any legitimate heirship claim to any property owned by William Humphries during his lifetime had to be made by someone claiming through those four children. Whatever property William and Polly owned at the time of their deaths, their surviving children now owned.

Before we revisit the children and grandchildren, and just because it's fun, let's take a peek at what William and Polly Humphries' own family thought their property consisted of in 1855. Keep in mind the fact that this bit of information comes from the people closest in time and the ones most likely to have accurate knowledge on the subject. Son-in-law Thomas McFadden's petition for guardianship identifies the property as

an interest as heirs of their mother, the said Polly Humphries decd in one third of a League of Land the Head Right of David Mchard situated in Panola County, also an interest in the Estate of their Grand Mother, To

wit the Estate of Jane McFadden decd, amt not known.
Also an interest in the Estate of Samuel McFadden
decd, who is the uncle of said minors amt of interest
unknown.

Because the focus of our inquiry is Spindletop, notice
that, at this early date, 1855, when the people with the
most knowledge would have had the best opportunity to
know about all of the property owned by William and Polly,
there is no mention of William's headright league of land
down in Jefferson County. The most logical and likely reason
for that, of course, is that William had disposed of the entire
Jefferson County league *before* he died. The property that
became Spindletop isn't mentioned as property of William's
children because William didn't own it when he died. It's
time now to revisit the children and grandchildren.

Jane

Sometime between 1850 and October 1855, Jane Humphries, William and Polly's oldest child, married her cousin,
Thomas J. McFadden. As we now know, Polly died in about
1855. Five years later, the 1860 Census records show that
Jane and Thomas, now the guardian of the minor Humphries children, also have two children of their own, five-
year-old Mary and two-year-old Adaline. Amanda, Holland,
and Mahaley are shown living with Jane and Thomas.

In 1880, an action to recover the property that would
years later become famous as "Spindletop," suit No. 682,
Heirs of William Humphries vs H.E. Simpson *et al.*, was
filed in the District Court of Jefferson County. This is the
first of the dozens of Humphries heirs' cases that will be
filed over the next 100 years, claiming ownership of the
Pelham Humphries league. Jane, Mahaley, and Amanda's
son Thomas Anderson are plaintiffs since "being informed"
they were the rightful owners of the Jefferson County land.

The *et al.* defendants included the heirs of William English and Steven Dozier.

To pay the legal fees for her portion of the lawsuit, on August 10, 1880, Jane, as an heir at law to the estate of William Humphries and "being informed that there is a body of land in Jefferson County, Texas, rightfully belonging to us," deeded to attorneys Tom J. Russell, J.W. Hays, and T.E. Boren, one-half of the Jefferson County land belonging to her as the heir of William Humphries. It's a safe bet that these attorneys "informed" the "rightful" owners.

Thomas E. Boren, one of Jane's and Mahaley's lawyers. Photo from *Panola County History.*

In the body of the deed, Jane's sister Mahaley, who was joined by her husband, Thomas Coble, was also shown to be deeding one-half of her interest in the land for legal fees. But neither Mahaley nor her husband actually signed that deed. Therefore, it was not effective as to Mahaley's interest.

Since Jane was not joined by her husband, Thomas McFadden, in the deed to Russell and the others, apparently he had died by that time. The next few years were unpleasant for Jane.

Through a February 21, 1883 deed from Jane, now Jane Wilkerson, we learn more about her family situation:

> I Jane Wilkerson, a daughter, and heir at law of William and Mary Humphries, deceased; and formerly the wife of Thomas McFadden, deceased; and later the wife of William Wilkerson . . . but who has later still abandoned me, taking with him, disposing of and appropriating to himself all community property, of the marriage; and all his separate property, and leaving the country, went to parts unknown, and left me in destitute circumstances . . . .

Who needs that at age forty-eight? William Wilkerson, by the way, may have been a stepcousin, if there is such a thing. Joseph Humphries' second wife, Sarah, was a Wilkerson.

In this 1883 deed Jane conveys all of her remaining right, title, and interest in her father's Jefferson County league to J.G. Hazlewood for $125. In this deed the property is more specifically identified as the same land that was granted to Pelham Humpries by George Antonio Nixon on February 14, 1835.

"J.G." Hazelwood purchased the last of Jane's interest in the Humphries league.

By the end of December 1883, suit No. 682 is partially settled by our then young friend, twenty-seven-year-old W.P.H. McFaddin, who purchased all of the ownership interest of Jane, Mahaley, and Thomas Anderson, the only child of the now deceased Amanda, as well as some of the defendants' ownership interests.

We need not trouble ourselves with sorting this business out, but it is still curious, since Jane had deeded half of her interest in the land to attorneys Russell, Hays, and Boren in 1880 and then all of her remaining interest in the land to Hazelwood in February of 1883, what did she have left for W.P.H. to purchase in December of 1883? To further complicate that issue, W.P.H.'s $800 payment for Jane's portion was paid one-half to "Jane McFadden or her Atty of record Tom J. Russell ... and the other four hundred to the firm of O'Brian & John. ... " O'Brian & John represented many of the defendants. Who knows, perhaps O'Brian & John represented Mr. Hazelwood, too, and they were just insuring that he got paid for what he purchased from Jane. But don't worry about Mr. Hazelwood. On Christmas day 1883 Hazelwood deeded his interest in the land to W.P.H. McFaddin for $125, exactly what he paid Jane. (Remember earlier we saw Rosine describe her grandfather, W.P.H., as an "empire builder," and she said: "Acquiring land was his art, and he always said that all he wanted was what was his and what was next to it." Apparently W.P.H., the artist, didn't let a little thing like Christmas get in the way of business.)

We leave Jane now, knowing that all of the interest, if any, that she may have had in the "Pelham Humphries league" was deeded away to her lawyers, to Mr. Hazelwood, and if anything was left, to W.P.H. McFaddin, all before her death. There was nothing left for any of *her* lineal descendants to fight over.

Amanda

Poor Amanda had husband trouble too. In 1862 she and her then husband, James Hughs, homesteaded 160 acres in Panola County under a preemption grant. Between 1866 and 1898 homesteaders were permitted to claim up to 160 acres of land. They were required to live on the land for three years and make improvements on it. In Amanda's May 22, 1871 affidavit proving up her claim, she states that she and her husband, James Hughs, settled on the land on the 24th of November 1862. *She* continued to occupy and improve the land for the next three years, but James left the county in 1863 and didn't return. Did Humphries women tend to drive men off? Surely not.

In 1873, at age thirty, Amanda married Jeptha Anderson. He died within a year, and in 1874 she married Garrison Anderson. The next year she and Garrison had one child, Thomas Ezekiel Anderson. The following year Amanda died.

Thus, whatever portion of the original William Humphries estate Amanda received as the heir at law of her father, William, and whatever portion of William's estate she received as the heir at law of her mother, Polly, as well as her share of what her deceased brother Jonathan and her sisters Tina and Polly would have received, if anything, now became the property of Amanda's son, Thomas. Amanda's husband Garrison would not be an heir at law because whatever interests she may have had in that property, she had prior to her marriage to Garrison.

Thomas E. Anderson

In the suit papers of case 682, and in the December 5, 1883, W.P.H. McFaddin settlement agreement, we learn that Garrison Anderson has also died and that attorney Thomas J. Russell, in addition to representing Jane and Mahaley, is serving as the guardian of Thomas Anderson, the minor son of the now deceased Amanda and Garrison

Anderson. As we saw earlier, Thomas Anderson's interest in what was to become Spindletop in just another seventeen years and thirty-six days was sold to W.P.H. McFaddin for $800. Attorney Russell got two hundred of it for his services as guardian and for prosecuting the case on Thomas' behalf. Thus, following the 1883 purchase by W.P.H. McFaddin, Thomas Anderson had nothing left of his interest in the Pelham Humphries league. Naturally, no one later claiming through Thomas could have a greater interest than Thomas himself had left, which was zero.

Holland

Following his mother's death in 1855, Andrew Holland Humphries lived with his older sister Jane and her husband, Thomas McFadden. As we have seen, Thomas McFadden served as Holland's guardian during Holland's age of minority.

At age twenty-two, in 1863, Holland married Sarah English in Panola County. Holland died, without children, a few years later. Thus, all of his interest in his mother and father's estates, and those of his prior deceased brother and sisters, now vested in his surviving sisters. Just as with Amanda's husband, Holland's wife Sarah would not be Holland's heir at law as to any of Williams Humphries' property, because Holland's interest was acquired before their marriage. That leaves us with Mahaley.

Mahaley

Mahaley, William and Polly's youngest child, married Lewis McMillan (sometimes spelled McMullen) on June 3, 1866. From the 1870 Census records we can see that she and Lewis have two children, three-year-old Andrew and four-month-old Elizabeth. In the same census report, Mahaley's older sister Amanda is recorded as living with them.

Remember, this is the time when James Hughs had abandoned Amanda, but before she married Jeptha Anderson.

Four years later, Lewis McMillan apparently having died (we hope he didn't simply abandon her), Mahaley McMillan is listed as married to G.W. Cobb. In the 1880 deed to Russell, which was not signed by Mahaley, she is referred to as Mahayla Cobel, wife of J.T. Coble. By 1883 the suit papers in case 682, as well as the McFaddin settlement agreement, refer to her as Mahaley Coble, the wife of Thomas Coble. From other court papers we learn that Mahaley had two other children by J.T. Coble, Mack Coble and Bazie Coble.

Cobb or Coble, it makes no difference. Whatever interest Mahaley had in the Pelham Humphries league she disposed of during her lifetime. The 1883 McFaddin settlement agreement shows that the interest of Mahaley *and Thomas Coble* (if Thomas Coble ever had any interest, he lost it here) was then "owned by one P.V. Thompson," and it was Mr. Thompson, as Mahaley's and Thomas' assignee, who was paid the $800 settlement amount for Mahaley's share.

Sorting It Out: Greed and Grasping

The Heirs at Law Postgusher Claims

As we have just seen, by virtue of deeds to lawyers (or others) and/or the 1883 settlement agreement in which W.P.H. McFaddin purchased their interests, none of the heirs at law of William Humphries had any interest left (if they had ever had any interest to begin with) in the Pelham Humphries league. We must report, however, that just because they had already sold and otherwise disposed of their interests in 1883, didn't mean they wouldn't try to resurrect them when they learned that the Lucas gusher came in on Grandfather Humphries' land.

Even the true heirs, those who had already received payment for their claims, if any, to the Pelham Humphries league, were blinded by visions of untold wealth. Perhaps they were emboldened by the final result of case 682.

On May 21, 1885, the plaintiffs in case 682: Jane, Mahaley (joined by her husband), and the late Amanda's only child, Thomas Anderson, prevailed against all the defendants and were adjudged to recover from the defendants all of the lands named in the petition, which was the Pelham Humphries league!

Wow! But, why did the case even continue after McFaddin had bought out their interests in 1883? Because McFaddin hadn't bought out the interests of *all* of the defendants in the suit, and he had warranty deeds from the Heirs and Assigns of William Humphries. One of the obligations of a person giving a warranty deed is to defend the title as to all claims. Two sets of defendants, the heirs of Steven B. Dozier and an M.W. Humphries, didn't sell to McFaddin and so were still making claims. So the Humphries heirs were meeting their warranty obligations. And they won. Since McFaddin had purchased all of Jane's, Thomas Anderson's, and Mahaley's ownership interests, the court's decision for William's heirs at law, and against all the other defendants, meant McFaddin now owned all of the league. The critical question of whether the remaining defendants had any ownership interest was decided against them. That meant McFaddin had title to the land and didn't have to deal with those defendants who were not part of the 1883 settlement agreement. The effect of the court's ruling was that those defendants had no title.

No doubt the court's ruling for the plaintiffs was made simpler by the fact that none of the defendants appeared in court. Its much easier for the plaintiffs' lawyer to be eloquent and persuasive when no one is arguing the other side of the case. Naturally, none of the defendants who had participated in the settlement agreement appeared to contest the case. They had already been paid and had no reason to further waste their time and energy over mere pasture land with a big hill in the middle of it, and W.P.H. wouldn't have wanted them to. Why M.W. Humphries and the heirs of S.B. Dozier didn't appear to press their claims is only speculation at this point. The common sense application of the laws of descent and distribution that we have already seen might tell you that M.W. Humphries, whoever that was, certainly was not one of the heirs at law and was thus destined to lose. The case of the heirs of S.B. Dozier is a little different.

On September 22, 1860, there was filed on the public records of Jefferson County a warranty deed purporting to convey the contested Pelham Humphries league to Stephen B. Dozier. The deed was supposedly from Pelham Humphries Jr. and his brother, William Humphries, as heirs and joint heirs of the estate of Pelham Humphries deceased ("our father") for $1200. The deed was signed in San Augustine County on September 26, 1859, by Pelham Jr. and William making their marks.

Since we now know that there was no "Pelham," and that William Humphries had no sons named Pelham Jr. or William, the deed to Dozier is clearly fraudulent. We must also suspect that in 1885, when the case came to trial and actual witnesses with first-hand knowledge would be available to testify, it would be a fairly simple matter to prove the deed was fraudulent. Perhaps that's why Mr. Dozier's heirs did not appear to present their case.

The case was tried to the judge rather than to a jury. When the defendants didn't appear, the plaintiffs, through their attorney (and guardian) waived a jury trial and submitted all matters of fact and of law to the court. Unfortunately for historians, the judge in case 682 was of little help on the issue of why the defendants didn't appear, because he didn't announce his specific findings of fact and the rules of law he relied upon. He merely uses the catch-all language, "the court having heard all of the pleadings of the Plaintiffs and of said Defendants read and having heard the evidence of Plaintiffs and considered the same...," and then found for the plaintiffs.

Well, that too should have finally ended the quest for the Pelham Humphries league for William's heirs at law. After all, they now had a moral victory when their position was vindicated in court, and they had already had a financial victory when they deeded it away for attorneys' fees and the settlement payments from W.P.H. McFaddin. Perhaps over the intervening sixteen years their memories faded? Doubtful. It's far more likely that after the Lucas gusher came in they thought they sold out too cheap. In any event, one of the true heirs at law, Thomas Anderson, was back at it. So were his cousins, the sons of his Aunt Mahaley, Andrew McMillian, and Mack and Bazie Coble. They were also joined by their stepcousins, the children and grandchildren of their uncle Thomas Humphries, and a whole passel of other people claiming to be the rightful heirs to the Pelham Humphries league.

As the discerning reader will instantly recognize, in 1901 Thomas Anderson could have no claim to Spindletop, having transferred his interest to W.P.H. McFaddin in 1883, and neither could his cousins, the children of Aunt Mahaley, because their mother (joined by her husband) also transferred her interest to W.P.H. during her lifetime. And, of course, the children of Uncle Thomas Humphries had no basis for a claim, as they were not heirs at law of their Uncle William.

The children of Thomas Humphries needed a new theory to support their claim that they were heirs to the Pelham Humphries league, and they found one. They claimed ownership to the Pelham Humphries league as the grandchildren and heirs at law of Joseph Humphries. To make that fly, they needed "Pelham" to be a separate individual who died during his father Joseph's lifetime. If that were true, then, under the laws of descent and distribution, upon Joseph's death, "Pelham's" estate, the Jefferson County property, would have gone to his parents. Since his mother was dead, that would mean that Joseph became the owner upon "Pelham's" death, and, as the children of Thomas, they became heirs at law of Joseph and they were now the rightful owners of the league at Spindletop.

It is the children of Thomas Humphries (and we should suspect, some unscrupulous but creative lawyer—after all, the theory spawned ninety years of litigation) who should be credited with first starting the claim that Uncle "Pel" was a separate individual who died after he got the Pelham Humphries headright grant for the Jefferson County league, but before his father Joseph died, and, of course, without a wife or children. To support that proposition, they offered seven affidavits.

Seven Affidavits: Uncle Pel's Best Case

Just four months after the gusher at Spindletop came in, on Friday May 24, 1901, Thomas Humphries' kids (or their lawyers) were hard at it. That day they obtained five affidavits to support their new "Uncle Pel" theory. In June they added two more. The affidavits didn't get the job done, but they are interesting reading nonetheless:

The State of Texas
County of Panola

On this day personally appeared before me the undersigned authority Sallie Wilkerson who being by me sworn says on her oath that she is now about sixty years old. That she has lived in Eastern Texas about sixty years. That she knew Joseph Humphries and Sallie Humphries who way [sic] my aunt that she knew William Humphries and Tiny Story was brother and sister and that they were children of Joseph Humphries by his first wife There was a Pelham Humphries in the family of Joseph Humphries I know that. Pelham Humphries was a brother of Tiny and William because the old folks said so and I have heard William Humphries and Tiny speak of their brother Pelham.

                          her
                  Sallie x Wilkerson
                         mark

Sworn to and subscribed before me this 24th day of
May 1901.

                        (seal)

              T.L. Anderson Justice of the Peace
              and Notary Public for Panola Co. Tex.

Let's do some simple math. We have no doubt that Ms
Wilkerson was a lovely lady trying to be truthful. But, at
sixty years of age, she would have been one year old when
Joseph Humphries died in 1842. Its hard to "know" someone when you're only one year old. Moreover, William died
sometime between 1846 and 1849. She would have been
between five and eight years old when she "heard William
and Tiny speak of their brother Pelham." I suppose she
could have some memory of that conversation, but when
she can't remember that her aunt's name is Sarah, not Sallie,
you have to wonder.

The affidavits of A.E. Anderson and A.S. Wall both are
offered to the effect that they know Sallie Wilkerson, and,
as Mr. Wall said, that she is an "illiterate old lady," but that
"she is an honest truthful old woman." A nice testimonial
to Sallie, but absolutely useless as to establishing a separate
"Pelham" as the son of Joseph Humphries.

Then there is the combined affidavits of Susie and Nannie
Wilkerson. The two ladies state that they knew Thomas
Humphries in his lifetime and that they both heard him
speak of his half brother Pelham.

To round out the Wilkerson families' contribution to this
issue, we next look at the affidavit of R.B. Wilkerson. Mr.
Wilkerson states that Sallie Wilkerson is his sister and ad-
justs her age to between sixty-five and seventy years old.

He gives us some useless but interesting information on his brother-in-law, Barry Wilkerson, and then states that he was "well acquainted with Joseph Humphries and his family" and that the last wife of Joseph was his aunt. He states that Joseph had three children by his first wife: "Pelham, William and Tuny; that he had three children by his second wife: Tom, Riley & Phill." He goes on to say that "I have for many years [been] of the impression that Pelham Humphries was killed by the Mexicans, this information has been handed down to me by my parents and that he died without issue and that his death occurred about 1838 or 1839."

We should not necessarily doubt the four Wilkersons' own belief in the existence of someone called "Pelham." But, God bless 'em, they're just wrong.

Then there is the affidavit of L.M. Truit. He gives his age as seventy-four (on July 1, 1901) and alleges he knew Squire Humphries during his lifetime. He says Squire was hung by the Regulators just below Logansport in the fall of 1841. That would be when Mr. Truit was fourteen years old. He says he knew Joseph Humphries and knew Pelham Humphries by reputation, and from his understanding they were from the same family or stock of people.

It's always interesting to learn more facts about the Regulators and Moderators, but, as we know, Mr. Truit is wrong about Squire Humphries and Joseph Humphries being from the "same family or stock of people." He adds nothing of substance to the question of whether there was a separate "Pelham."

Finally there is the affidavit of Ben Cannes. On June 11, 1901, Mr. Cannes gives his age as sixty-seven and says he was personally acquainted with Joseph Humphries and his family; he also knew that Joseph Humphries had two sets of children, and that Pelham was one of them. He does not mention George and also misses Mary, Joseph's daughter by his second wife, Sarah. Since Ben would be only eight years old when Joseph died, we should not give too much weight to his being "personally acquainted" with Joseph Humphries or otherwise privy to family details.

Well, how does this anecdotal information fit with what we already know? The parts about "Pelham" don't. But to the extent we can, we should try to give credence to what the Wilkersons and Mr. Truit said. It is probable that the name "Pelham" was being bandied about ever since the 1880s, when the litigation first began over the "Pelham Humphries" league. The Wilkersons and Mr. Truit may have confused their having heard of a "Pelham," which none of them knew personally, with their shadowy knowledge that Joseph did have a son who predeceased him. As we have already seen, the third child of Joseph Humphries and his first wife is not Pelham, it is George Humphries.

The affidavits offered no actual evidence of the existence of a Pelham. When considering the affidavits we need to balance them against what we learned in the previous "Pelham or William" discussion. That analysis, when weighed against these affidavits, or any other assertions made in the history of the Humphries heirs' cases, is conclusive. The person who received the league of land that became Spindletop was William Humphries, not Pelham. They are one and the same person. That conclusion is based upon documents which are contemporaneous with the event it relates to and appear on the public record, as opposed to the 1901 affidavits consisting of personal reminisces about circumstances and events that purportedly took place sixty or seventy years prior. There are other public records which discredit the "Pelham" theory and show that Thomas Humphries' lineal descendants would have no claim even if there was a Pelham.

Joseph Humphries' estate file is found on the public records of Harrison County. When an estate is filed with the probate court, as was done with Joseph Humphries, the administrator and administratrix, if there is one, must file an inventory listing all the property of the estate. Joseph's wife, Sarah, was appointed administratrix and S.P. January, administrator, of Joseph's estate. They made an accounting, inventorying the assets of the estate. If Thomas Humphries' children are right and Joseph had a son named "Pelham" who predeceased Joseph, then the Pelham Humphries league should be listed among the assets of Joseph's estate. It is not. Let's take a look at Joseph's assets and their estimated value at the time of his death:

Twelve hundred and thirty acres of land on the
West side of the Sabine River opposite Pulaski $613.00

Twenty two hundred and forty acres of land
the part of [the] Headright of said Joseph
Humphries unlocated (certificate only) $300.00

Ferry and Ferry boat the half
of said privilege and all the boat $300.00

1 sorrel horse	$75.00	1 handsaw	$ .75
1 grey horse	10.00	1 crosscut	5.00
1 drawing knife	.12½	1 whipsaw	5.00
75 bushels of corn	37.25	1 spade	1.00
27 head of hogs	54.00	1 axe	.75
2 chisels & 3 augers	1.50	1 plough	1.00
3 carpenters planes	4.00	1 wedge	.12½

On account of James Rowe	$32.00
Ditto John Coly	34.62½
Ditto C.H. McClure	49.00
Ditto on Daniel Naughen	115.00
Receipt on L. H. Dilliard	64.00
D. Shorro account	3.25

(It's interesting to see that the probate judge, L.H. Dillard, owed Joseph sixty-four dollars for something. This is the stuff conflicts of interest are made of.)

Thus, the theory of Thomas Humphries' children, that the property of Uncle "Pel," specifically the league of land now spouting oil and sprouting derricks at Spindletop was inherited by their grandfather Joseph, a critical element to their own claims, is dealt a serious blow. The property does not appear in Joseph's estate. Most logically, and consistent with the documents on the public record, that means that Joseph never had the property to begin with, and he never had it to begin with because there was no "Pelham" who ever owned the property. Of course, if Joseph's administrators didn't know about it, and thus didn't include it on the inventory in Joseph's estate, naturally it wouldn't be shown as part of the estate. Even if that were to be the case, Thomas Humphries' children and other lineal descendants would still have no claim to Spindletop.

Under their own theory, Thomas' children could have no interest in the Pelham Humphries league, because, as the clever reader will recall, on July 28, 1850, Thomas Humphries himself sold "all my interest in the estate of Joseph Humphries" to his neighbor, George Nippert. Since Thomas sold it all to George Nippert, there was none left for his own children to inherit. Thus, they could have no claim to Spindletop under their own theory. And, of course, they did not prevail.

As we know, in every lawsuit since the gusher blew in, the Humphries heirs have failed. And, as we also know, because of the rulings in the Humphries trilogy and especially since Judge Cobb fined Brown Peregoy and Max Wilson, none ever will. Nor should they. As we have just seen, the true legal heirs sold their interests in the land. Even Mahaley's husband signed away his possible interest. But, as our clever reader will recall, when discussing the ownership interests of the heirs at law in the Pelham Humpries league, we have always spoken in terms of their interests, *if any*. Remember Jane's remark in her 1880 deed to attorneys Russell, Hays, and Boren: She said "*being informed* that there is a body of land in Jefferson County, Texas rightfully belonging to us." From Jane's statement, and from the listing of the property of William Humphries we saw earlier in the 1855 petition for guardianship filed by Jane's husband, Thomas McFadden, it's clear they didn't know about the Jefferson County property. And they are the ones who should have known. The most likely reason they wouldn't have known is that William had disposed of the property during his lifetime. So the question is, did William convey away all of his interest in the Jefferson County league during his lifetime? If he did, then his heirs never had anything to sell in the first place. Let's look again at the public record.

Transfers of Spindletop, 1834-1883

It should be apparent to the reader that the Jefferson County league of land was merely a revenue source for William Humphries. There is no evidence whatsoever that William ever used the league for ranching or farming or, for that matter, that he ever set foot in Jefferson County, Texas, let alone on his league of land. He either used the land as collateral for loans or sold it for cash. Before we get to the transfers made by William Humphries during his lifetime, let's take a look at those transfers appearing on the public record prior to the 1883 transfers to W.P.H. McFaddin, but after William's death. It's apparent that others sought to use the league as a revenue source, too.

On September 7, 1857, David Snively, of Refugio County, Texas, paid $2,000 to someone calling himself "Pelham Humphries" and received a deed to the Jefferson County league of land. Had Mr. Snively done his due diligence, he would not have seen any intervening deeds. However, in land transactions, due diligence should also include knowing the person with whom you are dealing. And, of course, had he checked, Mr. Snively would have known that he was dealing with the wrong person. That's because, as the reader will recall, the affidavit and power of attorney to change the name from "Pelham" to "William" is on the public record. Snively didn't examine the chain of title. If he had examined the chain of title, he would have seen the power of attorney (just as we can see it today) and known that he should be dealing with a "William" Humphries, not "Pelham" Humphries. Since we know that no "Pelham Humphries" received the headright grant to the Jefferson County league from Commissioner Nixon, we know this deed is fraudulent.

Another red flag indication of fraud is that whoever the person posing as "Pelham Humphries" actually was, he was able to *sign* the name "Pelham Humphries" to the deed, instead of having to rely on merely making his mark as the illiterate William had to do. Had Snively checked the record, he could have seen that little problem, too. Although he could have protected himself, someone made a fast $2,000 at Mr. Snively's expense. Unfortunately, fraud is not uncommon. The public records serve as one of the methods of avoiding fraud, but you have to actually look at them.

Then there is the $1,200 deed to Stephen Dozier two years later. We have already seen that the deed to Dozier is fraudulent too. This is just another case where an unsuspecting purchaser was bilked out of his money. We know that there was no "Pelham Humphries Jr.," and that none of William Humphries' sons were named "William." We have already met all of William's children.

Both the deed to Snively and the deed to Dozier were plain old garden variety fraud. Snively and Dozier did not do their due diligence investigation thoroughly enough. While in those days the common-law doctrine of "buyer beware" (the familiar *caveat emptor*) was still a viable defense, it would not apply to blatant fraud such as this. Fraudulent deeds can be set aside by the court as long as it is done timely and no intervening legal doctrine has occurred such as adverse possession. That is what happened to Dozier's deed in case 682. It was set aside. When the Humphries' heirs won and Dozier lost case 682, Dozier's deed no longer had the legal effect of an ownership claim on the property. Dozier no longer had "muniments of title" as the documentary evidence of title are sometimes called. Although the Snively deed was filed on the public record on January 5, 1861, almost twenty years before case 682 was filed, for reasons not known now, Snively was not made a party to case 682. But no matter, adverse possession has long since destroyed his title, too.

In 1873 there is another transfer of an interest in the league. It is made by Alexander W. Holmes to M.W. Houghton, but the chain of Holmes' title started with Bailey Anderson, an heir of William Inglish. This one is not fraudulent, and it is best explained by looking at the transfers that William Humphries made during his lifetime.

William's Transfer Documents

There are three transfers of interests in the Spindletop property that were actually made by William Humphries himself. As we have seen, the first was the bond for title to William Inglish ("Inglish" is often seen spelled as "English") and Wyatt Hanks on the same day William Humphries acquired the headright entitlement from Commissioner Nixon, September 27, 1834. As the reader will recall, the bond for title provided that William had to repay the money, $1,999, if he didn't make a title to Inglish and Hanks as required by the agreement. He had ample opportunity to make the title as required by the bond. For example, immediately following his power of attorney to William Inglish to change the title from Pelham to William, he could have next done a deed making the necessary title to Inglish and Hanks. We know from examining the public records that he didn't do that then, or ever. Therefore, the only rational conclusion is that he repaid the money satisfying his obligation to Inglish and Hanks. That conclusion is bolstered by the next document, William's second transfer, a deed from William Humphries to William Inglish for the same Jefferson County league of land.

On February 14, 1836, William Humphries put his mark on a deed to William Inglish. The plain meaning of the language in the deed is that, for one thousand dollars, William Humphries conveyed to Inglish the entire league of land which is now the site of Spindletop. The most obvious conclusion to be drawn from this deed is that William's original bond for title obligation had been discharged. Had his original obligation not been satisfied, Inglish surely would not have continued to deal with William Humphries over the same land and for another large sum of money. Nor could this deed merely be fulfilling Humphries' original obligation to make a title to Inglish and Hanks, because Wyatt Hanks is not included and because it is for all of the league rather than the just the acreage contemplated by the bond for title. Plus, Inglish has to pay again.

Despite the apparent plain language of this document, it's doubtful that this "deed" was actually intended to be a deed absolute. The most likely intended effect of this document is that it was to operate as a mortgage securing a loan from Inglish to Humphries in the amount of one thousand dollars. In addition to Inglish being in the business of loaning money, there are several other strong arguments for this conclusion.

First, four years after the deed to Inglish was signed, on September 17, 1840, William Humphries made his third transfer when he sold five hundred acres of his league to a gentleman by the name of John G. Love. It is true that, had Humphries been of a mind to sell the same property twice, the deed to Inglish had not been recorded and thus John Love could not learn of it by his due diligence and review of the public records. But, in this case, Love had personal knowledge of the deed to Inglish.

On February 14, 1836, John G. Love was serving as Primary Judge of the municipality of San Augustine. The sworn acknowledgment of the deed from William Humphries to William Inglish was taken by Judge Love himself. Since the same John Love was now spending six hundred dollars for five hundred acres of the land that he already knew had been deeded to Inglish a few years earlier, he would have made certain that the deed document was no longer in effect.

Since there is no record of a deed from Inglish back to Humphries, the only reason that Humphries' deed to Inglish would no longer have any effect would be that Inglish had been repaid the thousand dollars he had loaned to Humphries. Had the deed to Inglish been a deed absolute, in other words a normal sale rather than a loan with the deed serving as a mortgage, the transaction would have been complete when the deed was delivered to Inglish. A section of the deed itself is another reason to believe it was intended to act as a mortgage rather than a deed.

The deed from Humphries to Inglish contained a later added section in which Polly Humphries was to sign away her interest in the Jefferson County league. Although the form language is there, Polly's name is not written in, and she did not sign or make her mark. There is merely a blank space for her first name: "_____" Humphries wife of Wm. Humphries...." That section of the deed is dated with the year "1837," an obvious later addition to the original document. The fact that Polly did not sign the document is yet another indication that it was merely a mortgage and that it was paid off. It is entirely likely that Inglish got paid after he put pressure on William to get Polly's signature on the deed. This is particularly true in light of William's later sale of five hundred acres to John Love. The fact that the deed to Inglish was not timely filed is yet another reason to believe it was intended to be a mortgage rather than a deed absolute.

As we know, to protect their considerable investment, it is in the best interest of a purchaser of land to file his new deed on the public record as soon as possible. Inglish did not do that. We must of course recognize that at the time the deed was executed, February 14, 1836, Texas was in turmoil. They were fighting a war with Mexico, and, just at that time (remember the Alamo), things weren't going real well. But we know that the land office reopened on February 1, 1838. The deed from Humphries to Inglish was not filed for another twenty-one years after that. The most logical reason that the deed was not filed as soon as it could have been was that it was actually serving as a mortgage, and, by the time it could have been filed, it was already repaid. We also know, even as a mortgage, it would have been filed on the public records, too. If it had been repaid, there was no reason to file it.

The Humphries to Inglish deed was eventually filed on December 26, 1860. This was long after the transaction was completed, and the parties to it were both dead. Apparently someone in the Inglish family found the original deed and filed it. William's failure to retrieve the original deed or have it destroyed created lots of future Spindletop legal work. More lawyers' relief.

Regardless of whether the deed document was intended to be a mortgage or a deed absolute, because of the times, William Inglish demonstrated great confidence in Texas. In February of 1836, Texas history was in the making. Just a week before William's deed to Inglish, on February 2, 1835, the Alamo fell to Santa Anna. That event marked the beginning of what came to be known as the "Runaway Scrape."

The Runaway Scrape was the eastward flight of the Texas population to escape Santa Anna's pursuing armies. To a significant degree it included even those people living in East Texas. It has been argued that William sold out for $1,000 to assist in his escape from the Mexican army (or to join the Texas army). That is a perfectly reasonable assumption. However, during those stressful, turbulent times, it was a gutsy move for Inglish to part with a thousand dollars of his cash for either the outright sale of land in Texas or as a loan secured by Texas land. In either case, if Santa Anna won the war there would be no "Texas," and very likely neither William Humphries nor William Inglish would have any right to the land, if they survived.

The fact that the transaction followed the formal conventions of such documents, even though it was done in those chaotic times, indicates the confidence of all concerned, but especially William Inglish, in the successful outcome of the war of independence. On the one hand Inglish stood to lose the most, both the land and his money. On the other hand, if Texas won, and William either would not pay or had been killed in the fighting, Inglish would have gotten the land at a bargain price: 4,428 acres for less than twenty-three cents per acre—a bargain befitting the potential risk.

Well, as we all know, there was no loss or windfall. Sam Houston defeated Santa Anna at the Battle of San Jacinto on April 21, 1836. William Humphries repaid the $1,000 to William Inglish and four years later sold 500 acres of the same land to John Love. But William left a housekeeping task undone when he didn't get the original deed back.

As the reader will realize, it was the continued existence of the deed from Humphries to Inglish, after the $1,000 had been repaid, that accounts for the December 1873 deed of the "Pelham Humphries" league from Alexander W. Holmes to M. W. Houghton mentioned earlier. Holmes purchased an interest in the league from Bailey English, and Bailey English acquired his interest as an heir at law of William Inglish, who acquired his interest in the 1836 deed from William Humphries.

It made no difference to W.P.H. McFaddin. In 1883 he also purchased M.W. Houghton's interest in the Pelham Humphries league when he bought the interests of the Humphries heirs and the heirs of English as part of the settlement of case 682. We must also add that McFaddin's 1883 purchase of the claims of all of the heirs of English didn't stop them from suing again after the Spindletop gusher came in, any more than it stopped the Humphries heirs from renewing their claims.

Having now examined the transfers of the Pelham Humphries league, beginning with the 1834 bond for title given on the day of the original headright grant from Commissioner Nixon and through the next nearly fifty years to the 1883 deeds to W.P.H. McFaddin, we are ready to answer some questions: Did William Humphries "bargain sell and transfer" all of his ownership interest in the Jefferson County league during his lifetime? Did those Humphries heirs suing after the Spindletop gusher came in ever have any rights to the Spindletop fortune? Naturally both questions are answered in typical lawyers' terms—yes and no.

The Definitive Answers: Yes and No

At least one thing may be said with certainty. None of the purported heirs claiming under "Pelham" Humphries ever had a legitimate claim to Spindletop, even if they had not been outmaneuvered by McFaddins' and Big Oil's motions to dismiss, summary judgments, or directed verdicts grounded on those pesky legal doctrines like adverse possession. The heirs were just plain wrong. No matter what Daddy told them and no matter how badly they wished for it, they never had a legal right to the Spindletop fortune. As has been made abundantly clear, the original owner of the league of land granted by Commissioner Nixon in 1834 was William, not Pelham. There was no person named Pelham Humphries who ever had an ownership interest in the league of land that became Spindletop.

There is no big mystery about it, and there surely is no conspiracy. The name "Pelham" appears on the original headright petition because of a mere scrivener's error. A simple mistake made by Commissioner Nixon when he wrote the name down. Get a grip Humphries heirs: when they write, people make mistakes. It happens. That's why pencils have erasers, someone invented white-out fluid, and computers have backspace and delete keys. It was just a mistake. A mistake that was recognized and corrected. That irrefutable fact is made plain by the official records that had been available to the public for more than sixty years *before* the first Humphries heirs' postgusher lawsuit was filed.

Having no Pelham to rely on shatters a lot of dreams. Rubin Medders may have been someone's brother-in-law, but it wasn't Pelham Humphries. Ernest's, Margaret's, and the Poor Sisters' $500 million dream, no matter how hard they prayed over it, just wasn't destined to come true.

Having no Pelham also eliminates the $200 billion claim by Brown Peregoy and his band of unfortunates, those thousands of association members from the fifty states and seven foreign countries who (quite literally) bought into Peregoy's song and dance. Much to the chagrin of the heir who complained to a newspaper reporter that they had been driving his car too long, the McFaddins are going to keep right on driving that Mercedes.

The collateral kin of William Humphries, his nieces and nephews, William's half brother Thomas' descendants, also relied on Uncle Pel for their entitlement. Their claims are particularly repugnant because, for their chance at big money, William's nieces and nephews had to (and were willing to) disregard the existence of their Uncle George Humphries and disregard their cousins' ownership of the land as the heirs at law of Uncle William. Of course William and George were only "half uncles," so no one needed to care about them. Then dear Uncle Pel would have been just a half uncle too. But since he was their ticket to oil dollars, they certainly cared about him! Family members have been doing hurtful things to each other since Cain and Abel, and disputes by heirs over money are commonplace, but this form of greed is still disgusting.

The answer to the question of whether William had anything left of the Spindletop league to leave to his heirs at law is just a bit more equivocal. The short answer is yes he did, because the court's 1885 ruling in case 682 said so. Plaintiffs sued as the heirs of William Humphries and won. Since the heirs of William English were defendants in that lawsuit, the court found against them and disregarded the effectiveness of the 1836 deed from Humphries to Inglish as a deed absolute. But case 682 was decided under unique circumstances.

We must remember that, at the trial of case 682, none of the defendants appeared to offer their own evidence. The court said that it heard the "evidence" of the plaintiffs. The trial in 1885 was almost fifty years after the transaction between Humphries and Inglish. The reader will recall that in the 1855 petition for guardianship for William's children, the Jefferson County league is not listed as part of the property of William. Then, too, in her deed to the attorneys for their fee, it was clear that Jane didn't know about the property; she said "*being informed* that there is a body of land in Jefferson County...." " Since the league wasn't listed as part of William's property and since his oldest daughter didn't know of it until she was "informed," more than thirty years after her father's death, it's reasonable to believe that offering admissible evidence that the Inglish deed was really just a mortgage that had already been satisfied, and thus had no legal effect, would be difficult. Very difficult. Almost fifty years after the transaction itself, with both parties to it long since dead and buried, the heirs would have to offer admissible evidence to overcome the plain language of the deed. As we saw in the case of *McBride v. Gulf Oil*, when so many years have passed and there is no direct testimony available, that is often impossible to do.

Following the rules of evidence applicable to every trial, just as in the *McBride* case, there are several objections that may be raised to block the admissibility of any "evidence" which attempts to refute or contradicts unambiguous language in a document appearing on the public record. For example, the hearsay rule would block the attempt of any person, except William Humphries or William Inglish themselves, from testifying as to what they intended to do and what they actually did. Without the testimony of the long deceased two Williams, the plain language of the deed to Inglish could only be overcome by a later document of equal dignity. By "equal dignity" we mean one with the same formalities in its execution with witnesses to the signing of the document and the signing being under oath, and being sworn to in front of a notary or judge, by the party with authority to execute the document. The document would need to be the equivalent of a satisfaction of mortgage, executed by William Inglish or his successors, identifying and actually releasing the league of land from the obligation of the deed. There is no such document. If such a document existed it would be on the public record, and the heirs of English would not have had even a colorable claim.

Had the trial in case 682 been fully litigated, with the all parties present offering their own evidence and objecting to inadmissable evidence, the result may well have been different. If William Humphries' heirs at law had been unable to offer admissible evidence to show that the Humphries and Inglish transaction had been merely a loan, which had been repaid, the Inglish deed would have been upheld. If the deed were upheld, the heirs at law of William would have no basis to claim the land. The language in the deed to Inglish is clear. William deeded away *all* of his ownership interest. But remember, the heirs at law of William Humphries were also the heirs at law of their mother, Polly Humphries.

Polly didn't deed away her interest in the Jefferson County land. The deed to Inglish contains a place for her to do that, but she never signed it. Polly not signing the deed to Inglish means that, claiming as *her* heirs at law, Polly's daughters Jane and Mahaley, along with Amanda's son Thomas Anderson, would be entitled to an undivided one-half of the entire league of land. An "undivided" one-half means they would have either amicably shared the land as tenants in common with the heirs of William English, or they could ask for a judicial partition in which the court divides the actual land or sells it and divides the proceeds between the parties.

Had the deed to Inglish been upheld, and the heirs at law of Polly became tenants in common with the heirs of Inglish, Messrs. Snively, Dozier, and M.W. Humphries would still be out. There is still one more deed to be considered. What is the status of John Love's deed and his potential claim to 500 acres of the Spindletop league?

John Love's deed identified 500 specific acres in a square survey set in the northeast corner of the Humphries league. Since none of Judge Love's heirs are identified as defendants in case 682, his interests in the league were not defeated in case 682. In fact, the decision helped him. Judge Love's deed was after the deed to Inglish. Had the Inglish deed been upheld, Love would be out and left to seek his remedy from the estate of William Humphries. But that didn't happen, so Love's interest such as it was, remained viable. Of course, since Polly didn't sign away her interest on the deed to Judge Love, she and Judge Love would have been tenants in common on the 500 acres. Polly's heirs at law end up being tenants in common with the heirs of Judge Love. That was lost to the heirs at law when they transferred their interests to their lawyers and to W.P.H. McFaddin.

We hasten to add that the foregoing analysis does not mean that the heirs of Judge Love have a claim to Spindletop today. Just as with the generation-skipping Humphries heirs,

Judge Love's interest was lost long ago by the doctrine of adverse possession.

Whether they transferred their interests as heirs of William or heirs of Polly made no difference to W.P.H. McFaddin. In the deeds McFaddin got, he got *all* their interests in the league. And he got all the interests they transferred to their lawyers to pay their legal fees. McFaddin got all of the interest the Humphries ever had.

The bottom line answer to the Spindletop question is this: no Humphries heir, neither the heirs at law nor any collateral kin, had any legitimate claim to Spindletop after the 1883 deeds to W.P.H. McFaddin. And, of course, no one ever had a claim through the nonexistent Pelham. Which leaves one other question. Who is responsible for the nearly one hundred years of litigation that should never have started in the first place?

"The first thing we do, let's kill all the lawyers"

Did Shakespeare have the right idea? Lawyers must carry the most responsibility for the unending litigation over the Pelham Humphries league at Spindletop. All of the documents supporting the legal analysis, which leads invariably to the conclusion that no Humphries heir had a legitimate claim to any part of the league at Spindletop since the 1883 deeds to McFaddin, have been on the public records since January 10, 1884. That's the date McFaddin recorded all of the deeds he obtained to acquire and consolidate his complete ownership of the Humphries' league.

A full seventeen years before the Lucas gusher blew in, it was all there, just as it is today. The lawsuits should never have been brought. None were ever won. None will ever be won. The heirs were driven by their own greed, and so were the lawyers. Greed caused the lawyers to ignore their professional responsibility to their clients, ignore their legal training, and risk Rule 11 sanctions.

We may not need to actually kill all the lawyers, perhaps just maiming one or two will do the job. Judge Cobb's Rule 11 sanction put a serious hurt on Max Wilson (somewhat analogous of those sharp clouts administered to the young boys watching a land transaction) and hopefully got the attention of any other lawyer contemplating another Humphries' lawsuit.

But having said all that, the murder of Joe Perkins is still troubling. Forget for a moment all the documents and legal analysis we just went through. Think like a homicide investigator. Rosine's trip to see Jim Petty in Salt Lake City needs a rational explanation. To a homicide investigator, the circumstances of her meeting with Jim Petty, flying out there just after bonding out for murder, without an appointment, bringing no family genealogy materials, and especially after having written an article on the McFaddin family genealogy herself years earlier, just doesn't ring true with her explanation for the trip. And so, to those who like nice neat packages, questions still remain. Do the McFaddins have something to hide? Did Joe Perkins know something that got him killed? Could "Daddy" have actually been right? We may never know.

But this we do know: the one hundredth anniversary of the Spindletop gusher is only a few short years away. How many trillions of dollars would the Humphries think were sitting in a trust account just waiting for them by then? And what a tempting symbolic date for the next generation of Humphries to file a new lawsuit. Mark your calendar.

Appendix A

Spindletop Chronology

Some of the sources for this chronology are identified by the following abbreviations:

MM	Margaret Medders (*Medders Story*)
RMW	Rosine McFaddin Wilson (*The McFaddin Family*)
GLO	Texas General Land Office
TCET	*Two Centuries in East Texas*
JCPR	Jefferson County Public Records
PCPR	Panola County Public Records
PCHS	Panola County Historical Society
HCPR	Harrison County Probate Records

1519	Cortes lands in Mexico.
5-22-1783	King Charles III of Spain promulgates the Mining Ordinance which applies to all Spanish Americans, except Peru.
1803	Louisiana purchase by United States.
1806	Neutral ground agreed upon between Arroyo Honda and the Sabine.

1816	Tenney Humphries (daughter of Joseph Humphries) born. Calculated from 1850 Census records, Panola County.
2-22-1819	Treaty making the Sabine the boundary between the United States and Spain.
1819	William McFaddin, father of W.P.H. McFaddin, born in Lake Charles, La. *The McFaddin Family*, Rosine McFaddin Wilson.
1820	Moses Austin applies for permission to colonize 300 families.
1-17-1821	Moses Austin's petition granted by Spanish.
1821	Mexican independence from Spain. Mexico adopts and applies the Mining Ordinance of 1783.
8-19-1821	Austin's colonization plan is adopted by the Mexican government and undertaken by son Stephen Austin when Moses dies on June 10, 1821.
1-4-1823	General colonization law promulgated (Louisianians only).
1823	William Humphreys (Humphries) arrives in Texas. Text in certificate 256, Shelby 1st class file 117 Texas Land Office Austin, Tx. GLO.
1824	George Humphries arrives in Texas. Text of certificate 280, Shelby 1st class 1/3 part of a league issued to Elizabeth Nail, administrator of the estate of George Humphries. GLO.
1824	Second colonization law enacted (removed Louisianians only provision).
3-24-1825	Law of Colonization. Gammel's Laws, Vol. 1. Coahuila and Texas become a Republic, 382 S.W.2d 277 (entry 9-1-1964).

1827	Thomas Humphries born to Joseph and Sarah Humphries.
3-29-1829	Contract for colonization enterprise between Empressario Lorenzo de Zavala and the Supreme Government of the State of Coahuila and Texas. (Text of title to land petition 118.) GLO.
1833	James and Elizabeth McFaddin, grandparents of W.P.H. McFaddin, settle in Jefferson County on the banks of the Neches River. RMW.
3-6-1834	The Municipality of San Augustine created by an act of the State of Coahuila and Texas. TCET.
9-27-1834	Certificate of character for "William Umphries," a man of a family consisting of two persons. Signed by Benjamin Lindsey, Alcade. Petition 118, Texas Land Office, Austin, Tx.
9-27-1834	Petition from "Pelham Humphries" (changed to "William Humphries") to Lorenzo de Zavala to be admitted as colonist and to concede one league of land. (Petition prepared and approved by land commissioner Jorge Antonio Nixon and signed by Humphries, who made his "mark" and couldn't read the "Pelham" instead of "William" error.) Petition 118. GLO.
9-27-1834	Decree approving "Pelham" Humphries' petition signed by Jorge Antonio Nixon and instructing him to proceed to the Empressario to report on the petition. Petition 118. GLO.
9-27-1834	Certificate that Humphries is one of the colonists introduced in fulfillment of the contract

with the government, signed by August Hotchkiss, attorney for Lorenzo de Zavala. Petition 118. GLO.

9-27-1834   Bond for title under which "William" Umphries (and John Crippen) contract with William Inglish and Wiatt Hanks in consideration of $1,999 (each) and the costs of surveying the land, Inglish and Hanks get to select the land too and get 2,000 acres. 11GOYH pp. 57-59 San Augustine County Public Records.

9-30-1834   Order for survey by surveyor Arthur Henrie issued by Commissioner Nixon. Petition 118. GLO.

1835   Jane Humphries, daughter of William and Polly Humphries, born.

2-14-1835   Survey field notes by surveyor Arthur Henrie. Petition 118. GLO.

2-14-1835   Order for title to issue. Commissioner Nixon. Petition 118. GLO.

2-14-1835   Title of possession of league of land in name of "Pelham Humphries," issued by Commissioner Nixon. GLO.

9-5-1835   Date of death of "Pelham Humphries" according to allegations of Glover v McFaddin Civ. A. No. 12511 filed in the US District Court E.D. Texas at Beaumont 1948.

10-6-1835   Affidavit and power of attorney by "William Umphries" appointing Wm Inglish to take out the land title and change the name from "Pelham to William." Affidavit taken by Anthony Hotchkiss, Primary Judge of the Municipality of San Augustine. Witnessed by Samuel McFadden, E. Rains, Jonathan Anderson, and Wm Inglish. GLO.

154

11-7-1835	The independent "Republic of Texas" assumes sovereignty. 13 Tex. Jur. p. 587, note 4.
2-2-1836	Texas Independence declared. The Republic of Texas established as a sovereign nation. The Republic of Texas adopts the Mining Ordinance of 1783.
2-6-1836	Alamo falls to Santa Anna. Runaway Scrape begins.
2-14-1836	Deed from William Humphries to William Inglish for $1,000, a certain league of land . . . attested to by John G. Love, Primary Judge of San Augustine. Vol. M, 399 JCPR.
4-21-1836	Battle of San Jacinto, Santa Anna defeated.
1829-1836	First Census of Texas: Andrew McFaden 50, Jane McFaden 50, Baley 17, Mandy 14, John 12, Andrew 10, Margarett 9, and Thomas 6.
	First Census of Texas: Samuel McFaden 37, Margarett McFaden 35, Johnathan 15, William 13, Joseph 11, Mary 9, Darius 7, James Dustin 4.
	First Census of Texas: William McFaden, 29, Clancy 26, Andrew 1.
1837	Tina Humphries, daughter of William and Polly Humphries, born.
1837	William McFaddin marries Rachel Williams. RMW.
1838	At least by this year, Eliza McFaddin, daughter of James and Elizabeth McFaddin and, consequently, aunt of W.P.H. McFaddin, marries McGuire Chaison. RMW.
2-16-1838	Certificate 256, Shelby Ct. Land Commission certifies that William "Humphreys" is entitled to labor of land. Shelby 1st class file 117. GLO.

1838	Benjamin Strickland certificate 267 issued to Amos Strickland, administrator for the 1/3 part of a league. GLO.
2-22-1838	Certificate 280 for 1/3 of a league issued to Elizabeth Nail as the administrator of the estate of George Humphries. GLO.
3-22-1838	Plat and field notes for file 117. GLO.
4-7-1838	Petition from Shelby County to House of Representatives of the Republic of Texas requests a new county be formed, signed by Joseph Humphries and C.H. McClure, among many others. Harrison County Historical Society.
5-11-1838	Amos Strickland assigns the 267 certificate to William Humphries (on back of certificate). GLO.
	William assigns the 267 certificate to Joseph Humphries (on back of certificate). GLO.
6-11-1838	No. 36 2nd class certificate for 1280 acres issued to Joseph Humphries by board of Land Commissioners for Shelby County. Humphries unable to prove up entitlement to league and labor. See judgement entered 9-10-1841. GLO.
1838	Amanda (Manda, Mandy) Humphries, daughter of William and Polly Humphries, born.
9-12-1838	Field notes by virtue of certificate 267 for survey made for C.L. McClure and Joseph Humphries, assignees of Benjamin Strickland of 8166808 square varas of land situated on Humphries Bluff on the east side of the Sabine River. GLO.
1-5-1839	Joseph Humphries transfers 1/2 of his right, title, and interest in Certificate 267 to

Chauncy H. McClure. Witnessed by David
McHeard and Sarah Humphries. GLO.

1-29-1839   Harrison County created from Shelby
County. Panola County history.

1-4-1840   Joseph Humphries receives 3rd class headright for 320 acres, Conditional certificate
130, file HAS 3-26. Arrived in the Republic
on 1-13-38 single man. GLO.

6-4-1840   Joseph Humphries files notice of intention to
apply for letter of administration on the
estate of David McHeard. HCPR.

6-15-1840   Joseph Humphries files a petition for letters
of administration on the estate of David
McHurd. HCPR.

7-16-1840   Joseph Humphries files bond as administrator of the estate of David McHeard.
HCPR.

8-7-1840   In Marshall, Texas, Joseph Humphries gives
power of attorney to David Hill to apply for
the patent on headright certificate 130. GLO.

9-17-1840   Warranty Deed William "Humphreys" to
John G. Love for $600, 500 acres of the Jef-
ferson County league of land. Vol. M, 344
JCPR.

1840   Jonathan Humphries, son of William and
Polly Humphries, born.

2-4-1841   Joseph Humphries conveys (makes a bond to
convey) the track of land on which the town
of Pulaski is situated and formerly known as
Walnut Bluffs on the east side of the Sabine.

3-1-1841   Joseph Humphries bond to make a warranty
deed to James T. Kelley for a lot or parcel of
ground in the upper Walnut Bluff on the

east side of the Sabine River sometimes called Humphries Bluff. Identifies Main, Water, and River Streets and a house built by Samuel McHenry.

3-15-1841   Joseph Humphries bond to make a warranty deed to James T. Kelley for the tract or parcel of land (50 acres) lying on the west side of the Sabine River and a part of the headright certificate of Joseph Humphries, about 200 yards from Humphries' old ferry,

1841   Andrew (Holland) Humphries, son of William and Polly Humphries, born.

1841   Regulators horsewhip Squire Humphries and, after looking for them in the vicinity of McFadden Creek, burn the homes of brothers William and Bailey McFadden, and James Strickland. PCHS.

1841   Regulators formed after Charles Jackson kills Joseph Goodbread. PCHS.

6-26-1841   Joseph Humphries petitions Harrison District Court establishing his emigration into Texas in 1823, as head of a family and entitled to one league and one labor of land from the government.

7-16-1841   Trial set for Regulator Charles Jackson in Pulaski. PCHS.

1841   Squire Humphries and the McFadden brothers (and others), all Moderators, kill Jackson. PCHS.

9-10-1841   Joseph Humphries gets jury verdict in his favor and the court gives judgment against the Republic of Texas for an additional 3,340 acres of land.

1841	Brothers William and Bailey McFadden hung by the Regulators. PCHS.
1842	Joseph Humphries dies at Pulaski.
6-27-1842	Harrison County Petition of Sarah Humphries (described as the wife of the late Joseph Humphries) and Samuel P. January, Joseph Humphries having died intestate, seek letters of administration for the estate of Joseph Humphries. HCPR.
July 1842	William Humphries petitions Harrison County court to be appointed as administrator of the estate of David McHeard, reciting that McHeard "before his death appointed one Joseph Humphries Executor by his last will and Testament of all and singular of his estate ... and the said Joseph Humphries by death having been prevented from carrying into execution the decedents last request ...." and praying that he (William) be appointed administrator. HCPR.
8-29-1842	Bond of William Humphries and S.P. January as administrators of the estate of David McHeard, approved. HCPR.
9-10-1842	Inventory of Joseph Humphries estate includes "1230 acres on the west side of the Sabine River opposite Pulaski ... one half of ferry (privilege) and ferry boat ... 2240 acres unlocated land in headright certificate...." HCPR.
1842	Polly Humphries, daughter of William and Polly Humphries, born.
1843	William McFaddin set about building a large cattle ranch in Jefferson County. RMW.

1843	Beazely v. Stinson, June term 1843. Affirms Harrison County District Court decision determining that Marshall not Pulaski, shall be the county seat of Harrison County.
8- -1844	President Houston sends troops and ends Regulator and Moderator war.
12-31-1844	Acknowledged debts of estate of Joseph Humphries listed: to David Hill... $41.12 1/2; to James T. Kelly 173.80 plus interest thereon of 47.49; to James T. Kelly "acpt" 9.53; and to ELIZABETH NAIL "apt"... "xxx xx."
12-29-1845	Texas Statehood. 9 Tex. Jur. 415.
3-30-1846	Panola County created by act of first legislature of Texas.
1846	Mahaly Humphries, daughter of William and Polly Humphries, born.
2-8-1846	Grant of headright from Republic of Texas to heirs and assigns of Benjamin Strickland. GLO.
5-16-1846	Letter from Elizabeth Nail to Dr. Rowe, requesting he lift her patent on the George Humphries 1/3 league and send it to her. Written in her own hand. GLO.
6-29-1846	Sarah Humphries conveys to James T. Kelley the lot or parcel on the east side of the Sabine River and known as Walnut or Humphries Bluff—the subject of the bond given to James T. Kelley on March 1, 1841.
6-29-1846	Sarah Humphries conveys to James T. Kelley the tract or parcel of land (50 acres) lying on the west side of the Sabine River and a part of the headright certificate of Joseph Humphries, about 200 yards from Humphries old

ferry, the subject of a bond given by Humphries to Kelley on March 15, 1841.

6-29-1846	Joseph Humphries estate closed. HCPR.
8-6-1846	Patent 90, Volume 3, file she-1-54, Certificate 280, issued to heirs of George Humphries. GLO.
9-1-1846	Panola County formed, Pulaski first county seat. History of Panola County. PCHS.
11-3-1849	Dempsey Blanks marries Mary S. Humphries. Panola County records.
1846-1850	William Humphries dies.
1850	Census records Panola County: Sarah Humphries, age 43 living with children Riley Humphries, 17, Philip Humphries 14, and "Mary" Humphries age 18.
1850	Census records Panola County: "James" Story and Tenny Story living with children Joseph, 13, Matilda 12, William 8, Robert 4, and Felena.
6-1-1850	Stephen B. Dozier marries Evelina Elliott. Panola County Records.
7-28-1850	Thomas Humphries sells all of his interest in the estate of Joseph Humphries to George Nippert for $150.
10-4-1850	Panola County, Texas Census record: Polly Umphries, widow, living with Jane 15, Tina 13, Manda 12, Jonathan 10, Andrew 9, Polly 8, and Mahaly 4.
12-27-1850	Having advertised it for sale, the Tax Assessor and Collector of Jefferson County sells and deeds the Pelham Humphries league to the State of Texas. Foster V. Gulf Oil Corporation 335 S.W. 845 (see entry 3-31-1960).

1-10-1853	Sarah Humphries conveys to Mary D. Robe all her right title and interest in the track of land on which the town of Pulaski is situated on and formerly known as Walnut Bluffs on the east side of the Sabine, but specifically not the interest of any of her children.
4-29-1853	Polly Humphries petition for guardianship of the "Heirs of William Humphries, Deceased," stating that his "headright" in Panola County needs to be sold for their support. (Plus incomplete but signed order.) Vol. C, 598 et seq PCPR.
1853	May Term of Panola County Court: Order granting Polly Humphries petition for letters of guardianship for heirs of William Humphries and appointing James T. Kelley, Andrew Robe, and Stephen L. Davis appraisers of the minors' estate. PCPR.
12-26-1853	Thomas Humphries marries Mary Witherspoon. PCPR.
7-30-1854	Field notes of 1280 acres on the west side of the Sabine of Joseph Humphries headright certificate 41 assigned to James T. Kelley. GLO.
12-14-1854	Texas Governor E.M. Pease grants title in Panola County (formerly Shelby County) labor of land (certificate 256) to William Humphries, his heirs and assigns. GLO.
10-30-1855	Petition of Thomas McFadden (husband of Jane Humphries McFadden) for guardianship of the heirs of William and Polly Humphries: Amanda Humphries, Holland Humphries and Mahala Humphries, minors and the owners, as the heirs of their mother Polly Humphries, in one third of a league of land the headright of David McHeard and in the

estate of their grandmother, Jane McFadden, and in the estate of their uncle Samuel McFadden. PCPR.

2-5-1856   William Perry Herring McFaddin born to William and Rachel McFaddin, called "Perry." RMW

9-7-1857   Warranty deed from "Pelham Humphries" to David Snively (of Refugio County, Texas) for $2,000, all interest in the Jefferson County league. JCPR.

This deed was executed in Bexan County, Texas and signed by "Pelham Humphries" (no "mark"). It was filed for record in Jefferson County on January 5, 1861. Vol. M, 401, 402, JCPR.

12-4-1857   Thomas Humphries sale of his interest in Joseph Humphries estate recorded on Panola County records.

9-26-1859   Warranty deed from Pelham Humphries Jr. and William Humphries and heirs and joint heirs of the estate of Pelham Humphries deceased ("our father"), to Stephen P. Dozier of Panola County, Texas, for $1200, the Jefferson County league. Signed in San Augustine County by making their marks. Filed for record in Jefferson County on September 22, 1860. Vol. M, 276, 277. JCPR.

1860   Census records Panola County: Amanda Humphries and Holland Humphries living with Jane and Thomas McFadden. Jane and Thomas have children Mary, age 5, and Adaline, age 2.

1860   Census records Panola County: Joseph and "Tinna" Story with children Joseph 23, Alexander 13, Ellen 10, Thomas 6, and Layla 3.

4-11-1861	Jeptha Anderson marries Sarah J. Cochran. Panola County Records.
11-24-1862	Amanda Hughs and husband James W. Hughs occupy 160 acres surveyed for them in Panola County. GLO.
1863	James Hughs leaves Panola County and does not return. Amanda Hughs affidavit-proof of settlement, File 3-869 GLO.
7-22-1863	Holland Humphries marries Sarah English. Panola County Records.
4-4-1864	Joseph Story marries Mary Parrish. Panola County Records.
1866	Texas adopts the Constitution Relinquishment Act, Art. VII, Sec. 39, releasing to the owners of the soil all mining and mineral substances.
6-3-1866	Mahaley Humphries marries L.M. McMullen. Panola County Marriage Records.
1870	Census records Panola County: Lewis McMillan and Mahala McMillan living in Panola County with children Andrew 3, Elizabeth 4 Months, and with Amanda Hughs.
1870	Census records Panola County: 50-year-old Sallie Humphries living next door to Mahala and Amanda.
1870	Census records Panola County: Thomas Humphries 35, Mary 27, Elizabeth 14, Thomas 7, Margaret 6.
1870	Census records Panola County: S.B. Dozier 50, living with William Dozier 14, and Stephen Dozier 6, (no wife).

5-22-1871	Amanda Hughs affidavit, proof of settlement 160 acres preexemption grant in Panola County. File 3-896 GLO.
6-16-1871	Letter patent to Amanda Hughs for the Panola County preexemption grant. GLO.
12-27-1873	Deed to W.P.M. McFaddin from M.W. Houghton, who was the grantee of Alexander Homes who was the grantee of B.B. Lacey, of an interest in the Pelham Humphries league, Lacey being the grantee of Baily English who acquired an interest in the league as the heir of William English. JCPR.
12-16-1874	Mahala McMillan marries G.W. Cobb. Panola County marriage records.
6-25-1880	Census records for Panola County: Thomas Humphries 54, wife Jane 31, son William T. (Thomas?) 16, daughter Margaret A. 15, daughter Bula 1.
8-10-1880	Deed from Jane McFadden of Panola County and J.T. Coble and Mahayla Coble of Smith County, as heirs at law to the estate of William Humphries . . . to Attorneys Tom J. Russell, J.W. Hays and T.E. Boren, 1/2 of the body of land in Jefferson County belonging to them as heirs of William Humphries in consideration of the attorneys bringing suit to recover the lands for them. Mahayla does not sign. JCPR.
1882	Cause 682, the heirs of Wm Humphries v. Simpson et al and heirs of Wm English; Court grants special exception 3 and strikes such portion of heirs of English pleadings that seek to attack title and possession of defendants Simpson, Engalls, and Dallas as set out in amended original answer of heirs of Wm English filed 5-10-1880. JCPR.

2-14-1883	Jane McFadden/Mahayla Coble deed to Russell et al, Recorded in Vol. V, 425. JCPR.
2-21-1883	Deed from Jane Wilkerson, daughter and heir at law of William and Mary Humphries deceased, and formerly the wife and later the surviving widow of Thomas McFadden and the wife of William Wilkerson, but who has later still abandoned me . . . for consideration of $125 convey to J.G. Hazelwood, all my right and claim be an undivided one third as heir at law the that certain league of land in Jefferson County. . . granted to William Humphries as "Pelham Humphries." JCPR.
	The deed to correct a deed to J.G. Hazelwood dated 2-10-1883 which contained erasures and other immaterial defects.
12-5-1883	Heirs of William Humphries v Simpson et al, cause 682 Jefferson County District Court: compromise in case but plaintiff Thomas Anderson is a minor. Tom J. Russell appointed as guardian for purposes of carrying out the terms of the compromise on behalf of Thomas Anderson: to receive $800 with Russell to get $200 for his services. JCPR.
12-10-1883	Deed from Tom J. Russell to W.P.H. McFaddin, for $400, to Russell's one fourth interest in the Pelham Humphries league acquired from the heirs of William Humphries as a fee for his services in recovering the land for them in suit 682 pending in the District Court of Jefferson County. The heirs of William Humphries are: Jane McFadden, Mahala Coble and her husband Thomas Coble, and Thomas Anderson, a minor represented by Tom Russell. JCPR.

12-10-1883   Deed from Thomas Anderson (by his guardian Tom J. Russell) to W.P.H. McFaddin for $800, for Anderson's one third interest in the Pelham Humphries league (as part of settlement of case 682). JCPR.

12-14-1883   Deed from James Ingalls to W.P.H. McFaddin for $800, for two tracts totaling 500 acres of the Pelham/William Humphries league in Jefferson County. JCPR.

12-19-1883   Deed from Henry F. Ring of Harris County and J.W. Thompson of Falls County for $400, to W.P.H. McFaddin, all of their interest in the Pelham Humphries league being that of Mahale Coble and her husband Thomas Cobel, one of three heirs at law of the original grantee (a one third interest) subject to a half interest in the third conveyed to Tom J. Russell, attorney, for services in prosecuting a suit for recovery of the league. JCPR.

12-24-1883   Deed from Thomas E. Boren to W.P.H. McFaddin for $400, to all right, title, and interest in the Pelham Humphries league, to wit: a one fourth interest conveyed as a fee for recovering the league, from the heirs of Pelham Humphries: Jane McFadden and Mahala Coble (and Thomas Coble, her husband). JCPR.

12-25-1883   Deed from J.G. Hazelwood to W.P.H. McFaddin in consideration of $125, all rights acquired by Hazelwood from Jane McFadden late Jane Wilkerson, daughter of William Humphries deceased, conveyed on February 21,1883. JCPR.

12-27-1883   Deed from M.W. Houghton to W.P.H. McFaddin for $50, for all right, title, and interest in the Humphries league as an assignee or grantee of the heirs of Wm English: Bailey English as heir of Wm English to B.B. Lacey, and Lacey to M.W. Houghton 12-27-1873. JCPR.

12-31-1883   Deed from R.E. Carswell (as agent for the "heirs of Wm English") to W.P.H. McFaddin for $390.25 being part of the $600 to be paid the heirs of English in compromise of case 682, all of their interest in the Pelham Humphries league in Jefferson County. JCPR.

1-10-1884   Deeds from Jane Wilkerson to J.G. Hazelwood recorded in Jefferson County.

1-10-1884   Deed from Hazelwood to W.P.H. McFaddin recorded in Jefferson County.

1-10-1884   Deed from "heirs of Wm English" to their interest in the Pelham Humphries league for $390.25, in compromise of Civil Suit 682, Heirs of Humphries vs. Heirs of Wm English, filed for record Vol. W, 322. JCPR.

1-10-1884   Deed from M.W. Houghton to W.P.H. McFaddin filed for record in Jefferson county, Vol. W, 326, 327.

1-10-1884   Deed from Thomas Anderson (by guardian Russell) to W.P.H. McFaddin received for filing in Jefferson County, Vol. W, 327, 328, 329.

1-10-1884   Deed from Thomas E. Boren to W.P.H. McFaddin received for filing Jefferson County Vol. W, 329, 330.

1-10-1884   Deed from Tom J. Russell to W.P.H. McFaddin filed for record in Jefferson County Vol. W, 331, 332.

1-10-1884	Deed from James Ingalls to W.P.H. McFaddin filed for record in Jefferson County Vol. W, 332, 333 and 334.
2-7-1885	Deed from W.P.H. McFaddin to T.J. Chaison and J.M. Hebert for $715.50, 530 acres of Pelham Humphries league. (West side of the big hill.) Vol. X, 224. JCPR.
5-21-1885	Case 682 Heirs of Wm Humphries v. Henry E. Simpson: Plaintiffs Jane McFadden, Mahala Coble, Thomas Anderson, minor son of Garrison Anderson and Amanda Anderson deceased, who was a daughter of Wm Humphries and defendants Simpson et al and heirs of English, M.W. Humphries, and the heirs of S.B. Dozier, all of which defendants filed answers and pleadings but not appeared at court nor made further defense; the court finds for the plaintiffs that they recover from the defendants all the lands and premises sought: the Pelham Humphries league in Jefferson County. JCPR.
12-26-1886	Deed from William McFaddin, W.P.H. McFaddin,V. Wiess and W.W. Kyle to D.W. Lewis of forty eight and fifty two hundredths acres of the Pelham Humphries league. Vol. 14, page 437. JCPR.
8-14-1887	Deed from W.P.H. McFaddin to Beaumont Pasture Company of 1887 for $5,000, 3898 acres of the Pelham Humphries league (and four other tracts of land). JCPR.
3-18-1888	J.B. Humphries marries Mary Parker. Panola County records.
10-15-1895	Deed from Beaumont Pasture Company of 1887 (in consideration of other land) to Wm McFaddin, W.P.H. McFaddin, V. Wiess, and W.W. Kyle, 3898 acres of the Pelham

Humphries league (and other lands). Vol. 11, page 174. JCPR.

10-22-1898 Thomas Humphries dies. Lived near McDaniels Ferry. McDaniels Ferry, also known as Hookers Ferry, located two miles north of the mouth of the Murvaul Bayou. Leila LaGrone Panola County obituary.

1-23-1899 W.P.H. McFaddin and Jas. A. McFaddin as executors of the wills of Wm McFaddin and Rachel McFaddin deed 957 1/2 acres of the P. Humphries league, to W.P.H., representing the undivided 1/4 interest of Wm McFaddin and Rachel in said league, after deducting 530 acres to Chaison and Hebert, 48 1/2 acres to Dan Lewis, and 19 1/2 acres to Sabine & East Texas Railway. Vol. 26, 272. JCPR.

5-14-1900 Oil lease from J.M. Hebert and Clara Chaison to A.F. Lucas of 500 acres of the P. Humphries survey. JCPR.

6-20-1900 10-year lease (with extension provisions if producing) for oil drilling and production (or any minerals) from W.P.H. McFaddin, V. Wiess, and W. W. Kyle to Anthony Lucas for all of the P. Humphries league containing 3850 acres more or less, for $1.00 and one tenth of all produced. JCPR.

1900 Census records for Panola County: Thomas Anderson, born 1870, living with wife Mary, son William 4, daughter Bertha 1.

1900 Census records for Panola County: Maggie Humphries 24, living with mother Mollie Blair 55, and Maggie's daughters, Gracie Humphries 5, and Mineloa Humphries 3.

1-10-1901 SPINDLETOP GUSHER

5-1-1901   Lease of 933 acres of the Pelham Humphries league from W.P.H. McFaddin, V. Wiess, and W.W. Kyle to J.M. Guffy, John H. Galey and Anthony F. Lucas (unrecorded ... see 5-16-1901 agreement). JCPR.

5-2-1901   J.T. Coble, Mack Coble, and Bazie Cobel of Limestone Ct., Texas, power of attorney to C.A. Kennedy to take possession of, sue, and recover our one third undivided interest in the Pelham Humphries survey, conveys to Kennedy an undivided one half interest in all their interest in the land. JCPR.

5-6-1901   Coble(s) to Kennedy filed for record in Jefferson County Vol. 47, page 219, 220. JCPR.

5-14-1901   Affidavit of L.M. Truit who will be 74 on the 11th day of June 1901, that he came to Texas in the year 1839, that he knew Squire Humphries during his lifetime, that Squire was hung by the Regulators in the fall of 1841; that he knew Joseph Humphries and "knew Pelham Humphries from reputation" that from what he heard of them they were from the same stock or family of people and that he has known Joe Story who now lives in Shelby County ever since he was a boy, and that his father's name was Joseph Story. Vol. 40, page 569, 569. JCPR.

5-15-1901   Power of attorney and conveyance from heirs of Thomas Humphries who was a son of Joseph Humphries: S.E. Milford and M.D. Milford, W.T. Humphries and J.S. Humphries, as grandchildren and heirs of Joseph Humphries, to James W. Truit and H.N. Nelson for an undivided one-half of the lands that they may recover of the Pelham

	Humphries land standing in Jefferson County. JCPR.

5-16-1901   Assignment of lease rights to 933 acres of the Pelham Humphries league from J.M. Guffy, John H. Galey, and Anthony F. Lucas d/b/a the J.M. Guffy Company to the J.M. Guffy Petroleum Company. JCPR.

5-24-1901   Affidavit from Salli Wilkerson of Panola County, age "about 60 years old" and lived in eastern Texas about 60 years, that she knew Joseph Humphries and Sallie Humphries were (Sallie Wilkerson's) aunt, that she knew William Humphries and Tunie Story were brother and sister, and that they were children of Joseph Humphries by his first wife.

"There was a Pelham Humphries in the family of Joe Humphries I know that Pelham Humphries was a brother of Tiny and William because the old folks said so and I have heard William Humphries and Tiny speak of their brother Pelham." Vol. 40, page 565. JCPR.

5-24-1901   Affidavit of A.E. Anderson, a commissioner of Panola County who states that he has known Sallie Wilkerson for 40 to 50 years, that she is the surviving wife of Benny Wilkerson, that her reputation for truth and veracity is good and that she is worthy of belief. Vol. 40, page 567. JCPR.

5-24-1901   Affidavit of A.S. Wall that he has known Sallie Wilkerson for 50 years, that she is 65 or 70 years old, and that she is honest and truthful old woman. Vol. 40, page 567. JCPR.

5-24-1901   Affidavit of Susie and Nannie Wilkerson of Panola County that they knew Thomas

Humphries during his lifetime, that they have both heard him speak of his half brother Pelham Humphries, and, further, that they have always been told that Thomas Humphries is a half brother of William Humphries and Tiny Story. Vol. 40, page 567, 568. JCPR.

5-29-1901   Deed from C.S. Bradley, R.C. DeGraffeuorid, A. Hull, A.N. Baker Jr. for $5,000, to Chaison(s) all their interest in the Pelham alias William Humphries league of 118.92 acres. Filed for record 5-31-1901 Vol. 42, pages 430-432. JCPR.

6-3-1901   Deed (and power of attorney) from M.A. Graves to J.E. Wall and A.R. Wall, in consideration of recovering and reducing them to possession, an undivided one half of all lands of Pelham Humphries in Jefferson County to which she is entitled as an heir of Pelham Humphries, M.A. Graves being one of four children of Thomas Humphries, said Thomas Humphries being one of three children surviving their father Joseph Humphries who was the father of Pelham Humphries. The other two children surviving Joseph Humphries being: William Humphries and Tuniny Story, wife of Joe Story. Vol. 40, page 565. JCPR.

6-4-1901   Affidavit of R.B. Wilkerson who states that he is acquainted with Sallie Wilkerson, his sister, who is 65 to 70 years old and the surviving widow of Berry Wilkerson; that he was well acquainted with Joseph Humphries and that the last wife of Joseph Humphries was the aunt R.B. Wilkerson, and that Joseph Humphries had three children by his first wife: Pelham, William and Teuny and three by his second wife: Tom, Riley, and

Phill. "I have for many years been of the impression that Pelham was killed by the Mexicans, this information handed down by his parents, and that he died without issue about 1838 or 1839." Vol. 40, page 570. JCPR.

6-8-1901   Deed from J.T. Coble, the surviving husband of Mahaley Coble, Andrew McMillan, Macko Coble, and Bazie Coble, the only heirs of Mahaley Coble and C.A. Kennedy, for $1,300, to Chaisons (et al), "our thirds interest in . . . two blocks of lands each being a part of the William or Pelham Humphries league Survey situated in Jefferson County." Vol. 43, pages 551-553, Recorded 6-10-1901. JCPR.

6-11-1901   Andrew McMillan et al v. A.F. Lucas et al: Defendants Chasion (et al) severed from case and settled by payment of $1,300 to plaintiffs in exchange for deed to two blocks of the "William (or Pelham) Humphries survey situated in Jefferson County containing 118.92 acres." (See deed from J.T. Coble . . . above.) Vol. 46, pages 565-567. JCPR.

6-11-1901   Affidavit of Ben Cannes (sp) that he is now 67 years old, was born in this part of the state, and was personally acquainted with Joseph Humphries and his family, and that Joseph Humphries had two sets of children, three by his first wife: Pelham, William and Tiny. He never heard of Pelham being married. Tiny married Joe Story and died leaving children Joseph Story, Alex Story, Ellen, and Jeannie. William Humphries died leaving four children: Jane, Holland, Mahala, and Amanda. Joseph Humphries had three children by his second wife: Thomas, Rile, and

Phill. Rile and Phill were never married and died leaving no children. Thomas Humphries left several children when he died. "I have always heard that Pelham Humphries was killed and that he died before his father did. I know that Joseph Humphries died at Pulaski on the Sabine River. I never heard of Pelham owning any land in this county." Vol. 40, page 568. JCPR.

7-25-1901   5-16-1901 Assignment of lease rights to J.M. Guffy Petroleum Company filed for record in Jefferson County Vol. 48, pages 536-539. JCPR.

8-14-1901   Power of attorney from John Humphries and Abe Humphries of Fulton County Georgia to their brother W.A. Humphries of McLennan County Texas to recover the interest they may have in the Pelham Humphries league. JCPR.

8-24-1901   Deed (and power of attorney) from Jennie Haliburton, S.P. Haliburton, S.E. Milford, M.D. Milford, W.T. Humphries, and James Humphries, in consideration of prosecuting a suit to recover the lands, to H.N. Nelson of Panola County an undivided one half interest in the lands standing in the name of the Pelham Humphries league in Jefferson County.

This instrument revokes the deed and POA executed to James W. Truit and H.N. Nelson on 5-10-1901. Vol. 53, pages 173, 174. JCPR.

10-15-1901   John and Abe Humphries power of attorney to W.A. Humphries filed for record in Jefferson County Texas. Vol. 54, pages 11-13. JCPR.

10-29-1901	Power of attorney from M.T. Humphries of Calhuan County Alabama to Lillie A. Mincey of Greenville, Hunt County, Texas, in regard to interests that he may be entitled to in regards to "any and all lands located at or near Beaumont or in Jefferson County" Texas. Vol. 54, page 257, 258. JCPR.
11-29-1901	Deed from H.N. Nelson to W.L. Crawford of a fractional interest in the Pelham Humphries league. Vol. 54, page 406. JCPR.
12-17-1901	Deed from Marcus T. Humphries to Lillie Mincey for one dollar and love and affection (his eldest daughter), all his interest in the "Pelham Humphries" survey in Jefferson County, Texas. JCPR.
1-2-1902	Warranty deed from Marcus T. Humphries to Lillie Mincey recorded on Jefferson County Public Records. Vol. 55, page 250, 251. JCPR.
6-14-1902	Deed from H.N. Nelson, W.L. Crawford, W.T. Humphries, S.E. Milford, M.D. Milford, James S. Humphries, and Jennie Halliburton to Hugh B. Short and John H. Broocks, an undivided fractional interest for legal services in reducing the Pelham Humphries land in Jefferson County to their possession. Vol. 61, pages 503-507. JCPR.
7-3-1902	Deed from H.N. Nelson et al to Short and Broocks filed for record Jefferson County. JCPR.
7-10-1902	Deed from Jennie Halliburton, Maggie Lingo, W.T. Humphries, M.D. Milford, Sarah Elizabeth Milford, and James Humphries to John H. Broocks and H.B. Short, an undivided one third one hundredths, and to H.M.

Nelson, an undivided interest of nine and one third one hundredths, and to W.L. Crawford an undivided thirty seven and one third one hundredths:

"It is the intention ... to convey ... to John H. Broocks and H.B. Short jointly and to ... H.M. Nelson and W.L. Crawford ... sixty percent of our interest in ... the pelham Humphries league ... and to retain unto ourselves ... forty percent of our said interest...." JCPR.

7-10-1902   Deed from Jennie Halliburton, Maggie Lingo, W.T. Humphries, M.D. Milford, S.E. Milford, and James Humphries for $4000, to P.A. Norris and Frank J. Phillips, thirty one hundredths of an undivided three fourth of the Pelham Humphries league (leaving us an undivided ten percent interest) and hereby sell forth percent which is our whole interest in that certain forty eight and fifty two hundredths acres of the said league which was conveyed to D.W. Lewis by McFaddin et al on 12-26-1896. JCPR.

7-10-1902   Irrevocable power of attorney from Jennie Halliburton, W.T. Humphries, James Humphries, S.E. Milford, joined by her husband M.D. Milford, and Maggie Lingo, as owners of ten one hundredths of three fourths of the Pelham Humphries league, except for forty eight and fifty two one hundredths of said league known as the D.W. Lewis tract, to H.B. Short to bargain, sell etc our entire remaining interest in the Pelham Humphries league, now in litigation in Jefferson County. JCPR.

7-12-1902	Above irrevocable power of attorney filed for record in Jefferson County Vol. 62, pages 458-462. JCPR.
7-12-1902	Deed of 7-10-1902 from Halliburton et al to Broocks et al, filed for record, recorded 7-14-1902. Vol. 63, pages 461-464 Jefferson County Records. JCPR.
7-12-1902	Deed of 7-10-1902 from Halliburton et al to P.A. Norris and Frank Phillips filed for record, recorded on 7-14-1902 Jefferson County Records Vol. 63, pages 464-467. JCPR.
10-8-1902	Power of attorney and grant of one half of his interest in land or monies from the sale of the land, from David T. Humphries of Greens County Tennessee to C.W. Howith and Charles R. Reynolds of Jefferson County Texas, to recover compromise title to sell... "all lands that I may be entitled to as an heir at law of Pelham Humphreys... more particularly that League of land... in Jefferson County." JCPR.
12-10-1902	David T. Humphries POA and deed to Howith and Reynolds filed for record in Jefferson County Vol. 69, pages 93, 94. JCPR.
4-25-1906	Thomas Anderson et al v. A.F. Lucas et al No. 2817 in the District Court of Jefferson County, Texas, the parties having entered into an agreement disposing of all matters in controversy between them, it is ordered and adjudged: Jennie Halliburton, W.T. Humphries, James Humphries, M.D. Milford and wife S.E. Milford, Maggie Lingo, H.N. Nelson, John H. Broocks, H.B. Short, W.L. Crawford, W.L. Crawford as trustee, P.A. Norris, and Frank J. Phillips take nothing

against defendants J. M. Hebut, Clara
Chaison, Charles J. Chaison, W.G. Chaison,
Lizzie Chaison Bryan and Husband Singleton Bryan, Jennie Chaison Houk and
husband W. Houk, Telara Brandon Russell,
Jeff Russell, Alberta Russell the executors of
the last will and testament of Hallie G.
Russell, and the defendants go hence without
day as regards the land in controversy in this
severed cause (a portion of the Pelham
Humphries survey, about 530 acres). JCPR.
Plaintiffs get no rents or profits from the
land, defendants get possession and title
quieted in their name. Each party to pay
their costs, in accordance with their agreement, defendants to pay plaintiffs
("complainants") the sum of $350.

4-25-1906   Thomas Anderson et al v. A.F. Lucas et al
No. 2817 in the District Court of Jefferson
County, Texas, the parties having entered
into an agreement disposing of all matters in
controversy between them it is ordered and
adjudged: Jennie Halliburton, W.T. Humphries, James Humphries, M.D. Milford and
wife S.E. Milford, Maggie Lingo, H.N.
Nelson, John H. Broocks, H.B. Short, W.L.
Crawford, W.L. Crawford as trustee, P.A.
Norris, and Frank J. Phillips take nothing
against by their suit against defendants the
Higgins Oil and Fuel Company and the
defendant go hence without day as regards
the land in controversy in this severed cause
(blocks 27-29, 33-35 of Spindle Top Heights
sub-division including a portion of the
Pelham Humphries Survey, as recorded in
book one page 25 of the Map records of
Jefferson County). JCPR.

Plaintiffs get no rents or profits from the land, defendants get possession and title quieted in their name. Each party to pay their costs, in accordance with their agreement, defendants to pay plaintiffs ("complainants") the sum of $250.

9-1-1906   Judgment(s) in Thomas Anderson et al vs. A.F. Lucas et al filed for record in Jefferson County Vol. 91, pages 479-478-483. JCPR.

6-30-1923   Affidavit of W.P.H. Mcfaddin to the effect that he purchased the whole of the Pelham Humphries sometimes known as the William Humphries survey, in 1883, that in January 1884 he fenced the whole of the league except a portion that he had theretofore sold to other parties, and that it had been continuously fenced and in use since that time. JCPR.

That in 1894 his agent D.W. Lewis moved on the property and commenced cultivation of a small portion and looked after stock thereon. The land has been continuously in use for raising farm products and grazing. He and his successors have continuously claimed to own and have paid taxes on the land.

Affidavit attested to as true by Henry Davison, employee of McFaddin, Wiess, Kyle Land Company.

7-3-1923   Affidavit of W.P.H. McFaddin filed for record in Jefferson County Vol. 230, pages 7, 8. JCPR.

1927   Rosine McFaddin born, daughter of Caldwell McFaddin (W.P.H. McFaddin's son), later marries Will Wilson and becomes Rosine McFaddin Wilson.

11-10-1948   No. 1511, Glover et al v. McFaddin et al. 81 F. Supp 426, District Court for E.D. of Texas: Suit to recover title and possession of land, for an accounting and damages related to the Pelham Humphries survey, filed by L.B. Glover and others against Mrs. W.P.H. McFaddin and others.

Plaintiffs allege they are the heirs at law of William Humphries, Betsy Jane Humphries Foust, and Elisha V. Humphries "who Plaintiffs say were the sole heirs at law of Pelham Humphries, the original grantee of such tract of land." Plaintiffs seek damages of five hundred million dollars.

Plaintiffs also allege that defendants claim under Jesse Humphries, a son of Elisha V. Humphries, Jr. and that, therefore, they are tenants in common with defendants on the tract. Plaintiffs seek to recover not only for themselves, but on behalf of a large number of other tenants in common, i.e., heirs of said Pelham Humphries similarly situated.

Defendants motion to dismiss, considered by the court as a motion for more definite statement, granted with leave to amend to name other tenants in common and their place of residence.

Plaintiffs may only recover for tenants in common who are parties to the suit and in their own interest in the land or damages, if any.

4-23-1951   No. 1511, Glover et al v. McFaddin et al 99 F Supp 385: Approximately 1,000 parties appear as plaintiff or intervenors and 20 appear as defendants.

Defendants moved to dismiss for want of diversity and to have the claims of various intervenors determined. Judge Ben Connally held intervenors who sought to align themselves with plaintiff and who had complete diversity would be allowed, but intervention by parties who presented new and different issues from the main action are denied for unduly delaying disposition of the action.

Plaintiff's attorneys: Herman R. Parker, C. Howard Bozeman, Francke Sandford, and Hugh C. Simpson of Knoxville, E. GARLAND BROWN of Corpus Christi and M. Herbert Oldham of Beaumont.

Defendants: Mrs. McFaddin, Mrs. Houck, Perry McFaddin, Caldwell McFaddin, Unity Oil Co., Magnolia Petroleum Co., Stanolind Purchasing Co., Gulf Oil Corporation, Gulf Refining Co., Gulf States Utilities Co., Kansas City Southern Ry. Co., Sun Oil Co., Sun Pipe Line Co., Texas & New Orleans R. Co., Reconstruction Finance Corp., Defense Plant Corporation, Lynn Magill, Fred M. McSpadden, Mrs. Louise H. Taylor, Charles E. English.

The court divided the intervenors into three groups:

Group I, those who claim to be additional collateral kin of Pelham Humphries, claim the same chain of title, and adopt the original plaintiff's pleading except that of their heirship;

Group II, those whose allegations which are completely inconsistent with those of the plaintiffs and other groups of intervenors or with each other, and each of them describes the original patentee under whom they claim in a manner to indicate that, despite the name, he was in fact a different individual from the original patentee, they allege a different table of genealogy;

Group III, a group represented by Charles E. "English" and who contend that Pelham Humphries and William Humphries are one and the same individual, that the deed from William Humphries to William English was genuine, but that the original deed did not convey the "mineral interests," and that the mineral interest remained in the sovereign until they passed to Bailey English, son of William English, by constitutional amendment in 1866.

Allegations of plaintiffs:

They are the collateral kin of Pelham Humphries who died intestate 9-5-1835, single and without issue, survived by a brother William Humphries, sister Betsy Jane Humphries Foust, and a half-brother, Elisha V. Humphries Jr.; that during their entire lives William, Betsy Jane, and Elisha resided in Tennessee and were not aware of their inheritance on the death of their brother Pelham; that as part of a fraudulent conspiracy by strangers to their title, after the death of Pelham, the name "Pelham" was stricken and replaced by the name "William" in the original title papers and likewise a forged and fraudulent power of attorney from William Humphries to William English was prepared under which the title ostensibly was conveyed to others; that title has actually reposed in the descendants of William, Betsy Jane, and Elisha during all of the intervening years.

Further alleged: That the defendants in possession purchased from collateral kin of the original patentee and hence plaintiff and defendants are tenants in common.

Plaintiffs pray for title and possession, an accounting of the oil extracted therefrom, and appointment of a receiver to take possession of the land, the refineries and other improvements and for damages.

6-5-1953   Glover V. McFaddin 205 F2d 1 (5th Cir) E. GARLAND BROWN for appellants.

Affirmed summary judgment that "brothers and sister of patentee from Mexico" took no interest by inheritance at patentee's death in 1835 since they were aliens to Mexico and Mexican law precluded inheritance by aliens. Property would have escheated to Mexico on death of owner.

ADMITTED that appellees, or their predecessors in title, have been in actual possession since November 17, 1860, that they fenced the land in 1884 and have paid all taxes on the land since 1884, Appellants having never been in possession or paid taxes.

12-1-1955   McBride et al v. Gulf Oil Corporation et al, 292 S.W.2d 151 (Tex. Ct. App. Beaumont) Rehearing denied May 23, 1956, further rehearing denied June 27, 1956.

Appeal from a jury trial in Jefferson County, Texas. Plaintiff's claimed as heirs of William Humphrey who was born in the State of North Carolina in 1786. William Humphrey never married, never had any children, and never had a "family." Plaintiff's claims are at odds with the facts recited in the application for grant of land in question. The circumstances and descriptive recitations appearing in the application for grant and in the certifi-

	cate must be accepted as true. Directed verdict for defendants affirmed.
1959	Ernest Medders answers notice in Tuscaloosa, AL, paper looking for heirs of "Ruben Medders, the brother-in-law of Pelham Humphries." MM.
3-31-1960	Foster v. Gulf Oil Corporation et al, 335 S.W.2d 845 (Tex. Ct. App. Beaumont) rehearing denied 4-27-1960.
	Vacancy suit involving the Pelham Humphries league in Jefferson County brought by the plaintiff (after his application for a mineral lease on the land was denied in 1953 by the General Land Office Commissioner) for adjudication of the question as to whether the land is or is not vacant and unsurveyed school land. District Court of Jefferson County, Judge Harold R. Clayton's judgment for defendants affirmed.
1961	W.T. Weir files Jones et al v. W.P.H. McFaddin et al in the 58 District Court in Jefferson County. Ernest Medders a plaintiff in this action.
1961	Subiaco Priests loan Medders $20,000 for move to Texas. MM.
12-10-1961	Medders move to Texas. MM.
9-15-1962	Ernest Medders receives $15,000, the first in a series of loans from the Sisters of St. Francis eventually totaling 1.94 million. MM.
8-20-1963	Jones et al v. W.P.H. McFaddin et al pending before Judge Brookshire 58 District Court (Jefferson County): Judge enters summary judgment for defendants on statute of limitations and adverse possession theories. Beaumont Enterprise article 8-21-1963.

9-1-1964   Jones et al v. W.P.H. McFaddin et at, 328 S.W.2d, (Tex. Ct. App. Texarkana): Plaintiffs, heirs of original landowner suit, to try title to surface and mineral estates against heirs of subsequent landowners.

Appellants/Plaintiffs' Attorneys W.T. Weir, Philadelphia, Miss., William Glover, Houston, and W.W. Hewitt, Meadowville, Miss.

Plaintiff sued on behalf of approximately 3,000 heirs of Pelham Humphries against W.P.H. McFaddin and 300 other defendants, alleging defendants removed approximately one-half billion dollars of minerals from the Pelham Humphries league.

The Jefferson County District Court Judge, Jack Brookshire, granted summary judgment for defendants on theories of statutes of limitations and adverse possession. The Court of Civil Appeals affirmed finding the record supported the finding that McFaddin had unbroken, continuous, peaceful and adverse possession of all the Humphries league of land since 1883, over 75 years!

Plaintiffs argued that the mineral estate was severed from the surface estate by the Spanish Mining Ordinance of 1783; that the mineral estate was reserved to the Crown of Spain and subsequently to the State of Texas and that, each being fee simple estates, could not be merged by the Constitutional Release of 1866, further, that possession of the surface, although sufficient to cure limitation to the surface, would not mature limitation title to the severed mineral estate.

The Court found that, since the record shows a deed from Humphries to English was on 2-14-1836, and the Constitutional

Release was not executed until 1866, according to their own theory, the Humphries have never been the owners of the mineral estate and have no cause of action.

Moreover, in 1883, still prior to the Constitutional Release of 1886, English conveyed "all the right, title, and interest that they had in and to the league of land" to McFaddin, and, since the intention of the parties governs as to whether of not the mineral estate merged with the soil, the deed evidences such intention and the minerals merged into a fee simple estate with the surface and, if necessary, the mineral estate is subject to limitation title by possession of the minerals since the year 1901.

10-11-1965   Jones et al. v. W.P.H. McFaddin et al., 382 U.S. 15: Appeal dismissed for want of a substantial federal question.

4-9-1968   Green et al v. Texas Gulf Sulphur Company et al 393 F.2d 67 (5th Circuit). The Circuit Court affirms the US District Court for Eastern Division of Texas, Chief Judge Joe J. Fisher's dismissal of commissioner of general land office and entry of summary judgment in a declaratory judgment action seek an adjudication that a tax deed was invalid, on the theory that plaintiffs and predecessors had made no claim or use of the land for 125 years, and had paid no taxes thereon and could not successfully claim title against those who actively used and possessed the land and paid taxes thereon for such a period.

Heirs of Humphries claim only a mineral interest. They argue that an 1850 tax deed vested title in the State of Texas, and, if it were set aside, they would be entitled to the minerals rather than the appellees.

If the tax deed did vest title in Texas, the doctrine that a party must recover on the strength of his own title, not on the weakness of his opponents, would preclude recovery.

4-9-1968   Beasley et al v. W.P.H. McFaddin, Jr., et al, 383 F.2d 68 (5th Cir.). The Humphries heirs in this case claim only an interest in the land. They argue that the original grant was to Pelham and not to William Humphries. They argue that the William Humphries who conveyed to Inglish in 1836 was not the heir of Pelham and had nothing to convey. For purposes of determining this case, the court did not need to discuss those issues. Appellees gained title by adverse possession.

4-9-1968   M.T. Humphries et al v. Texas Gulf Sulphur Company et al, 393 F.2d 69 (5th Cir.). Trial court granted summary judgment reasoning that the deeds from Humphries to Inglish in 1836 and the deed from "Pelham" Humphries to Snively in 1857 were valid and divested Humphries heirs of title.

Moreover, on the Texas "lost deed" presumption, the court adopts a conclusive presumption that the 125 years of adverse possession justifies the imposition of a conclusive presumption that the Humphries heirs have lost their title. This is a way to put a judicial stop to the Pelham Humphries litigation. These endless suits have been an harassment to the land and mineral owners as well as a useless expense of time and money by litigants and courts.

8-18-1986	Rosine McFaddin Wilson (59) kills former caretaker Joseph Albert Perkins (56) at 9:00 P.M. with a .22 caliber gunshot wound to the chest.
	Shooting takes place at entrance to Wilson's "M Half Circle Ranch" on Texas 73, Jefferson County Texas, while Perkins is in a pickup.
	Unknown to Rosine, the shooting is witnessed by Perkins' wife, Marie, who is a passenger in the truck, but who, in the dark, was apparently not seen by Rosine.
	Rosine drives off after the shooting.
8-19-1986	At her home, Rosine McFaddin Wilson removes the bullets (putting them in a "tool drawer"), wraps the murder weapon in newspaper, and throws it in the garbage.
	Rosine tells Jefferson County sheriff's deputies (Sgt. Jay White, a female deputy, and Sgt. John Gowling) she has no knowledge of Perkins' death.
	Later that day Sgt. White again questions Rosine who denies being at the ranch Monday night and says that she was playing bridge until 7:00 P.M. that night and did not go out after that.
	Sgt. White tells Rosine that they have the statement of Marie Perkins that Rosine was at the ranch; Rosine calls her a liar and suggests that Marie may have killed Perkins because she was going to get a divorce and leave her husband, and, now that Perkins was dead, Marie has an "instant divorce."
	Rosine refuses to give a written statement without speaking to her husband.

8-20-1986	Rosine, accompanied by her lawyer Joseph "Lum" Hawthorn, gives a written statement to deputies White and Gowling saying the shooting was "accidental."
9-3-1986	Rosine indicted for first degree murder.
12-1-1986	*Houston Chronicle* runs "Spindletop/Humphries" regarding Brown Peregoy and the Humphries Heirs Trust Association (5,000 members), quotes Jim Petty, Salt Lake City genealogist hired by Humphries to prove heirship with William Humphries.
1986	Rosine visits Jim Petty in Salt Lake City, knowing who he is and questioning him about his progress in proving the Humphries' claims. She is a mean, hard woman.
1-27-1987	Sometime after 10:30 P.M., Rosine takes an overdose of pills with alcoholic beverage.
1-28-1987	Rosine McFaddin Wilson found unconscious in her bedroom and is hospitalized for drug overdose at St. Elizabeth Hospital in Beaumont.
2-7-1987	Rosine released from the hospital.
4-13-1987	Defense change of venue hearing begins in Wilson case.
4-14-1987	At change of venue hearing, "Many witnesses testified that they had heard rumors in the community that [Rosine] was having an affair with Perkins..." *Houston Chronicle* 4-15-1987.
5-15-1987	Judge Gist orders venue of the trial changed from Jefferson County to Harris County (Houston).

8-18-1987	After grant of change of venue motion, Rosine McFaddin Wilson's trial begins in Houston, Texas.
8-26-1987	Rosine found guilty of involuntary manslaughter, gets five years probation and $5,000 fine, $100 court costs.
2-14-1989	Brown Peregoy (and three others) file complaint in the United States District Court for Western Tennessee seeking 200 billion dollars as the legal heirs of Pelham Humphries.
9-27-1989	In re B.L. Peregoy, 885 F2d 349 (6th Cir.) appeal from the District Court of Tennessee entry of order of transfer, heirs petitioned for writ of mandamus, petition denied finding that transfer to the Eastern District of Texas was appropriate for convenience of parties and witnesses and in the interest of justice.
6-18-1990	Peregoy v. Amoco Production Co., a Division of Standard Oil of Indiana; Mobile Oil Corporation; Phillips Petroleum Co.; Texaco Inc., Chevron, Inc., 742 F. Supp 372 (US District Court, Eastern District Texas).
	District Court Judge Cobb dismissed case on doctrines of stare decisis, collateral estoppel and res judicata. Citing to the Humphries "trilogy" of claims (Green, Beasley, and Humphries), Judge Cobb said: "This case is meritless. A simple and cursory examination of the table of cases in the Federal Digest System would have revealed the result which this court reached..." Judge Cobb set a hearing for possible sanctions against the plaintiffs and lawyer under rule 11.
	"Lest there be any further misunderstanding as to this court's ruling, take heed: there is no claim available to any heir of Pelham

Humphries as to any part, parcel, or portion of the league of land commonly known as the Humphries Survey, nor the minerals extracted therefrom . . . . "

4-23-1991   Peregoy et al v. Amoco et al 929 F2d 196, (5th Cir.) Affirms Judge Cobb's dismissal on summary judgment.

Appendix B

A Selected Abstract of Title

9-27-1834	Bond for title under which "William" Umphries (and John Crippen) contract with William Inglish and Wiatt Hanks for all but 1,000 acres the league(s) of land just petitioned for, in consideration of $1,999 (each) and the costs of surveying the land, Inglish and Hanks get to select the land too. 11GOYH pp. 57-59 San Augustine County Public Records.
2-14-1835	Title of possession of league of land in name of "Pelham Humphries," issued by Commissioner Nixon.
10-6-1835	Affidavit and power of attorney by "William Umphries" appointing Wm Inglish to take out the land title and change the name from "Pelham to William." Affidavit taken by Anthony Hotchkiss, Primary Judge of the Municipality of San Augustine. Witnessed by Samuel McFadden, E. Rains, Jonathan Anderson, and Wm Inglish.

2-14-1836	Warranty deed William Humphries to William Inglish for $1,000, a certain league of land...attested to by John G. Love, Primary Judge of San Augustine. Vol. M, 399. JCPR.
9-17-1840	Warranty deed William "Humphreys" to John G. Love for $600, 500 acres of the Jefferson County league of land. Vol. M, 344. JCPR.
12-27-1850	According to the 1960 case of Foster v. Gulf Oil Corporation 335 S.W. 845, the Tax Assessor and Collector of Jefferson County purportedly sells and deeds the Pelham Humphries league to the State of Texas. (See Appendix A entry for 3-31-1960).
9-07-1857	Warranty deed from "Pelham Humphries" to David Snively (of Refugio County) for $2,000, all interest in the Jefferson County league.
	This deed was executed in Bexan County, Texas and signed by "Pelham Humphries (no "mark"). It was filed for record in Jefferson County on January 5, 1861. Vol. M, 401, 402. JCPR.
9-26-1859	Warranty deed from Pelham Humphries, Jr., and William Humphries and heirs and joint heirs of the estate of Pelham Humphries deceased ("our father"), to Stephen P. Dozier of Panola County, Texas, for $1200, the Jefferson County league. Signed in San Augustine County by making their marks. Filed for record in Jefferson County on September 22, 1860. Vol. M, 276, 277. JCPR.
12-27-1873	Deed from B.B. Lacey to M.W. Houghton of an interest in the Pelham Humphries league, Lacey being the grantee of Baily English who acquired an interest in the league as the heir of William English.

8-10-1880   Deed from Jane McFadden of Panola County and J.T. Coble and Mahayla Coble of Smith County, as heirs at law to the estate of William Humphries... to attorneys Tom J. Russell, J.W. Hays, and T.E. Boren, 1/2 of the body of land in Jefferson County belonging to them as heirs of William Humphries in consideration of the attorneys bringing suit to recover the lands for them.

2-14-1883   Jane McFadden/Mahayla Coble deed to Russell et al, recorded in Vol. "V" 425 Jefferson County Records.

2-21-1883   Deed from Jane Wilkerson, daughter and heir at law of William and Mary Humphries deceased, and formerly the wife and later the surviving widow of Thomas McFaddin and the wife of William Wilkerson, but who has later still abandoned me... for consideration of $125 convey to J.G. Hazelwood, all my right and claim be an undivided one third as heir at law that certain league of land in Jefferson County... granted to William Humphries as "Pelham Humphries."

The deed to correct a deed to J.G. Hazelwood dated 2-10-1883 which contained erasures and other immaterial defects.

12-10-1883   Deed from Tom J. Russell to W.P.H. McFaddin for $400, to Russell's one fourth interest in the Pelham Humphries league acquired from the heirs of William Humphries as a fee for his services in recovering the land for them in suit 682 pending in the District Court of Jefferson County. The heirs of William Humphries are: Jane McFadden, Mahala Coble and her husband Thomas Coble, and Thomas Anderson, a minor represented by Tom Russell.

12-10-1883	Deed from Thomas Anderson (by his guardian Tom J. Russell) to W.P.H. McFaddin for $800, for Anderson's one third interest in the Pelham Humphries league (as part of settlement of case 682).
12-14-1883	Deed from James Ingalls to W.P.H. McFaddin for $800, for two tracts totaling 500 acres of the Pelham/William Humphries league in Jefferson County.
12-19-1883	Deed from Henry F. Ring of Harris County and J.W. Thompson of Falls County for $400, to W.P.H. McFaddin, all of their interest in the Pelham Humphries league being that of Mahale Coble and her husband Thomas Cobel, one of three heirs at law of the original grantee (a one third interest) subject to a half interest in the third conveyed to Tom J. Russell, attorney for services in prosecuting a suit for recovery of the league.
12-24-1883	Deed from Thomas E. Boren to W.P.H. McFaddin for $400, to all right, title, and interest in the Pelham Humphries league, to wit: a one fourth interest conveyed as a fee for recovering the league, from the heirs of Pelham Humphries: Jane McFadden and Mahala Coble (and Thomas Coble, her husband).
12-25-1883	Deed from J.G. Hazelwood to W.P.H. McFaddin in consideration of $125, all rights acquired by Hazelwood from Jane McFadden late Jane Wilkerson daughter of William Humphries deceased, conveyed on February 21, 1883.
12-27-1883	Deed from M.W. Houghton to W.P.H. McFaddin for $50, for all right, title, and interest in the Humphries league as an

assignee or grantee of the heirs of Wm English: Bailey English as heir of Wm English, to B.B. Lacey, and Lacey to M.W. Houghton 12-27-1873.

12-31-1883   Deed from R.E. Carswell (as agent for the "heirs of Wm English") to W.P.H. McFaddin for $390.25, being part of the $600 to be paid the heirs of English in compromise of case 682, all of their interest in the Pelham Humphries league in Jefferson County.

1-10-1884   Deeds from Jane Wilkerson to J.G. Hazelwood recorded in Jefferson County.

1-10-1884   Deed from Hazelwood to W.P.H. McFaddin filed in Jefferson County.

1-10-1884   Deed from "heirs of Wm English" to their interest in the Pelham Humphries league for $390.25, in compromise of Civil Suit 682, Heirs of Humphries vs. Heirs of Wm English, filed for record Vol. W, 322 Jefferson County.

1-10-1884   Deed from M.W. Houghton to W.P.H. McFaddin filed for record in Jefferson County, Vol. W, 326, 327.

1-10-1884   Deed from Thomas Anderson (by guardian Russell) to W.P.H. McFaddin received for filing in Jefferson County, Vol. W, 327, 328, 329.

1-10-1884   Deed from Thomas E. Boren to W.P.H. McFaddin received for filing Jefferson County Vol. W, 329, 330.

1-10-1884   Deed from Tom J. Russell to W.P.H. McFaddin filed for record in Jefferson County Vol. W, 331, 332.

1-10-1884	Deed from James Ingalls to W.P.H. McFaddin filed for record in Jefferson County Vol. W, 332, 333, and 334.
2-7-1885	Deed from W.P.H. McFaddin to T.J. Chaison and J. M. Hebert for $715.50, 530 acres of Pelham Humphries league. (West side of the big hill.) Vol. X, 224. JCPR.
5-21-1885	Cause 682 Heirs of Wm Humphries v. Henry E. Simpson: plaintiffs Jane McFadden, Mahala Coble, Thomas Anderson, minor son of Garrison Anderson and Amanda Anderson deceased, who was a daughter of Wm Humphries, and defendants Simpson et al. and heirs of English, M.W. Humphries, and the heirs of S.B. Dozier, all of which defendants filed answers and pleadings but not appeared at court nor made further defense; the court finds for the plaintiffs that they recover from the defendants all the lands and premises sought: the Pelham Humphries league in efferson County. JCPR.
12-26-1896	Deed from William McFaddin, W.P.H. McFaddin, V. Wiess and W.W. Kyle to D.W. Lewis of forty eight and fifty two hundredths acres of the Pelham Humphries league. Vol. 14, page 437. JCPR.
8-14-1887	Deed from W.P.H. McFaddin to Beaumont Pasture Company of 1887 for $5,000, 3898 acres of the Pelham Humphries league (and four other tracts of land).
10-15-1895	Deed from Beaumont Pasture Company of 1887 (in consideration of other land) to Wm McFaddin, W.P.H. McFaddin, V. Wiess, and W.W. Kyle, 3,898 acres of the Pelham Humphries league (and other lands). Vol. 11, 174 JC Records.

1-23-1899   W.P.H. McFaddin and Jas. A. McFaddin as executors of the wills of Wm McFaddin and Rachel McFaddin deed 957 1/2 acres of the P. Humphries league, to W.P.H., representing the undivided 1/4 interest of Wm McFaddin and Rachel in said league, after deducting 530 acres to Chaison and Hebert, 48 1/2 acres to Dan Lewis, and 19 1/2 acres to Sabine & East Texas Railway. Vol. 26, 272. JCPR.

5-14-1900   Oil lease from J.M. Hebert and Clara Chaison to A. F. Lucas of 500 acres of the P. Humphries survey. JCPR.

6-20-1900   10 year lease (with extension provisions if producing) for oil drilling and production (or any minerals) from W.P.H. McFaddin, V. Wiess, and W.W. Kyle to Anthony Lucas for all of the P. Humphries league containing 3850 acres more or less, for $1.00 and one tenth of all produced.

1-10-1901   SPINDLETOP GUSHER

5-1-1901   Lease of 933 acres of the Pelham Humphries league from W.P.H. McFaddin, V. Wiess, and W.W. Kyle to J.M. Guffy, John H. Galey, and Anthony F. Lucas (unrecorded ... see 5-16-1901 agreement).

5-2-1901   J.T. Coble, Mack Coble, and Bazie Cobel of Limestone Co. Texas, Power of Attorney to C.A. Kennedy to take possession of, sue, and recover our one third undivided interest in the Pelham Humphries survey, conveys to Kennedy an undivided one half interest in all their interest in the land.

5-6-1901   Coble(s) to Kennedy filed for record in Jefferson County Vol. 47, page 219, 220.

5-15-1901   Power of Attorney and conveyance from heirs of Thomas Humphries who was a son of Joseph Humphries: S.E. Milford and M.D. Milford, W.T. Humphries and J.S. Humphries, as grandchildren and heirs of Joseph Humphries; to James W. Truit and H.N. Nelson for an undivided one half of the lands that they may recover of the Pelham Humphries land standing in Jefferson County.

5-16-1901   Assignment of lease rights to 933 acres of the Pelham Humphries league from J.M. Guffy, John H. Galey, and Anthony F. Lucas d/b/a the J.M. Guffy Company to the J.M. Guffy Petroleum Company.

5-29-1901   Deed from C.S. Bradley, R.C. DeGraffeuorid, A. Hull, A.N. Baker Jr. for $5,000, to Chaison(s), all their interest in the Pelham alias William Humphries league of 118.92 acres. Filed for record 5-31-1901 Vol. 42, pages 430-432.

6-3-1901   Deed (and power of attorney) from M.A. Graves to J.E. Wall and A.R. Wall, in consideration of recovering and reducing them to possession, an undivided one half of all lands of Pelham Humphries in Jefferson County to which she is entitled as an heir of Pelham Humphries, M.A. Graves being one of four children of Thomas Humphries, said Thomas Humphries being one of three children surviving their father Joseph Humphries who was the father of Pelham Humphries. The other two children surviving Joseph Humphries being: William Humphries and Tuniny Story, wife of Joe Story. Vol. 40, page 565 Jefferson County Records.

6-8-1901   Deed from J.T. Coble, the surviving husband of Mahaley Coble, Andrew McMillan, Macko Coble, and Bazie Coble, the only heirs of Mahaley Coble and C.A. Kennedy for $1300, to Chaisons (et al), "our thirds interest in . . . two blocks of lands each being a part of the William or Pelham Humphries league survey situated in Jefferson County." Vol. 43, pages 551-553, Jefferson County Records. Recorded 6-10-1901.

7-12-1901   Irrevocable power of attorney from Jeanne Halliburton. W.T. Humphries, James Humphries, S.E. Milford joined by her husband M.D. Milford, and Maggie Lingo, as owners of ten one hundredths of three fourths of the Pelham Humphries league except for forty eight and fifty two one hundredths of said league known as the D.W. Lewis tract, to H.B. Short, to bargain, sell, etc., our entire remaining interest in the Pelham Humphries league, now in litigation in Jefferson County.

7-12-1901   Above irrevocable power of attorney filed for record in Jefferson County Vol. 62, pages 458-462.

8-24-1901   Deed (and power of attorney) from Jennie Haliburton, S.P. Haliburton, S.E. Milford, M.D. Milford, W.T. Humphries, and James Humphries, in consideration of prosecuting a suit to recover the lands, to H.N. Nelson of Panola County an undivided one half interest in the lands standing in the name of the Pelham Humphries league in Jefferson County.

This instrument revokes the deed and POA executed to James W. Truit and H.N. Nelson on 5-10-1901. Vol. 53, pages 173, 174 Jefferson County Records.

11-29-1901	Deed from H.N. Nelson to W.L. Crawford of a fractional interest in the Pelham Humphries league. Vol. 54, page 406 Jefferson County Records.
12-17-1901	Deed from Marcus T. Humphries to Lillie Mincey for one dollar and love and affection (his eldest daughter), all his interest in the "Pelham Humphries" survey in Jefferson County, Texas.
1-2-1902	Warranty Deed from Marcus T. Humphries to Lillie Mincey recorded on Jefferson County Public Records. Vol. 55, page 250, 251.
6-14-1902	Deed from H.N. Nelson, W.L. Crawford, W.T. Humphries, S.E. Milford, M.D. Milford, James S. Humphries, and Jennie Halliburton to Hugh B. Short and John H. Broocks, an undivided fractional interest for legal services in reducing the Pelham Humphries land in Jefferson County to their possession. Vol. 61, pages 503-507, Jefferson County Records.
7-3-1902	Deed from H.N. Nelson et al to Short and Broocks filed for record Jefferson County.
7-10-1902	Deed from Jennie Halliburton, Maggie Lingo, W.T. Humphries, M.D. Milford, Sarah Elizabeth Milford, and James Humphries to John H. Broocks and H.B. Short an undivided one third one hundredths, and to H.M. Nelson, an undivided interest of nine and one third one hundredths, and to W.L. Crawford, an undivided thirty seven and one third one hundredths:

"It is the intention ... to convey... to John H. Broocks and H.B. Short jointly and to ... H.M. Nelson and W.L. Crawford ...

> sixty percent of our interest in . . . the pelham Humphries league . . . and to retain unto ourselves . . . forty percent of our said interest . . . . "

7-10-1902   Deed from Jennie Halliburton, Maggie Lingo, W.T. Humphries, M.D. Milford, S.E. Milford, and James Humphries for $4,000, to P.A. Norris and Frank J. Phillips, thirty one hundredths of an undivided three fourth of the Pelham Humphries league (leaving us an undivided ten percent interest) and hereby sell forth percent which is our whole interest in that certain forty eight and fifty two hundredths acres of the said league which was conveyed to D.W. Lewis by McFaddin et al on 12-26-1896.

7-12-1902   Deed of 7-10-1902 from Halliburton et al to Broocks et al, filed for record, recorded 7-14-1902. Vol. 63, pages 461-464 Jefferson County Records.

7-12-1902   Deed of 7-10-1902 from Halliburton et al to P.A. Norris and Frank Phillips filed for record, recorded on 7-14-1902 Jefferson County Records Vol. 63, pages 464-467.

10-8-1902   Power of attorney and grant of one half of his interest in land or monies from the sale of the land, from David T. Humphries of Greens County Tennessee to C.W. Howith and Charles R. Reynolds of Jefferson County Texas, to recover, compromise title to sell . . . "all lands that I may be entitled to as an heir at law of Pelham Humphreys . . . more particularly that League of land . . . in Jefferson County." JCPR.

12-10-1902   David T. Humphries POA and deed to Howith and Reynolds filed for record in Jefferson County Vol. 69, pages 93, 94.

4-25-1906   Thomas Anderson et al. v. A.F. Lucas et al. No. 2817 in the District Court of Jefferson County, Texas, the parties having entered into an agreement disposing of all matters in controversy between them, it is ordered and adjudged: Jennie Halliburton, W.T. Humphries, James Humphries, M.D. Milford and wife S.E. Milford, Maggie Lingo, H.N. Nelson, John H. Broocks, H.B. Short, W.L. Crawford, W.L. Crawford as trustee, P.A. Norris and Frank J. Phillips take nothing against defendants J.M. Hebut, Clara Chaison, Charles J. Chaison, W.G. Chaison, Lizzie Chaison Bryan and Husband Singleton Bryan, Jennie Chaison Houk and husband W. Houk, Telara Brandon Russell, Jeff Russell, Alberta Russell, the executors of the last will and testament of Hallie G. Russell, and the defendants go hence without day as regards the land in controversy in this severed cause (a portion of the Pelham Humphries survey, about 530 acres).

Plaintiffs get no rents or profits from the land, defendants get possession and title quieted in their name. Each party to pay their costs, in accordance with their agreement, defendants to pay plaintiffs ("complainants") the sum of $350.

4-25-1906   Thomas Anderson et al v. A.F. Lucas et al No. 2817 in the District Court of Jefferson County, Texas, the parties having entered into an agreement disposing of all matters in controversy between them it is ordered and adjudged: Jennie Halliburton, W.T. Humphries, James Humphries, M.D. Milford and wife S.E. Milford, Maggie Lingo, H.N. Nelson, John H. Broocks, H.B. Short, W.L. Crawford, W.L. Crawford as trustee, P.A. Norris, and Frank J. Phillips take nothing against by their suit against defendants the Higgins Oil and Fuel Company and the defendants go hence without day as regards the land in controversy in this severed cause (blocks 27-29, 33-35 of Spindle Top Heights sub-division including a portion of the Pelham Humphries survey, as recorded in book one page 25 of the map records of Jefferson County).

Plaintiffs get no rents or profits from the land, defendants get possession and title quieted in their name. Each party to pay their costs, in accordance with their agreement, defendants to pay plaintiffs ("complainants") the sum of $250.

9-1-1906 Judgment(s) in Thomas Anderson et al vs. A.F. Lucas et al filed for record in Jefferson County Vol. 91, pages 479-478-483.

Appendix C

Selected Documents

Due to fading inks, fragile papers, and the general ravages of time, many of the old documents did not successfully survive the reproduction process necessary to appear in this collection. The reader is encouraged to view or obtain his or her own copies of the following documents from the locations indicated. It is a rewarding task.

The Texas General Land Office, Archives and Records Division, Stephen F. Austin Building Room 800, 1700 North Congress, Austin Texas 78701-1495, is the source for the following:

The affidavit and power of attorney from William Humphries to William Inglish.

The authorization for survey of the William Humphries headright certificate of one labor of land.

The authorization for survey of one third of a league for Benjamin Strickland issued to Amos Strickland.

The authorization for survey of one third of a league for George Humphries issued to Elizabeth Nail.

The patent on William Humphries labor.

At the Jefferson County Clerk's Office, 1141 Pearl Street P.O. Box 1151, Beaumont, Texas 77704, the researcher will find the deeds from William Humphries to William Inglish and from William Humphries to John Love, along with the affidavits from the Wilkersons, and Messrs. Anderson, Wall, Truit and Cannes.

The Harrison County Clerk's Office, 200 West Houston, Marshall, Texas 75670, is the place to find Joseph Humphries Bond to James T. Kelley, Joseph's petition to administer the David McHeard estate, and William Humphries' petition to administer the David McHeard estate following Joseph's death.

The bond of Thomas Humphries to George Nippert will be found at the Panola County Clerk's Office, Room 201, Courthouse, Carthage, Texas 75633.

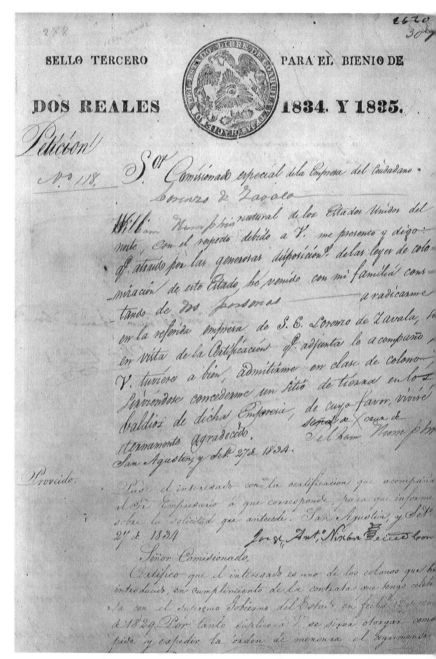

Original Spanish petition (four pages)

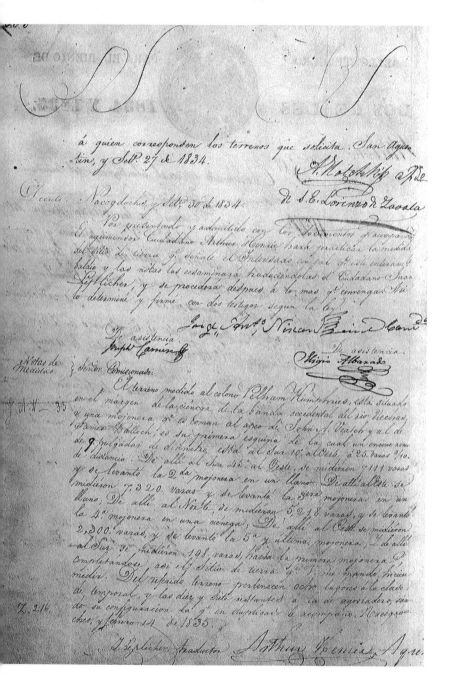

á quien corresponden los terrenos que solicita. San Agustin, y Sel.º 27 de 1834.

A. Molchile Azte
de S.E. Lorenzo de Zavala

Nacogdoches, y Sel.º 30 de 1834:

Por presentado y admitido con los documentos y acompaña El agrimensor Ciudadano Arthur Henrie hará practicar la medida del sitio de tierra q.ᵉ señalo el Interesado en tal q.ᵉ esta interam.ᵗᵉ baldio y las notas las esaminara traduciendolas el Ciudadano Juan Feplicher, y se procederá despues a lo mas q.ᵉ convenga Asi lo determine y firme con dos testigos segun la ley.

Jorge S.mtº Niscar Lain de Camd.
De asistencia.
Juseph Camire.

De asistencia.
Higio Alvarado

Notas de Medidas:

Señor Comisionado:

El terreno medido al colono Pelham Humphries, esta situado en el margen de la cienega, de la banda occidental del rio Necnas, y una mojonera, q.ᵉ es comun al ageo de John A. Veatch y al de Jamer Ballech, es su primera esquina de la cual un encino nom de 9. pulgadas de diametro, esta al Sur 10. al Oeste á 25. varas ¾⁄10. de distancia. De alli al Sur 45. al Oeste, se midieron 7111. varas y se levanto la 2.ᵈᵃ mojonera en un llano. De alli al Este se midieron 7,320. varas y se levanto la 3.ᵉʳᵃ mojonera en un llano, De alli al Norte, de midieron 5,218. varas, y se levanto la 4.ᵃ mojonera en una cienega; De alli al Oeste se midieron 2,300. varas, y se levanto la 5.ᵃ y ultima mojonera, Y de alli al Sur se midieron 198. varas, hasta la primera mojonera, completandose asi el sitio de tierra q.ᵉ V me mando hiciese media. Del referido terreno pertenecen ocho labores a la clase de temporal, y las diez y siete restantes a la de agostadero, siendo su configuracion la q.ᵉ en duplicado le acompaño. Nacogdoches, y febrero 14 de 1835.

J. Zeplicher, traductor   Arthur Henrie, Agro.

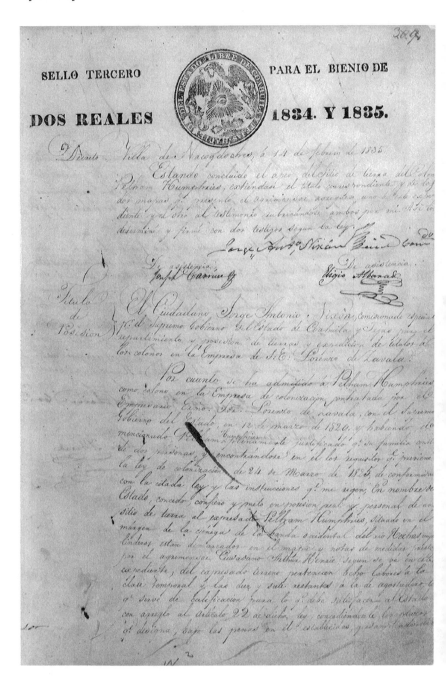

310.

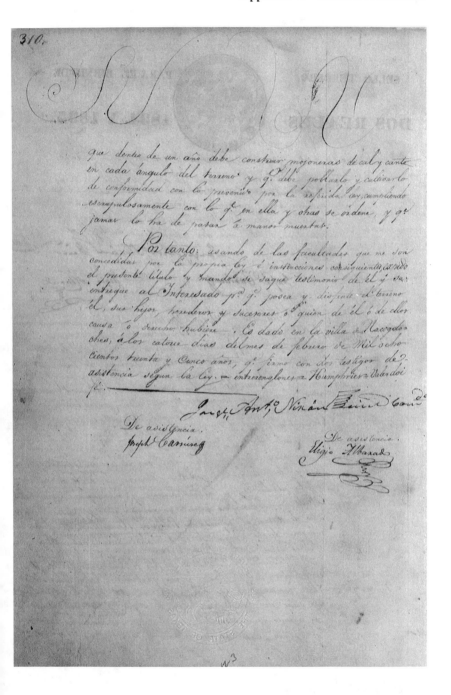

qe dentro de un año debe construir mojoneras de cal y canto
en cada angulo del terreno, y qe debe poblarlo y cultivarlo
de conformidad con lo prevenido por la referida Ley, cumpliendo
escrupulosamente con lo qe en ella y otras se ordene, y qe
jamas lo ha de pasar á menor cuenta.

Por tanto: usando de las facultades que me son
concedidas por la propia Ley é instrucciones consiguientes, estiendo
el presente titulo y mando se saque testimonio de el y se
entregue al Interesado pa qe posea y disfrute el terreno
el, sus hijos, herederos y sucesores ó quien de el ó de ellos
causa ó derecho hubiere. Es dado en la villa de Nacogdoches, á los catorce dias del mes de febrero de Mil ocho-
cientos treinta y cinco años, qe firmo con dos testigos de
asistencia segun la Ley. = entrerenglones = Humphries = vale doi
fe.

Jorge Antº Nixon

De asistencia.
Joseph Carricos

De asistencia.
Eligio Albarado

THIRD SEAL	[Seal of the Treasury of the Free State of	FOR THE BIENNIUM
TWO REALES	Coahuila and Texas]	OF 1834 AND 1835.

Petition
No. 118

Honorable Special Commissioner of the Enterprise of Citizen Lorenzo de Zavala:

         William
[I,] Pelham* Humphris, a native of the United States of the North, with due respect appear before you and say: That, attracted by the generous provisions of the colonization laws of this State, I have come with my family, consisting of two persons, to settle in the aforesaid enterprise of His Excellency Lorenzo de Zavala if you should see fit in view of the attached certificate to admit me as a colonist, being pleased to concede to me one league of land in the vacant tracts of said Enterprise, for which favor I shall live eternally grateful.

Mark of the X cross of
Pelham Humphrie

San Augustine, Sept. 27, 1834.

Order:

Let the interested party proceed with the accompanying certificate to the corresponding Honorable Empresario in order that he may report on the foregoing petition. San Augustine, Sept. 27, 1834.

Jorge Ant.° Nixon [Rubric] Com.^r

Report:

Honorable Commissioner:

    I certify that the interested party is one of the colonists I have introduced in fulfillment of the contract I made with the Supreme Government of the State on March 12, 1829. Therefore, I pray that you may be pleased to grant as he asks and issue the order of survey to the surveyor assigned the lands he requests. San Augustine, Sept. 27, 1834.

A. Hotchkiss, atty.
[Rubric]
of H[is] E[xcellency] Lorenzo de Zavala

Decree:

Nacogdoches, September 30, 1834.

    [The petition] Having been presented and admitted, along with the accompanying documents, the surveyor, citizen Arthur Henrie, shall have the survey made of the league of land designated by the interested party, provided it be entirely vacant, and he shall examine the notes, which are to be translated by Citizen Juan Leplicher, proceedings to follow as may be most suitable. Thus I decided and signed with two witnesses according to law.

Jorge Ant.° Nixon [Rubric] Com.^r

English translation of Spanish petition

212

Assisting Witness

Joseph Carriere [Rubric]

Assisting Witness

Eligio Albarado

[Rubric]

Field
Notes:

Honorable Commissioner:

The tract surveyed for colonist Pelham Humphries is situated on the margin of the marsh on the west side of the Neches River, and a landmark common to the John A. Veatch and James Bullock surveys is the first corner, from which a post oak 9 inches in diameter bears south 10° west 25 3/10 varas distant. Thence south 45° west surveyed 7,111 varas and raised the 2nd landmark in a prairie. Thence east surveyed 7,320 varas and raised the 3rd landmark in a prairie. Thence north surveyed 5,218 varas and raised the 4th landmark in a marsh. Thence west surveyed 2,300 varas and raised the 5th and last landmark. Thence south surveyed 198 varas to the first landmark, thus completing the league of land you ordered me to have surveyed. Of the aforesaid tract eight labors belong to the class of arable land and the remaining seventeen to that of pasture land, its configuration being that which in duplicate I send you herewith. Nacogdoches, February 14, 1835.

J. Leplicher, Translator

[Rubric]

Arthur Henrie, Surveyor

[Rubric]

THIRD SEAL	[L.S.]	**FOR THE BIENNIUM**
TWO REALES		**OF 1834 AND 1835**

Decree:

Town of Nacogdoches, February 14, 1835.

The survey of the league of land for colonist Pelham Humphries having been concluded, let the corresponding title be issued; and of the two plats presented by the surveyor let one be added to this file and the other to the testimonio, both being signed by me with my rubric. Thus I decided and signed with two witnesses according to law.

Jorge Ant.^{o} Nixon [Rubric] Com.^{r}

Assisting Witness

Joseph Carriere [Rubric]

Assisting Witness

Eligio Albarado

[Rubric]

Title
of
Posses-
sion:

Citizen Jorge Antonio Nixon, special commissioner of the Supreme Government of the State of Coahuila and Texas for the distribution and possession of land and the issuance of titles to the colonists in the enterprise of His Excellency Lorenzo de Zavala:

Whereas Pelham Humphries has been admitted as a colonist in the colonization enterprise contracted by the Empresario, the Most Excellent Lorenzo de Zavala, with the Supreme Government of the State on March 12, 1829, and the said Pelham ^{Humphries} having fully established that his family consists of two persons, and finding in him the requisites prescribed by the Colonization Law of March 24, 1825, in conformity with the aforesaid law and the instructions that govern me, in the name of the State I concede to, confer upon, and put the said Pelham Humphries in real and personal possession of one league of land situated on the margin of the marsh on the west side of the Neches River, the boundaries of which are delineated on the plat and in the field notes set down by surveyor Citizen Arthur Henrie, as is seen in this file of documents. Of the said tract eight labors belong to the class of arable land and the remaining seventeen to that of pasture land, which serves as classification for the amount he shall pay the State according to Article 22 of said law, conceding to him the terms it designates under the penalties therein established; he being notified that within one year he shall construct stone masonry landmarks at each corner of the tract, that he shall settle and cultivate it in conformity with the provisions of said law, complying scrupulously with what is ordered therein and elsewhere, and that he shall never convey it in mortmain.

Therefore, exercising the authority vested in me by the same law and the consequent instructions, I issue the present title and order a testimonio made of it and delivered to the interested party in order that he may possess and enjoy the tract, he, his children, heirs and successors, or whoever from him or from them shall have cause or right. Given in the Town of Nacogdoches on the fourteenth day of February, 1835, which I sign with two assisting witnesses according to law. Interlined - Humphries - valid - I certify.

Jorge Ant.^o Nixon [Rubric] Com.^r

Assisting Witness   Assisting Witness
Joseph Carriere [Rubric]   Eligio Albarado
                                     [Rubric]

* [Note: At this place in the original document, the name "William" has been written directly over the name "Pelham," which is the name appearing originally in the text.]

214

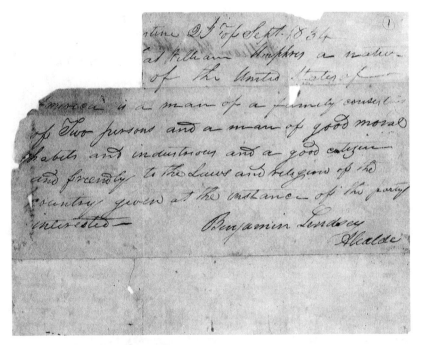

Benjamin Lindsey Certificate of Character

Before me Benjn. Lindsey Sole and Constitutional Alcalde
of the Municipality of San Augustine and three Instrumental
Witnesses who were by me appointed for that purpose besides
two assisting Witnesses with whom I associate for want of
a notary public according to Law, on this 27th day of
September in the year of our Lord one thousand eight hundred and thirty four,personally came and appeared John
Crippen & Wm Humpries residents of said municipality,
whom I certify that I know, and who declared, that they
acknowledged themselves, and who by these presents do
acknowledge themselves justly indebted to Wm Inglish
and Wyatt Hanks in the sum of nineteen hundred and ninety
nine dollars each, for the payment of which said sum of
nineteen hundred and ninety nine dollars as aforesaid,
well and truly to be made, on the immediate failure of
the conditions herein after expressed he hereby binds
themself their heirs executors administrators and assigns
jointly and severally firmly by these presents, with
all their property present and future of whatsoever nature
it may be, hereby renouncing all and every law in favor
of obligors and confessing a judgment against thereselves
with all Interests damages and costs which might accrue,
the same as if there had been a judgment rendered before
the proper tribunal, having obtained the authority, <u>de re
judicata</u> hereby renouncing- submitting theirselves to the
jurisdiction and authority of all the judges justices and
tribunals of the State-municipality- State and particularly to those of the municipality renouncing likewise
their own proper privileges, domicil and residence, the law

William Humphries Bond for Title (three pages)

216

si convenerit de jurisdictione omnium judicum and

all others, in due form, - The conditions of the above
obligations is such that whereas the aforesaid John
Crippen Wm Umfries have been received as settlers and
colonists in the colony of Zavala and whereas, they have
obtained from the agent of said Zavala an order of
Survey for 2 leagues of land, Now therefore If the aforesaid Wm Inglish and Wiatt Hanks shall well and truly and
privily-by-these-presents- faithfully select and surverey
the said land and pay all the expences incident thereto
until the said John Crippen and William Umfries shall
make or cause to be made a good title to the whole of said
two Leagues of land excepting one thousand acres to the
aforesaid William Inglish and Wiatt Hanks and to their
heirs or assigns to be divided according to quantity and
quality and value, as soon as the laws of the State will
permit the same, hereby obligating and binding himself
theirselves their heirs executors and administrators to
make the said title, in due form of law with all the
renunciations required by the laws, usages and customs
of the Country, then and in that case the above first
mentioned obligation of the payment of nineteen hundred
and ninety nine dollars, to be void or else remain in
full force and virtue, anything in the laws not-with -
standing- usages and customs of the Country notwithstand-
ing- - - - -

     Done and passed in the Town of San Augustine on the
27th day of September in the year of our Lord one thous-
and eighteen- hundred and thirty four in presence of
James W Bullock Henry Teel and Saml Raines as instrumental Witnesses present and residents by me the afore-

said Alcalde with Jos S Johnston and Edwin O Legrand
assisting witnesses with whom I associate for want of a
notary

according to law

          his
John x Crippen
      mark
         his
William x Umfries
        mark

Benjamin Lindsey Alcalde

Jos. S.Johnston,Edwin O Legrand

Assisting Witnesses

Field Notes of a Survey made for C. H. McClure and Joseph Humphrys assignees of Benjamin Strickland of 8,166,808 Square Varas of Land Situated on Walnut Bluff on the East bank of the Sabine River about 12 miles above the mouth of Muried Bayou it being a part of the land to which they the Said McClure & Humphrys are entitled by virtue of Certificate No 267 issued by the board of Land Commissioners for the County of _____ Certifying that the Said _____ is entitled to One Third part of a League of Land

Beginning at a Stake on Line Bank on a Conditional line between Said McClure & Humphrys and David McHugh from which S62 W 3 Var is a White Oak 30 in diam & N68 W 25 Var is a White Oak 24 in diam Each MrK 1 DS Thence with Said Conditional _____ to _____ from which N88 E 6 Var is a Pine 24 in diam & S31 W 35 Var is a Pine 24 in diam Each MrK 1 DS Thence North 1450 Var to a Corner Stake from which North 3 Var is a Maple 10 in diam & N12 W 3 Var is a Post Oak 6 in diam Each MrK 1 DS Thence _____ Gibbs Lake at 1172 Var _____ a Stake from which S _____ is a Pine 34 in diam _____ Pine 24 in diam _____ S35 W 9 Var is a Beech 30 in diam MrK 1 DS & N65 W 6 Var is a Sugar tree _____ N5 Thence N10 E _____ 1000 Var to the N W Corner of Said Labor a Stake from which N66 E 12 Var is a Hickory 12 in diam MrK 1 DS & S 86 17 Var is a Pine 24 in diam MrK 1 DS & N5 Thence S80 E 1000 Var to the _____ Corner of Said Labor a Stake from which S 52 E 25 Var is a Hickory 10 in diam MrK 1 DS & N5 & N 52 45 Var is a Hickory 10 in diam MrK 1 DS Thence N10 E 1450 Var to a Corner Stake _____ from which S 23 W 5 Var is a Red Oak 18 in diam & N 33 W 10 Var is a Hickory 14 in diam Each MrK 1 DS

Benjamin Strickland Survey (two pages)

Thence a width Sabine Lake West 600 Var to F. Coffin's
Corner a Stake from which N85W 11 Var is a Pine, 24 in diam &
S42W 9 Var is a Red Oak 20 in diam each MR 135 Thence
with said Coffin's line S55W 1340 Var to said Coffin's Corner
a Stake from which N50W 4 Var is a Red Oak 36 in diam
MR 135 + JLC + S28W 10 Var is a Hickory 10 in diam MR 135
Thence S73W 2380 Var to a corn Stake on J line V Bank from
which S55W 5 Var is a Sweet Gum 24 in diam & S53E 9 Var
is a White Oak 6 in diam each MR 135
Thence following down River S38W 627 Var Thence S40E
500 Var Thence S83E 1580 Var Thence S34E 270 Var Thence
S20E 460 Var Thence South 380 Var Thence S25E 300 Var
to Corner of the Begining Containing 8146808 Square Var
of which one half is arable the other

                Surveyed Sept. 6th

&Joseph Story&
Samuel Harrison Chainmen

    Field Notes of a
    Survey made for
    C H McClure and
    Joseph Humphreys by
    H Benj'n Strudwick

   Notice for Examination
   Sep. 12th 1838.

Joseph Humphries petition for remainder of headright entitlement (four pages)

The State of Texas } Be it Remembered
County of Harrison } that at the September
Term of the District Court for Harrison County
in said State the following proceedings were
had in the following cause — viz
Joseph Humphries }
vs } No 46.
Republic of Texas }

The Republic of Texas } Harrison District Court
County of Harrison } Septr Term in AD 1841

Petition filed
June 21st
46 1841

To the Honorable John M Hansford Judge
of the Seventh Judicial District Holding Sessions
for said County On the first Monday in Septr
AD 1841 — Your Petitioner Joseph Humphries
a citizen of said County and Republic afore
=said would with Respect Represent & Show
to your Honor that he Emigrated to the Repub
=lic of Texas in the year of our Lord One Thou
=sand Eight hundred and Twenty three
and that he has Remained in the Republic
Ever since his Emigration and was a citizen
of the same at the date of the declaration
of Independence and the head of a family
whose family did reside with him in Texas
at that time and by the laws & Constitution
he considers himself entitled to One League
and one Labor of Land from the Govern-
=ment of Texas — And petitioner further
represents to your Honor, that he made
an application to the Board of Land Comm-
=issioners when in Session for the County
of Shelby & Republic of Texas, and was not
at that time able to make the proof that said
Board required him to make and therefore

would not grant him an unconditional certificate for one League and one Labor of Land
as he did consider himself entitled to by the
Laws and Constitution of the Republic of Texas
but did grant him a constitutional certificate
for Twelve hundred and Eighty one of land,
And therefore your petitioner considers himself
injured and aggrieved in the proceedings and
prays your Honor to grant him a certificate
for the additional quantity of one League
and Labor of land which is three thousand
three hundred and forty one acres of land
which he does consider himself entitled to
by the Laws and Constitution all of which
facts and matters set forth in this petition
Petitioner is ready to verify and prove according to Law, And in granting the same petitioner in duty bound will Ever pray &c

        A P. Vaughan Attorney
           for Plaintiff

The Republic of Texas)
County of Harrison) Personally appeared
before me the undersigned authorized
Authority Joseph Humphries and after
being duly Sworn in due form of Law says
that the matters and facts set forth in
the foregoing Petition is Just and True Sworn
to and Subscribed to before me this 26th day of
June AD 1841   Joseph h x Humphries
Attest Samuel Stinson Clk

And at the Said Term of the Court on the
10th day of September 1841 the following
Judgment was entered.
           To wit—

Joseph Humphries ⎫ Petition for Land —
as ⎬ " In this case came the
Republic of Texas ⎭ Parties by their Attornies
" and thereupon came a jury of Twelve
" good and lawful men to wit, James Asher
" James Stout, David Gilleland Howard
" Dilliard, Benjamin Page James Dilliard, Jerem
" iah White Samuel McFadden James Lugrine
" Thomas D. Matthews James L Matthews and
" Drury Reid — who being duly sworn to well &
" truly try the issue joined and a true account
" render of the same returned into open
" court the following Verdict to wit, We the jury
" find in favor of the plaintiff Signed James
" A. Dilliard foreman
" It is therefore Considered by the Court that
" the plaintiff recover of the Republic of Texas
" Three thousand three hundred & forty
" one acres of land & that the plaintiff
" Joseph Humphries be taxed with the cost
" of Suit & that Execution issue "

The State of Texas ⎫
County of Harrison ⎬ I J M Henderson Clerk
of the District Court of Said County do
hereby Certify, that the foregoing contains
a full true & complete Transcript of the rec
-ords of the foregoing named cause wherein
Joseph Humphries is Plaintiff & the Republic of Texas
Defendant, Test J M Henderson Clk
of Said Court & Seal of Same at Mar-
-shall this 18th March AD 1853 —
J M Henderson Clk
By Alex Beazley Depy

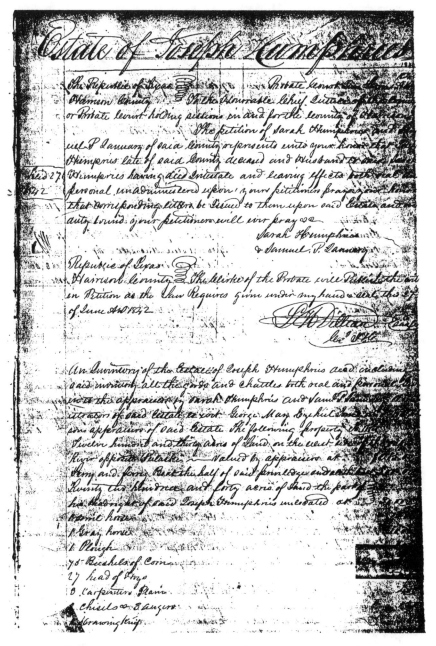

Estate of Joseph Humphries, Sarah Humphries and S.P. January Administrators (first page of nine)

The State of Texas } Know all men by these presents
County of Bexan } that I Pelham Humphries of the
Republic of Mexico for and in consideration of the sum of
Two thousand dollars to me in hand paid by David
Snively of the county of Refugio and State aforesaid
the receipt whereof is hereby acknowledged have
this day granted, bargained sold aliened and conveyed
and do by these presents grant, bargain, sell, alien
and convey unto him the said David Snively all
my right title interest and claim in and to a
certain League of Land Granted to me by the Government
of Coahuila and Texas on the 14th day of February
A. D. 1835 Situated on the West bank of Neches River
in the county of Jefferson and State of Texas. For a
fuller description of said land reference is hereby made
to the original title on file in the General Land
office of said State and which said Grant is
hereby made a part of this instrument, To have
and to hold all and singular the right, hereditaments and appurtenances to the same belonging or in
any wise appertaining thereto unto him the said
David Snively his heirs, executors administrators and
assigns and I the said Pelham Humphries for
myself my heirs executors, administrators and assigns
will forever warrant and defend, the right and Title
of the right and Title of the same against the claims
of myself my heirs executors administrators and assigns
or against any other person or persons claiming the same
or any part thereof in through, by or under me. In
testimony whereof I have hereunto set my hand and Seal
using Scroll for Seal this 7th day of September A. D. 1851.
Witness present.   Pelham Humphries (Seal)
Thos D. Pearce }
Wm Stoner }
The State of Texas
County of Bexan. } Before me H. Canterbury a
Notary Public in and for said county came Pelham
Humphries with whom I am personally acquainted and
acknowledged that he Signed, Sealed and delivered
the within and foregoing instrument of writing for
the purposes and considerations therein Stated.
Given under my hand and seal of office

Deed from "Pelham Humphries" to Snively (page 401)

Deed from "Pelham Humphries Jr. and William Humphries" to Dozier (page 276)

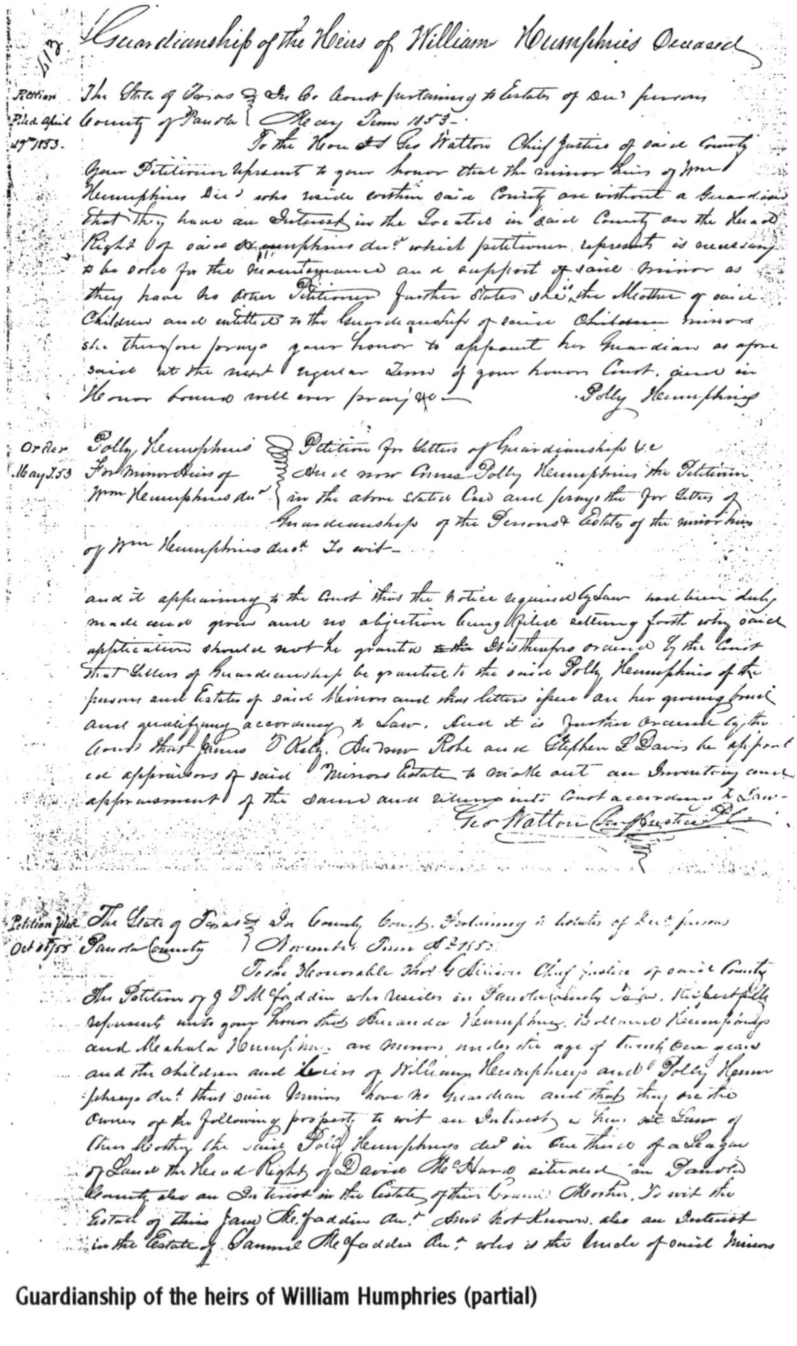

513 Guardianship of the Heirs of William Humphries Deceased

Petition Filed April 29th 1853.

The State of Texas } In Co. Court pertaining to Estates of Dec'd persons
County of Panola } May Term 1853.

To the Hon. Geo Watton Chief Justice of said County
Your Petitioner represents to your honor that the minor heirs of Wm
Humphries Dec'd who reside within said County are without a Guardian
that they have an Interest in the Located in said County on the Head
Right of said Humphries dec'd which petitioner represents is necessary
to be sold for the maintenance and support of said minor as
they have no other Petitioner further states she is the Mother of said
Children and entitled to the Guardianship of said Children minors
she therefore prays your honor to appoint her Guardian as afore
said at the next regular Term of your honors Court, and in
Honor bound will ever pray &c. — Polly Humphries

Order May T. 53

Polly Humphries For minor Heirs of Wm Humphries dec'd } Petition for Letters of Guardianship &c
And now Comes Polly Humphries the Petitioner
in the above stated Case and prays the for Letters of
Guardianship of the Persons & Estates of the minor heirs
of Wm Humphries dec'd To wit —

and it appearing to the Court that the Notice required by Law had been duly
made and given and no objection being filed setting forth why said
application should not be granted It is therefore ordered by the Court
that Letters of Guardianship be granted to the said Polly Humphries of the
persons and Estates of said Minors and that letters issue an her giving bond
and qualifying according to Law. And it is further ordered by the
Court that James T. Kelly, Andrew Rohe and Stephen L. Davis be appoint
ed appraisers of said Minors Estate to make out an Inventory and
appraisement of the same and return into Court according to Law —
Geo Watton Chief Justice P.C.

Petition filed Oct 18/55

The State of Texas } In County Court. Pertaining to Estates of Dec'd persons
Panola County } November Term A.D. 1855

To the Honorable Thos G Allison Chief Justice of said County
The Petition of Jas D McFaddin who resides in Panola County Texas, Respectfully
represents unto your honor that Amanda Humphreys, [illegible] Humphreys
and Mahala Humphreys are Minors under the age of twenty one years
and the children and heirs of William Humphreys and Polly Hum
phreys dec'd that said Minors have no Guardian and that they are the
Owners of the following property to wit an Interest [illegible] of
their Mother the said Polly Humphreys dec'd in One third of a League
of Land the Head Right of David McHard situated in Panola
County also an Interest in the Estate of their Grand Mother, To wit the
Estate of [illegible] Jane McFaddin dec'd [illegible] not known. also an Interest
in the Estate of Samuel McFaddin dec'd who is the Uncle of said Minors

Guardianship of the heirs of William Humphries (partial)

Tom J. Russell et al
agrent with
W.P.H. McFaddin

The State of Texas } Know all men by these presents that We,
County of Jefferson } Tom J. Russell of the first part; representing
the plaintiffs in a suit now pending in the district Court of
said county of Jefferson entitled No 682, Heirs of Wm Humphries vs Henry E. Simpson et als. which said plaintiffs are Jane McFadden, Mahala Coble, and her husband
Thomas Coble, whose interest in said suit, is now owned
by one P. V. Thompson, and Thomas Anderson a minor represented by said Tom J. Russell, as his Guardian,
or Attorney ad litem by the appointment of said Court,
each of said heirs owning a third interest in the
~~Court~~ Claim of plaintiffs and the firm of O'Brien &
John; parties of the second part, representing the defendants
in said suit namly James Ingalls. Molly Simpson
Langham only heir of Henry E. Simpson, decd and her husband J. B. Langham Jr. and the estate of Elisha O. Brewer
and the Heirs of James L. Dallas; decd whose names
appear of record, and the heirs of one Wm English;
decd all of whose names appear of record in said
suit, and claiming several distinct and seperate
interests in the subject matter of said suit namly, the
league of land situated in said County of Jefferson, granted to Pelham Humphries by the government, in 1835.
and W.P.H. McFadden party of the third part. Now it
is agreed by and between the parties of the first part,
and the second part that they will sell to the party
of the third part all of said league of land, and make
titles there to, said titles to be made ~~to~~ and signed
by the respective claimants of all of their seperate rights
titles interests and claims, unto said W.P.H. McFadden
of the third part for and in consideration of the
sum of six thousand dollars, to be paid to them
by said W.P.H. McFadden one half to be paid
now, and the other half of said sum to be paid

in one year from date of execution hereof, without interest
to be divided among the several parties of the first and
second parts as agreed upon among them, namly — To
Mahala Coble & her assign P. V. Thompson eight hundred
dollars, to Thomas Anderson or his guardian Tom J.
Russell eight hundred dollars; to Jane McFadden or
her Attes of record Tom J. Russell four hundred dol-

Case 682 settlement with W.P.H. McFaddin (two pages)

lars, one half of her claim the other four hundred to be
paid to the firm of O'Brien & John or to whom they may
direct, to James Ingalls the sum of $800 ºº to Mrs Molly
Langham the sum of $640 ºº to the heirs of James
L. Dallas or their attys O'Brien & John the sum of
$1960ºº to the heirs of Wm English or their attorney
in fact the sum of $600 ºº And it is agreed by W. P. H. Mc
Faddin party of the third part, that he will pay to the several parties of the first part and of the second part, the a-
mounts due them according to the terms of this agreement
upon the tendering to him of their several titles, one half
of the amount now, and the other half one year from
date hereof ~without interest~ and the said ~John J. Russell
party of the first part reserves the right to withdraw
from this agreement if the same is not fully carried
into effect and the ~same~ ~another~ before the first day
of January A.D. 1874.~
All interlineations and   John J. Russell, Atty for Wliffe
erasures made before signing. and guardian for Thomas Ludlow
                              O'Brien & John Attys for Ingalls,
                              Langham, Heirs of English & Heirs &c
                              ~W. P. H. Mc Faddin~
                              W. P. H. Mc Faddin
The state of Texas) Before me S. S. Miller Clerk of the Coun
County of Jefferson) ty Court of said County on this day
personally appeared John J. Russell, George W. O'Brien and
W. P. H. Mc Faddin known to me to be the persons whose
names are severally subscribed to the foregoing instrument
in writing or agreement, and they each for themselves
And for the parties respectively represented by them, acknowledged to me that they executed said Instrument
for the purposes and Considerations therein expressed
and in the Capacity therein set forth. Given under
My hand and the seal of the County Court of said
County at office in Beaumont this 7th day

Jane McFaddin
to
Tom J. Russell

The State of Texas }
Panola County } Know all men by these presents
that we Jane McFaddin of Panola County Texas and J. T. Coble
and Mahayla Coble of Smith County Texas heirs at law
to the estate of William Humphreys deceased being in
formed that there is a body of land in Jefferson County

Texas rightfully belonging to us a the heirs of the said William
Humphreys deceased have this day and by these presents do employ
Tom J. Russell of Jefferson County Texas an Attorney at law
and J. N. Hays and T. E. Boren Attorneys at Law of Panola
County Texas as our attorneys and Counsellors at law to
bring and institute suit in the District Court of Jefferson
County Texas for the recovery of all lands situated in said
County formerly and now belonging to our father William
Humphries decd. for us and in our names as such heirs we hereby
agreeing to give grant and Convey unto our said attorneys all
of one half of all Lands which they shall as our said Attorneys recover by suit or otherwise in said County for us as
heirs of said William Humphries and that this Conveyance is to
serve as a fee simple deed to such portion of land as here-
inbefore mentioned to them their heirs and legal assigns forever Witness our hands this the 10th day of August A.D.
1880   her
                              Jane X McFaddin
Witness   mark
S. W. Morris
J. N. Hays
The State of Texas } Before me J. H. Long J. P. and Ex Officio
County of Panola } Notary Public in and for Panola County
Texas this day personally appeared Jane McFaddin known
to me to be the person whose name is subscribed to the fore-
going instrument and acknowledged to me that she had
signed and executed the same for the purposes and Con-
siderations therein expressed. Given under my hand
and seal this August 10th 1880   J. H. Long
Seal   J. P. O. E. T.
No. Jane McFaddin Et al. so ½ Conveyance to Tom J.
Russell J. N. Hays and T. E. Boren Attys &c. to ½ —
acres Land in Jefferson County Texas Filed for Record at 3
P. M. Feby 19 1883   D. L. Miller C.C. &c.
The State of Texas } I D. L. Miller Clerk of the County Court
County of Jefferson } of said County do hereby certify that the
above instrument of writing dated 10th August 1880 with

Deed from Jane (Humphries) McFadden to Thomas Russell et al.

The State of Texas } Know all men by those presents that
County of Panola } I, Jane Wilkerson, a daughter, and
heir at law of William & Mary Humphries, deceased, and
formerly, the wife, and later, the surviving widow of
Thomas McFaddin, deceased, and later, the wife of William
Wilkerson, of the state and county aforesaid; but who has later
still abandoned me, taking with him, disposing of, and appropri-
ating to himself all community property, of the marriage,
and all his seperate property, and leaving the county and
country, went to parts unknown, and left me in destitute circumstances, and without support, unless I act for myself, and
resort to the management and disposition of my seperate estate
for a subsistence (wherefore I act and convey as a single woman
herein) for, and in consideration of the sum of One hundred &
Twenty Five (125) dollars, to me in hand paid, by J. G. Hazelwood, of the state and county aforesaid, have this day, by these
presents, granted, bargained, sold and conveyed, unto the said
J. G. Hazelwood, and his heirs, or assigns, all and singular
of my right, title, interest share, and claim, being an undivided ... heirs at law as aforesaid, in and to that

certain leagues or sitio of land, lying and situate in the County
of Jefferson in said state fronting on the west side of the Neches, or snow, River and marsh, beginning at a corner common to it, the John A. Veatch and James W. Bullock surveys, and
being the same tract of land that was, on the 14th day of February A.D. 1835, by George Antonio Nixon, then commissioner at
Nacogdoches for Coahuila and Texas, and the government of
Mexico, granted to my father, in the name of Pelham Humphries, as a colonist, in the colony of Lorenzo De Zavalla,
for a more particular and specific description of which
land, the said original grant, to Pelham Humphries, is
hereby referred to, and made a part hereof; being of record in
the general land office, at Austin and in Jefferson County.
The same land having been by me conveyed, with Covenant
of general warranty, to the said Hazelwood, on the 10th day of
February A.D. 1883, with erazures made therein before signing, and other immaterial defects of form, this deed is made to
correct and ratify the same, for the same consideration.)
To have, and to hold the above described lands and premises,
together with all the rights, members, hereditaments, and
appurtenances, to the same belonging, or in any wise incident, unto the said J. G Hazelwood, and his heirs, and
assigns, forever. And I do hereby bind myself, and
my heirs, executors, and administrators, to warrant and

Deed from Jane (Humphries) McFadden Wilkerson to J. G. Hazelwood

J. G. Hazlewood
to
W. P. H. McFaddin

The State of Texas, } Know all men by these presents: That
County of Panola } I, J. G. Hazlewood of the County of Panola and State aforesaid, in consideration of the sum of One Hundred and Twenty Five Dollars, to me in hand paid by W. P. H. McFaddin of the County of Jefferson, and state aforesaid, the receipt whereof is hereby acknowledged have Granted, Bargained, Sold, and Conveyed, and by these presents do Grant, Bargain, Sell and Convey unto the said W. P. H. McFaddin and his heirs and assigns, the following described property, to-wit: All the right, title, interest and claim which I own in and to the land and premises hereinafter mentioned - my said interest being the entire interest which Jane McFaddin, late Jane Wilkinson, daughter of William Humphries, Decd, conveyed to me on the 21st day of February A.D. 1883, by deed of that date, her said interest being an undivided (1/3) one third, as heir at law, as aforesaid, in, to and of that certain league or sitio of land, lying and situate in the county of Jefferson in said state of Texas, fronting on the West side of the Neches, or Snow, River and Marsh - Beginning at a corner common to it, the John A. Veatch and James W. Bullock Surveys and being the same tract of land that was

on the 11th day of February A. D. 18[illegible]5 by George Antonio Nixon, then Commissioner, at Nacogdoches for Coahuila and Texas, and the government of Mexico, granted to William Humphries as Pelham Humphries, as a colonist in the colony of Lorenzo De Zavalla, for a more particular and specific description whereof, the original title to Pelham Humphries, of record in the general Land office and Jefferson county, is hereby referred to and made a part hereof together with all and singular the rights, members, improvements, hereditaments and appurtenances to the same belonging, or in anywise appertaining. To have and to Hold, all and singular, the said premises above mentioned unto the said W. P. H. McFaddin and his heirs and assigns, forever. And I do hereby bind myself my heirs, executors and administrators to Warrant and Forever Defend, all and singular, the said premises unto the said W. P. H. McFaddin and his heirs and assigns, against every person whomsoever, lawfully claiming or to claim the same or any part thereof, by, through or under me - this deed being a quit claim only of all right, title and interest therein, acquired, of Jane McFaddin. Witness my hand at Carthage this 25th day of December A. D. 1883.

J. G. Hazlewood

Deed from Hazelwood to McFaddin

R E Carswell
to
W P H. Mc Faddin

State of Texas } Be it known that we Elizabeth Anderson joined
County of Wise } by her husband Holland L. Anderson, J. H. Tate,
B. W. Tate, and H. W. Tate, of Panola County said state Marianna
Epps (feme sole) Salina Whetstone joined by her husband Harvest
Whetstone, Hannah Anderson joined by her husband William Ander-
son, of Freestone County formerly, now of Navarro County said
state, G. W. Smith, Jas. E. Smith, John M. Smith Isaac W. Smith
Malissa A. Hale, joined by her husband W. S. Hale and Sallie
Hooks joined by her husband R. S. Hooks Richard B. English,
George T. English, Elizabeth English (feme sole) & J. E. Stubblefield
joined by her husband J. E. Stubblefield, of Houston County said
state, children grand children, and heirs of William English
and his wife Myra English (sometimes written Inglish) deceased
and also heirs of our brother George English deceased son of the
said William English or Inglish who died without issue and all
represented in this Conveyance by R. E. Carswell our agent and
attorney in fact, resident of Decatur in Wise County, said state
our powers of attorney to him being herewith delivered, for and
in Consideration of the sum of Three Hundred and Ninety nine
dollars and twenty-five cents (being our part of the Consideration of $600 to be paid the English or Inglish heirs in Comp-
nance of Civil suit No. 682, styled Heirs of Wm. Humphries vs Heirs
of Wm. English on the docket of the district Court of Jefferson County
and therein pending) have bargained sold Conveyed and released
and do this day by these presents, grant bargain sell convey
and release, unto W. P. H. McFaddin, of the County of Jefferson said state, (by whom said Consideration money, is to us
in cash paid at the delivery hereof). All and singular of
that certain league of land situated on the west side of the
Neches River, in the said County of Jefferson, said state originally
Granted by George Antonio Nixon Special Commissioner of the state
of Coahuila and Texas, on the 14th day of February, A. D. 1835 to
Pelham (alias William) Humphries, as a Colonist in the Colony
of Lorenzo de Zavalla, said league being surveyed and described
as follows to wit: Begins at the Common Corner of the James W.
Bullock John A. Veatch and Humphreys Survey from which

a hm of men in dia, brs South 10°. st. 23 varas distant, Thence
South 45° West 7111 varas to 2d Corner, mound and stake in prairie
Thence East 5320 varas, made 3d Corner, mound and stake in
prairie, Thence North 5218 varas, made 4th Corner in a marsh
Thence West 2300 varas to 5th Corner and Thence South 1418 varas to
place of beginning — being the same tract of land which was
on the 14th day of February A D 1836 Conveyed by William Hum-

Deed from Carswell to McFaddin

H.F. Ring et al
to
W.P.H. McFaddin

The State of Texas }
County of Harris } Know all men by these presents that we
Henry F. Ring of said County and J. M. Thompson of Falls
County Texas in Consideration of the sum of Four Hundred
dollars, the receipt of Two Hundred of which is hereby acknowledged, the remaining two Hundred dollars to be paid on
the 1st of January 1885 according to the terms of two certain
promissory notes executed by W.P.H. McFaddin of Jefferson
County both of said notes falling due on said first day of
January 1885, one of said notes being for the sum of Fifty
dollars and in favor of the said Henry F. Ring and the
other being in favor of the said J.M. Thompson and for the
sum of one hundred and fifty dollars to secure the payment
of which said notes the vendors lien on the land herein after
conveyed is expressly retained have this day granted bargained
sold and Conveyed and by these presents do Grant bargain
sell and Convey unto the said W.P.H. McFaddin his
heirs and assigns the following discribed property to wit:
All our right title and interest in and to the league of land
situated in Jefferson County state of Texas Granted by the
Government to Pelham Humphries on the 14th day of February
A.D 1835 and discribed as follows beginning at a corner common to the leagues of J.W. Bullock and John A Veatch an oak
Tree 9 in. in dia brs S. 10° W. 25 varas Thence S.45° W. 7111
is made second Corner by mound and stake in prairie, Thence
East 7320 vars made third Corner by Mound and stake in
prairie Thence N. 5218 varas made fourth Corner in a March
Thence West 2300 varas to fifth Corner Thence south 198 vars
to place of beginning making one league, the interest
herein conveyed is that of Mahala Coble an heir of said
Pelham or William Humphreys as the case may be, and her
husband Thomas Coble one of three heirs at law of the original
Grantee or a one third interest of said league, subject to a lien
interest in said third Conveyed to Tom J. Russell of said County

of Jefferson for services as Attorney in the prosecution of a suit for
the recovery of said league together with all and singular the rights
members improvements hereditaments and appurtenances to the
same belonging or in any wise appertaining, To have and hold
all and singular the said premises mentioned unto the said
W.P.H. McFaddin his heirs and assigns forever. And we
do hereby bind ourselves our heirs Executors and administrators to warrant and forever defend all and singular the
said premises unto the said W.P.H. McFaddin his heirs

Deed from Ring to McFaddin

M.H. Houghton
to
W.P.H. McFaddin

The State of Louisiana] Know all men by these presents
Parish of Caddo] That I. M. W. Houghton of the
Parish of Caddo and state aforesaid in consideration of the
sum of Fifty dollars to me in hand paid by W. P. H.
McFaddin of the County of Jefferson, State of Texas, the receipt whereof is hereby acknowledged have Granted bargained sold and conveyed, and by these presents do Grant
bargain sell and convey unto the said W. P. H. McFaddin
and his heirs and assigns the following described property
to wit. All of my right title interest and claim in and
to, and of that certain league of land situate and being in
Jefferson County in the State of Texas and near the Neches
River about three and a half miles S. and S.E. of the City
of Beaumont and which was originally granted by the
Government of Medico on the (14) fourteenth day of February A. D. 1835 to one Pelham Humphries as a Colonist
in the Colony of Lorenzo de Zavalla, the original title
of record in the General land office, and in Jefferson
County being referred to and a part hereof, for description
of said league which is sometimes described as the Grant
of W.m Humphries, the interest hereby Conveyed being
that which I purchased from Alexander W. Holmes who
purchased December 27th 1873 from B. B. Lacey of Panola
County Texas who purchased of Bailey English as will appear
from a deed of record in Book P of the land records of Jefferson County Texas on pages 344 etc. The said Bailey English
conveying as an heir of W.m English deed or W.m English
died, together with all and singular the rights members
improvements hereditaments and appurtenances to the same
belonging or in any wise appertaining To have and to
hold all and singular the said premises above mentioned
unto the said W. P. H. McFaddin and his heirs and assigns
forever, And I do hereby bind myself & heirs executors
and administrators to warrant and forever defend all
and singular the said premises unto the said W.P.H.
McFaddin and his heirs and assigns against every
person whomsoever, lawfully claiming or to claim the
same or any part thereof, Witness my hand at

Shreveport La this 27th day of December. A D 1883
M. W. Houghton

Deed from Houghton to McFaddin

Thos Anderson
Minor by Gdn.
to
W. P. H. McFaddin

The state of Texas } Know all men by these presents that
County of Jefferson } I Tom J. Russell, Guardian Ad litum
of Thomas Anderson a minor by appointment of the
district Court as hereinafter described, of the County of
Jefferson and state aforesaid, in Consideration of the sum
of Eight hundred dollars four Hundred, of which is paid
to me by W. P. H. McFaddin, on execution and delivery of
this deed, the receipt of which is herein acknowledged, and
the promissory note of said McFaddin delivered to me and
payable to me on the 1st day of January A.D. 1885 in the
sum of Four hundred dollars as part payment of the purchase money on the land herein Conveyed, the vendors
lien to which is reserved for the unpaid portion of purchase money, have Granted bargained sold and Conveyed, and by these presents do grant, bargain sell and
Convey unto the said W. P. H. McFaddin his heirs and

assigns the following described property to wit: A one-
third interest in and to the league of land originally
Granted to Pelham Humphreys, and situated in said County
of Jefferson and described as follows Beginning at a corner
Common to John A. Yeates and J. W. Bullock leagues from
which an oak tree bears South 10° West 25 varas distant
Thence South 45° West 7111 varas made second Corner by
mound and stake in prairie Thence East 1320 varas made
third Corner by mound and stake in prairie Thence North
5218 varas made fourth Corner in the river marsh Thence
West 2300 varas to fifth Corner Thence south 198 varas to
place of beginning. Containing one league. This interest is
Conveyed by me as the Guardian and Attorney ad litum
of said Minor Thomas Anderson by appointment of the district Court of said County of Jefferson in a suit therein
pending numbered and entitled No 682 Heirs of Wm Humphreys vs Henry E. Simpson et als, in which suit Thomas
Anderson Minor, is a party plaintiff and the other heirs
of said Wm Humphreys, are Jane McFaddin and Mahala
Coble and her husband Thomas Coble which said suit is now
Compromised between the different claimants and the order of
the said Court made and entered at the November Term thereof
A.D. 1883, approving the Compromise on the part of said Minor
Thomas Anderson and authorizing said Tom J. Russell Guardian as aforesaid, to make and execute deeds for said Minor in
the Compromise of said suit. Together with all and singular
the rights members improvements hereditaments and appurtenances to the same belonging, or in anywise appertain-

Deed from Thomas Anderson to McFaddin

Thos E. Boren
to
W.P.H. McFaddin

The state of Texas } Know all men by these presents that County of Jefferson } I Thomas E Boren of the County of Panola and State aforesaid in Consideration of the sum of Two Hundred dollars to me in hand paid by W. P. H. McFaddin and the further sum of Two hundred dollars as evidenced by the promissory note of the said McFaddin payable on the first day of January A D 1885 and the receipt of the amount of money and the note are hereby acknowledged have Granted bargained sold and Conveyed and by these presents do Grant bargain sell and Convey unto the said W. P. H. McFaddin his heirs and assigns the following described property to wit. A claim to one fourth interest of the Pelham Humphreys league of land as Conveyed to me by the heirs as a fee for recovering said league which is described as follows Beginning at a Corner that is Common to the J. W. Bullock and John A Veatch leagues on the west side

of the Neches river in Jefferson County from which an oak tree bears south 10° West 25 varas constant Thence south 45° W. 7111 varas, made second Corner by mound and stake in prairie Thence East 7310 varas made third Corner by mound and stake in prairie Thence North 5218 varas made fourth Corner in a marsh Thence West 2300 varas to fifth Corner Thence south 198 varas to place of beginning Containing one league, The interest I convey is derived from Jane McFaddin and Mahala Coble and Thomas Coble her husband heirs of Pelham Humphries together with all and singular the rights members improvements heredita- ments and appurtenances to the same belonging or in any wise appertaining So have and to hold all and sin- gular the said premises above mentioned unto the said W. H. P. McFaddin his heirs and assigns forever and I do hereby bind my heirs executors and Administrators to war- rant and forever defend all and singular the said prem- ises unto the said W. P. H. McFaddin his heirs and as- signs against every person whomsoever lawfully claiming or to claim the same or any part thereof through by or under me Witness my hand at Carthage this 24th day of December A D 1883   Thos E. Boren

Deed from Boren to McFaddin

Tom J. Russell
to
W. P. H. McFaddin

The State of Texas } Know all men by these Presents that County of Jefferson } I Tom J. Russell of the County of Jefferson and State aforesaid in Consideration of the sum of Four hundred dollars Two hundred of which is now paid to me, Cash in hand by W. P. H. McFaddin of said County and the delivery to me of his promissory note of the sum of Two hundred dollars payable to me on the first day of January A.D. 1885, as a part payment of the purchase Money of the land hereinafter described for which a vendors lien is retained have Granted bargained sold and Conveyed and by these presents do Grant, bargain sell and Convey unto the said W. P. H. McFaddin his heirs and assigns the following described property, to wit: a one fourth interest in the Pelham Humphries League of land situated in said County of Jefferson and described as follows to wit: Beginning at a corner that is common to the leagues of land Granted one to J. M. Bullock and the other to John A. Veatch from which an oak tree 9 inches diameter bears south 10° West 25 varas distant Thence South 45° West 7111 varas a stake and mound for second Corner, Thence East 7320 varas made third Corner by mound and stake in prairie Thence North 5218 varas made fourth Corner in river marsh Thence West 2300 varas to fifth Corner Thence south 198 varas to place of beginning Containing one league of land, This interest is Conveyed to me by the heirs of the original Grantee of the league for my services for them as an Attorney at Law for recovering the land for them in a suit now pending in the district Court of Jefferson County aforesaid entitled No 682 Heirs of Wm Humphries vs Henry E Simpson et als the said having now been Compromised between the various Claimants, The Heirs of said Wm Humphries are Jane McFaddin Mahala Coble and her husband Thomas Coble and Thomas Anderson a Minor represented by Tom J. Russell Guardian and Attorney ad litem of said Minor together with all

and singular the rights members improvements heredita-ments and appurtenances to the same belonging or in any wise appertaining To have and to hold all and singular the said premises above mentioned unto the said W. P. H. McFaddin his heirs and assigns forever, And I do hereby bind my heirs executors and Admin-istrators to warrant and forever defend all and singu-

Deed from Russell to McFaddin

The State of Texas } Know all men by these presents that I
County of Jefferson } James Ingalls Sr. of the County of Jefferson
and State aforesaid, in Consideration of the sum of Eight
Hundred (800) dollars, cash to me in hand paid by

W. P. H. McFaddin of the same County and state the receipt
whereof is hereby acknowledged, have Granted bargained sold and
Conveyed, and by these presents do Grant bargain sell and Convey unto
said W. P. H. McFaddin and his heirs and assigns the following
described property to wit: Five Hundred (500) acres of land in two seperate tracts which are parts of that certain league of land in Jefferson
County said state of Texas, originally Granted by the Government of Mexico
on the 14th day of February A.D. 1835 to Pelham (alias William) Humphrey or
Humphreys and said two tracts of land are described as follows to wit:
The First begins on the west line of the Pelham Humphreys league where
it crosses the (old) Eastern Texas Railroad and on the east line of a survey made for James Ingalls Jr Thence S. 45° W. with Ingalls east
line 25 7/0 varas to the S. E. Corner of said Ingalls Jr survey post in
a pond for 2d Corner Thence S. 45° E. 439 varas to stake and
mound in the marsh for 3d Corner Thence North 45° E. (2570)
Twenty five Hundred and seventy varas to the Railroad (Grade) afore-
mentioned Thence North west with the Course of said Railroad (Grade)
to the place of beginning Containing 200 acres - be the same more
or less, The 2d Tract owned and claimed by grantor and hereby
Conveyed is as follows to wit: Beginning at the N. E. Corner of the
H. E. Simpson part of said league at a stake and mound
in the Neches Marsh and on the North line of said league.
Thence East (632) six hundred and thirty two varas, to the 2d
Corner of this tract, stake and mound thence south 2718 varas
to stake and mound for 3d Corner, on the North line of a 1/4
league once surveyed for Spicer, Thence west on said line 632 varas
to stake and mound for 4th Corner; Thence North 2718 varas to the
place of beginning, Containing 300 acres more or less, being the
same lands Conveyed to me by David Snively on the 2d day of July
A.D. 1868 and recorded on the 28th day of September 1869 in Book
O pages 353 & 354 of the land records of Jefferson County. together
with all and singular the rights, members, improvements,
hereditaments, and appurtenances, to the same belonging, or in
anywise appertaining. To Have and to Hold, all and singular
the said premises above mentioned unto the said
W. P. H. McFaddin and his heirs, and assigns, forever. And
I do hereby bind myself, my heirs, executors, and admin-

Deed from Ingalls to McFaddin

Heirs of William. alias Abham
Humphries Deceased
682
vs
Henry E. Simpson et al

11th day of the Term
District Court Jefferson County.
May Term, May 21st 1885. And now
on this day came the plaintiffs The
Jane McFaddin (widow) Mahala Coble, and her husband Thomas Coble, by their Attorney Tom J. Russell, and Thomas Anderson minor son of Jamison. Anderson, and his wife Amanda Anderson Deceased. who was a daughter of Wm. Humphries deceased) by his special Guardian and Attorney ad titum J J. Russell, and announced ready for trial, and the defendants all came not, viz James. Ingalls. Sr. Mattie E. Langham wife of James B. Langham Jr, who joined her in this suit, and duly heirs of Henry E. Simpson Deceased, and Mary Brewer, surviving wife of Elisha C. Brewer deceased. the heirs of James L. Dollas deceased viz. J. H. Dollas. J. C. Dollas. W. A. Dollas and Mary Epsie Dwyer (formerly dollas joined in this suit by her husband W. E. Dwyer. the heirs of William English (alias Inglish) deceased. viz W. B. English, George English, Elizabeth. English, Howard. Anderson. Elizabeth Anderson, (William L Fitz, Pamela Fitz, Marana Epsie Soliva Whitstone, Warnick. Whitstone, Miranda Smith. William. English, Fletcher English, William. W. English, John. B. English, Evalina Davis. and her husband Thomas L. Davis, and the defendant M. W. Humphries and the heirs of S. B. Dozier, deceased, viz W. A. D. Dozier, Billie Dozier, A. S. Huriott and Lucy. Huriott all of which defendants had filed answers and pleadings in this cause, as appear of record, but having appeared not, and made no further defense and the said plaintiffs heirs of William. Humphries. by their attorney, and Guardian as aforsaid having waived a Jury and Submitted the cause, and the matter of fact, as well as of law to the court, and the Court having heard all the pleadings of the plaintiffs and of said defendant read and having heard the evidence plaintiffs, and considered the same, finds the and the law to be for the plaintiffs. Whereupon Court

[illegible]
2. of the day of May
17 day of Term

Judgment in Case 682 (two pages)

ordered adjudged and decreed that the said above named plaintiff do have and recover of said above named defendants, all and singular of the lands and premises described in plaintiffs petition to wit: One League of land situate in the County of Jefferson, and State of Texas, and being the same which was, on the 1st day of February A D 1835, granted by the government of Mexico. Pelham, (alias William) Humphries the ancestor of Plaintiffs and is described as follows to wit: on the west bank of the River Neches, and beginning at the corner of J. W. Bullock and John A. Veatch Surveys, An oak tree, 9 inches in diameter bears South 10° West 25 varas distant. Thence South 115° West 1700 varas. Made second corner by mound and stakes in prairie; thence East 7320 varas made third Corner, Mound and Stakes in prairie thence North 5215 varas made the fourth Corner in a Marsh: thence West 2300 varas to fifth Corner and thence West 198 varas to the place of beginning— together with all the rights members hereditaments and appurtenances to said league of land belonging or in any wise incident— and it is ordered and adjudged that said plaintiff have their undisturbed possession and have restitution of said premises and have and recover of said defendants all the costs in this behalf expended. and that execution may issue for the same in favor of the plaintiffs and in favor of the officers of the Court. And it is further ordered and decreed that the plaintiffs and defendants respectively be permitted to withdraw from the records of this Court their title papers filed in this Cause, upon their leaving on file certified Copies in lieu thereof.

Whereupon Court adjourned until tomorrow Morning at 9 O'clock

(18 day)
Thursday Morning May 28th Court Met pursuant to adjournment at 9 o'clock A. M. Same present as on Yesterday

Agreement of Lease made, and entered this the 20th day of June A. D. 1900 By and between W. P. H. McFadden, V. Weiss and W. W. Kyle, all of the city of Beaumont, County of Jefferson, and State of Texas, as parties of the first part, and Anthony F. Lucas of the city of Washington D. C. as party of the seconds part. Witnesseth that the said parties of the first part, for and in Consideration of One Dollar to each of them in hand paid, by party of the second part, receipt of which is hereby acknowledged, and for the further consideration and the Covenants and agreements hereinafter mentioned, does Covenant and agree to lease, and by these presents has leased and granted the exclusive rights unto the party of the second part, his heirs or assigns for the purpose of operating and drilling for petroleum, gas, or any other minerals, to lay pipe lines, and erect necessary buildings, and derricks, on all that certain tract of land, situated in the County of Jefferson and State of Texas, and known as the P. Humphrey league, and containing three thousand and eight hundred and fifty (3850) acres more or less. The party of the second part to have and to hold for and during the period of ten years from date hereof, and so long thereafter as oil, gas or other mineral substances can be produced in paying quantities, provided, the party of the second part has operated continuously during said terms. This extension not to exceed fifteen years. Party of the second part, his heirs, or assigns agrees to give to the parties of the first part one Tenth (1/10) part of all oil, gas or other mineral substances as produced in a crude state. Said oil or other mineral substances to be set apart to the credit and for the benefit of the said parties of the first part, it being optional with the parties of the first part to market and sell said one tenth at their own pleasure, or together with the product belonging to the party of the second part, in which latter case, party of the second part, agrees to sell all said oil at the best obtainable market value, and also agrees to furnish duplicate receipts to parties of the first part, showing

Lease of Humphries league from McFaddin, Weiss, and Kyle to Lucas (three pages)

amount and price obtained. Parties of the first part, have the same right of storage and use of pipe lines, as party of the second part to shipping points, or to refinery should one be erected in the neighborhood, and pipe lines connected with the same, and said tract of land. If party of the second part sells said oil, settlements to be made, and the cash paid as the proceeds of sale are collected, in proportion to each parties interest. Party of the second part to notify in writing the parties of the first part at the end of each thirty days, the amount of oil produced, and the amount sold during that time. Parties of the first part, are to fully enjoy said premises for the purpose of tillage, irrigating and subdeviding, or pastures, except such part as shall become necessary for said mining purposes, including rights of ingress and egress over and across said premises to the place of mining operations, which is hereby granted, to the party of the second part, and no portion of said land shall be utilized for any other purpose except what is found necessary for the operations conducted on said land. Should party of the second part be unsuccessful in finding oil or other mineral substances, in paying quantities; but instead find a source of good water, then it is hereby agreed by both parties hereto, that at the option of the parties of the first part, said parties will have the privilege to purchase the casing of said well or wells, and pay for same at market value, and parties of the first part, shall have the right at any time to inspect said work as it proceed along, and ascertain for their own behalf, what stratas has been passed by the tool of the boring outfit, so that in case of a good strata of water bearing sand is encountered, parties of the first part shall have the privilege of learning of its existence of said water stratas, so that they can utilize this knowledge if so desired by boring for water in their own behalf. Party of the second part is to have the privilege of using sufficient water and gas, should the latter be found, to run their necessary machinery, also the rights to remove at any time, all their machinery fixtures, and buildings placed on said premises. Party of the second part agrees to commence operations within twelve months from the execution of this lease, and continue in good faith. Should party of the second part, stop or quit operations for the period of six months after beginning, then this stoppage will be construed as the abandonement and forfeiture of said lease. Parties of the first part, reserve the right, to at any time request the party of the second part, to bore additional wells, if said parties of the first part have good cause to think willful neglect by party of the second part, and if said party of the second part fails to do so, after having been served with due notice in writing, then three months after serving said notice, parties of the first part shall have the right to bore on the neglected territory for their own exclusive use and benefit. It is further agreed that in case all or part of said tract of land should be tilled for rice, or other produce, and should one or more pipe lines be obstructing said tillage, then it is agreed hereby by the party of the second part, to remove said obstructions, by placing said pipes under-ground. In the event this lease is sold or assigned by party of second part, his assigns shall carry out all the conditions incumbent on him herein. The party of the second part, shall have the right to surrender at any time this lease, and be released from all conditions unfulfilled, and from that time, this lease shall be null and void, and no longer binding on either parties. Witness our hands and seals in duplicate originals.

W. P. H. McFaddin
V. Wiess
W. W. Kyle
Anthony F. Lucas

THE STATE OF TEXAS,) W. P. H. McFaddin being duly sworn on oath states that in the
COUNTY OF JEFFERSON.) year 1883 he purchased the whole of the Pelham Humphries Survey
sometimes known as the William Humphries survey, in Jefferson County, Texas, That in
January 1884 affiant fenced the whole of said league, except that portion of same
lying west of the Sabine & East Texas Railroad, which portion of the league he had there
tofore sold to other parties. That the fence there used in connection with fences with
which it joined, made an enclosure of said land so continued to be owned by affiant, and
other lands then owned and controlled by affiant. That said fences in connection with
natural boundaries where sufficient to turn stock, and affiant and his successors in
title, have had said land continuously fenced and in use since said time. In 1894 affiant's agent, D. W. Lewis moved on said property and commenced the cultivation of small
portions thereof, and looking after stock thereon. That affiant, and his successors,
through agents have continued the cultivation of portions of said league, except that
portion that was sold, continuously from that time until the present. That the cultivation of the land thereon from 1894 to 1901 was not extensive, but was continuous
each year. That since 1901 large areas of same have been planted to rice. That each
year since 1901 said land has been extensively used in the raising of farm products as
well as portions of same being used for grazing purposes. That during this time the
fences on said land had been kept up so as to keep cattle in and to keep other cattle
out. That from the time of his purchase of said land in the early eighties until this
time affiant and his successors in title have continuously claimed to own the whole of
said land, and have paid taxes thereon. That affiant and his successors in title have
had the exclusive use of said land during the whole of said period. That while some
suits have been filed against affiant and his successors in title pertaining to said land
none of said suits have been successful, he having defeated all of them with the excep-
tion of one suit involving a very small interest, which is still pending and has been
pending for a long period of time without effort upon the part of the plaintiff to try
same, and it is the belief of the affiant that said suit is without merit.

                    W. P. H. McFaddin,

Subscribed and sworn to before me, this 30th day of June, A. D. 1923.
(Seal) Will E Orgain Notary Public in and for Jefferson County, Texas.
THE STATE OF TEXAS,) Henry Davidson, being duly sworn on oath states that he had been
COUNTY OF JEFFERSON) in the employ of McFaddin, Wiess, Kyle Land Company, since 1901,
who were the successors intitle to W. P. H. McFaddin, That he has read the foregoing
affidavit and all of the facts therein stated concerning the use and occupancy of said
land since 1901 are true and correct.

                    H. Davison.

Sworn to and subscribed before me, this 30th day of June, A, D. 1923.
(Seal) D. M. Anderson Notary Public, inand for Jefferson County, Texas.

Affidavit of W. P. H. McFaddin, Filed for record W. A. COWARD, County Clerk, Jul, 3,
1923 at 10:55 o'clock a. m. By T. C. Land, deputy, Recorded this 9th day of July A. D.
1923 at 11:25 a. m. W. A. COWARD, County Clerk, Jefferson County, Texas, By
E. Thruston, Deputy

//////////////////////

Affidavit of W.P.H. McFaddin

246

Bibliography

"Appeals Court Upholds Transfer of Spindletop Suit to Texas." *Houston Chronicle* (September 23, 1989).

"Attorneys End Testimony in Change of Venue Hearing." *Beaumont Enterprise* (April 24, 1987).

"Attorney for Beaumont Socialite Objects to Murder Charge Publicity." *Houston Chronicle* (January 21, 1987).

"Attorney: No Appeal Seen for Wilson." *Beaumont Enterprise* (September 29, 1987).

"Attorneys Settle Lawsuit." *Houston Chronicle* (October 18, 1988).

"Ball Is Over at Muenster, Home of the Medderses." *Memphis Press-Scimitar* (February 27, 1967).

"Banker Say Medders Got $310,000 Loan on Cattle." *Memphis Press-Scimitar* (June 28, 1967).

Beasley v. McFaddin, 393 F. 2d 68 (1968).

"Beaumont Civic Leader Accused in Slaying." *Houston Chronicle* (August 23, 1986).

"Beaumont Murder Case Defendant Hospitalized." *Houston Chronicle* (January 29, 1987).

"Beaumont Socialite Goes on Trial in Caretaker's Death." *Houston Chronicle* (August 18, 1987).

"Beaumont Socialite Kills Former Employee." *Houston Chronicle* (August 21, 1986).

"Beaumont Socialite's Trial Delayed." *Houston Chronicle* (October 30, 1986).

"Beaumont Socialite Testifies, 'I Did Not Mean to Shoot Man.'" *Houston Chronicle* (August 21, 1987).

"Beaumont's 'Red-Neck Mentality' Cited in Change of Venue Hearing." *Houston Chronicle* (April 15, 1987).

"Beaumont Woman Calls Fatal Shooting Accidental." *Beaumont Enterprise* (August 21, 1986).

"Both Sides Rest in Wilson Murder Trial." *Beaumont Enterprise* (August 22, 1987).

Bradshaw, Steve and Joyce Duncan. *Heirs To Misfortune.* Johnson City, Tn: The Overmountain Press. 1987.

"Change of Venue." *Beaumont Enterprise* (April 14, 1987).

"Charges Are Dismissed Against Mrs. Medders." *Memphis Press-Scimitar* (December 16, 1976).

"Civic Leader Gets Probation, Fine in Manslaughter." *Houston Chronicle* (August 27, 1987).

"Claimed Spindletop Heirs Await Magistrate's Verdict." *Beaumont Enterprise* (November 30, 1984).

Clark, James A. and Michel T. Halbouty, *Spindletop*. New York: Random House. 1952.

Clark v. Amoco Production Co., 794 F. 2d 967 (1986).

Clark v. Amoco Production Company, 908 F. 2d 29 (1990).

"Convicted Civic Leader to Quit Board Positions." *Houston Chronicle* (August 27, 1987).

"County JP Arraigns Wilson in Murder." *Beaumont Enterprise* (August 26, 1986).

Cowles, Calvin D., ed. *Atlas To Accompany The Official Records Of The Union And Confederate Armies.* Board of Publications. Washington D.C. 1891-1895.

"Credit-Card Accusations Denied." *Memphis Press-Scimitar* (October 11, 1976).

"Creditors Begin Bankruptcy Move Against Medders." *Memphis Press-Scimitar* (February 24, 1967).

Crocket, George Louis. *Two Centuries In East Texas.* Dallas, Texas: The Southwest Press. 1932.

"DA's Office Agrees to Delay Wilson Trial." *Beaumont Enterprise* (October 9, 1986).

"DA Wants Early Trial for Beaumont Socialite." *Houston Chronicle* (September 5, 1986).

"Defendants in Oil Case Win." *Beaumont Journal* (August 21, 1963).

"Deputies Investigate Man's Shooting Death." *Beaumont Enterprise* (August 20, 1986).

"Dreams of Travel explode into Nightmarish Riches-To-Rags Story." *Memphis Press-Scimitar* (October 11, 1976).

"Drug Overdose Hospitalized Defendant Wilson." *Beaumont Enterprise* (January 29, 1987).

"87 Years Later, Treasure Hunt Continues for Spindletop Royalties." *The Houston Post* (January 31, 1988).

"Exclusions Cut Medders' Loss." *Memphis Press-Scimitar* (April 20, 1967).

"Family Continues Decades-Old Fight for Texas Oil Well." *Atlanta Journal and Atlanta Constitution* (November 19, 1989).

"Family of Beaumont Civic Leader Wilson Historically Linked." *Houston Chronicle* (August 26, 1987).

"Family Seeking a Piece of Spindletop." *Beaumont Enterprise* (September 26, 1982).

"Family-tree Sleuths Join Spindletop Case." *Houston Chronicle* (March 3, 1989).

"FBI Enters Probe of Mrs. Medders' Financial Activities." *Memphis Press-Scimitar* (October 13, 1976).

"Federal Court Bans Law Suit on Spindletop." *Beaumont Journal* (February 4, 1948).

Fehrenbach, T.R. *Lone Star.* New York: MacMillan Publishing Company. 1968.

"Firms Seek Dismissal of Case Filed by 435 Alleged Oil Heirs." *Beaumont Enterprise* (June 15, 1985).

Foster v. Gulf Oil Corporation, 335 S.W. 2d 845 (1960).

Foy, Jessica H. and Judith W. Linsley. *The McFaddin-Ward House.* Austin, Texas: Texas State Historical Association. 1992.

"Gay Medders Party Recalls Glitter of Pre-Bankrupt Days." *Memphis Press-Scimitar* (March 27, 1969).

"Gist Grants Change of Venue Hearing in Wilson." *Beaumont Enterprise* (April 30, 1987).

Glover v. McFaddin, 205 F. 2d 1 (1953).

Glover v. McFaddin, 99 F. Supp. 385 (1951).

Glover v. McFaddin, 81 F. Supp. 426 (1948).

"Gracious Living Still a Medders Hallmark." *Memphis Press-Scimitar* (February 21, 1976).

"Grand Jury Indicts Mrs. Medders." *Memphis Press-Scimitar* (October 7, 1978).

"Grand Jury In Dallas Indicts Mrs. Medders." *Memphis Press-Scimitar* (November 30, 1976).

"Grand Jury Looks at Shooting Death." *Beaumont Enterprise* (September 5, 1986).

Green v. Texas Gulf Sulphur Company, 393 F. 2d 67 (1968).

"Group Says Genealogist to Sort Out Real Heirs." *Beaumont Enterprise* (1989).

Halley, James L. *Texas From the Frontier to Spindletop.* New York: St. Martin's Press. 1985.

Hansen, Harry., ed. *Louisiana: A Guide to the State.* New York: Hastings House. 1941.

"Heart Attack Kills Ernest Medders." *Memphis Press-Scimitar* (November 15, 1975).

"Heir Aspirants Deluge County Offices for Records." *Beaumont Enterprise* (August 28, 1985).

"Heirs Battle Oil Firms for Ancestors' Legacy." *Beaumont Enterprise* (March 9, 1984).

"Heirs Hustle for Share of Spindletop Oil Fortune." *Beaumont Enterprise* (January 13, 1985).

"Heirs Renew Spindletop Claims." *Houston Chronicle* (August 29, 1986).

"Hines Sorts Out Claims of Would-be Spindletop Heirs." *Beaumont Enterprise* (September 21, 1985).

"Hopefuls Gather for Spindletop Pleas/Humphries Claimants Fight Dismissal of Oil Royalty Suit." *Houston Chronicle* (December 7, 1989).

"Hospitalized Area Socialite Is Recovering." *Houston Chronicle* (January 30, 1987).

"House Here Sold by Mrs. Medders." *Memphis Press-Scimitar* (March 1, 1967).

"How Mr. and Mrs. Medders Amazed Texas; $3,000,000 Sham." *Life* (April 7, 1967), pp. 82-85.

"Humphries Heirs Want Fortune." *Beaumont Enterprise* (December 7, 1989).

Humphries v. Texas Gulf Sulphur Company, 393 F. 2d 69 (1968).

In re Peregoy, 885 F. 2d 349 (1989).

"Investigator Says Nuns Admitted Medders Loan of Near 2 Million." *Memphis Press-Scimitar* (February 23, 1967).

"Investigator Says Wilson Shifted Blame." *Houston Chronicle* (August 20, 1987).

"It's Sad Day for Medders." *Memphis Press-Scimitar* (February 24, 1967).

"I Want Her to Face the System; Beaumont Shocked by Fatal Shot Fired by Socialite." *Houston Chronicle* (September 1, 1986).

Jones v. McFaddin, 382 S.W. 2d 277 (1964).

Jones v. McFaddin, 382 U.S. 15 (1965).

"JP: Deputies Gave Wilson Preferential Treatment in Probe." *Beaumont Enterprise* (August 22, 1986).

"JP Issues Second Warrant for Wilson." *Beaumont Enterprise* (August 24, 1986).

"JP Issues Warrant for Wilson's Arrest in Shooting Death." *Beaumont Enterprise* (August 23, 1986).

"Judge Denies Bid to Dismiss Murder Indictment Against Wilson." *Beaumont Enterprise* (February 6, 1987).

"Judge Denies Probation for 'Millionairess' Margaret Medders." *Memphis Press-Scimitar* (December 19, 1978).

"Judge Moves Socialite's Trial to Houston." *Houston Chronicle* (May 19, 1987).

"Judge Orders Move for Socialite's Trial." *Houston Chronicle* (April 30, 1987).

"Judge Orders Murder trial of Socialite Moved From Beaumont." *Houston Chronicle* (April 30, 1987).

"Judge Rejects Suits Seeking Share of Spindletop Fortune." *Houston Chronicle* (February 13, 1986).

"Judge Studies Arguments in Oil Fortune Suit." *Port Arthur News* (December 12, 1989).

"Judge Throws Out Lawsuit Over Spindletop Fortune." *Beaumont Enterprise* (May 8, 1985).

"Judge to Hear Request to Move Wilson Trial." *Beaumont Enterprise* (February 11, 1987).

"Jurors Find Wilson Guilty." *Beaumont Enterprise* (August 26, 1987).

"Jury Deadlocked in Wilson Case." *Houston Post* (August 27, 1987).

"Jury Expected to Get Medders Case Today." *Memphis Press-Scimitar* (May 4, 1977).

"Jury Indicts Mrs. Medders." *Memphis Press-Scimitar* (November 30, 1976).

"Jury Starts Deliberating Medders Case Verdict." *Memphis Press-Scimitar* (May 4, 1977).

"Jury Struggles to Determine Wilson Penalty." *Beaumont Enterprise* (August 27, 1987).

"Lamar Professor Says 90 Percent of Voters Know of Wilson's Case." *Beaumont Enterprise* (April 23, 1987).

"Lawyer Briefs Spindletop Heirs." *Beaumont Enterprise* (July 13, 1985).

"Lawyer May Ask Rejection of Wilson's Indictment." *Beaumont Enterprise* (September 5, 1986).

Lowe, John S. *Oil And Gas Law*. St. Paul, Mn: West Publishing Company. 1984.

McBride v. Gulf Oil Corporation, 292 S.W. 2d 151 (1956).

"McFaddin's Have Bust Proof Title." *The Dallas Morning News* (July 24, 1960).

"McGrath Briefs Grand Jurors on Shooting Death Groves Man." *Beaumont Enterprise* (September 4, 1986).

"Medders' Bankruptcy Asked by 7 Creditors." *Memphis Press-Scimitar* (February 23, 1967).

"Medders Barn to Have New Role Going, Going, Gone! (Almost)." *Memphis Press-Scimitar* (May 19, 1967).

"Medders Case Goes to Jury." *Memphis Press-Scimitar* (August 1, 1967).

"Medders Case Jury Chosen." *Memphis Press-Scimitar* (December 5, 1967).

"Medders Case Studied Anew? Medders Files Deposition." *Memphis Press-Scimitar* (February 28, 1967).

"Medderses Admit Being Bankrupt." *Memphis Press-Scimitar* (March 10, 1967).

"Medderses Indicted on Defraud Intent." *Memphis Press-Scimitar* (April 12, 1967).

"Medders Farm in Texas Sold." *Memphis Press-Scimitar* (April 10, 1969).

"Medders Indicted On Cattle Sale." *Memphis Press-Scimitar* (April 12, 1967).

"Medders Lose Summer Home." *Memphis Press-Scimitar* (July 21, 1967).

Medders, Margaret. *The Medders Story.* Memphis, Tn: Marest Publishing Co. 1973.

"Medders Party in Memphis Was Lavish and Listed 'Pd.'" *Memphis Press-Scimitar* (February 25, 1967).

"Medders Owes Memphis Bank $310,000." *Memphis Press-Scimitar* (April 8, 1967).

"Medders Riches Began on Loans of Holy Order." *Memphis Press-Scimitar* (February 22, 1967).

"Medders Rites to Be Today." *Memphis Press-Scimitar* (November 17, 1975).

"Medders Road to Muenster." *Memphis Press-Scimitar* (February 22, 1967).

"Medders Says He Got Riches By Borrowing." *Memphis Press-Scimitar* (April 8, 1967).

"Medders Story: Or Rags To Riches To Rags." *Memphis Press-Scimitar* (September 7, 1973).

"Medders Trial Opens In Dallas." *Memphis Press-Scimitar* (May 3, 1977).

"Medders Walked on a Tangled Trail to Texas." *Memphis Press-Scimitar* (February 22, 1967).

"Misbegotten Fortune Begetting Misfortune." *Memphis Press-Scimitar* (October 6, 1978).

"'Missing Link' Unlocked for Spindletop Claimants." *Houston Chronicle* (October 9, 1987).

"Mistrial is Ruled in Medders Case." *Memphis Press-Scimitar* (June 30, 1967).

"More Potential Heirs Enter Fight for Spindletop Fortune." *Beaumont Enterprise* (May 28, 1985).

"Mrs. Medders' Arrest Reported in Forgery Case." *Memphis Press-Scimitar* (October 10, 1976).

"Mrs. Medders Arraigned on Dallas Charge." *Memphis Press-Scimitar* (February 2, 1977).

"Mrs. Medders Called to Trial." *Memphis Press-Scimitar* (December 4, 1967).

"Mrs. Medders Faces Jail Term." *Memphis Press-Scimitar* (May 5, 1977).

"Mrs. Medders Fine—Daughter Needs Food Stamps." *Memphis Press-Scimitar* (January 28, 1975).

"Mrs. Medders Gets 5 Years." *Memphis Press-Scimitar* (May 14, 1977).

"Mrs. Medders Gets Five Years for Unpaid Bill." *Memphis Press-Scimitar* (May 14, 1977).

"Mrs. Medders Held In LA; Memphians Ask Detainer." *Memphis Press-Scimitar* (January 29, 1977).

"Mrs. Medders Indicted Again on Check Count." *Memphis Press-Scimitar* (March 25, 1967).

"Mrs. Medders Released on Parole." *Memphis Press-Scimitar* (May 18, 1979).

"Mrs. Medders Tells Story of Rise to Money, Trouble." *Memphis Press-Scimitar* (February 23, 1967).

Mullins, Marion Day. *The First Census Of Texas, 1829-1836 To Which Are Added Texas Citizenship Lists, 1821-1845 And Other Early Records Of The Republic Of Texas.* Washington, D.C. National Genealogical Society Quarterly. 1959.

"Murder Cases Begin Pre-trial Motions." *Beaumont Enterprise* (January 20, 1987).

"Murder Trial of Prominent Beaumont Woman Delayed." *Houston Chronicle* (October, 30, 1986).

"$975,000 Is Asked by Nuns in Suite Against Medders." *Memphis Press-Scimitar* (August 1, 1967).

"1987/The Year in Review." *Houston Chronicle* (February 27, 1987).

"Officer Says Wilson Denied Going to Ranch." *Beaumont Enterprise* (August 20, 1987).

"Officials Call Would-be Oil Heirs Victims of 'Con-game.'" *Beaumont Enterprise* (August 29, 1985).

"Oil Suit comes Up Dry/Spindletop Case Called Frivolous." *Houston Chronicle* (November 3, 1990).

Olmsted, Frederick Law. *Journey Through Texas.* New York: Burt Franklin. 1860.

"One of Several Spindletop Lawsuits Dropped." *Houston Chronicle* (March 21, 1987).

"Pair Say Deeds Prove Claims on Spindletop." *Houston Chronicle* (February 3, 1989).

Peregoy v. Amoco Production Company, 929 F. 2d 196 (1991).

Peregoy v. Amoco Production Co., 742 F. Supp. 372 (1990).

Petty, James W. *Pelham Humphries, The Myth—William Humphries, The Man: Uncovering The Identity of Pelham Humphries.* Unpublished manuscript. Salt Lake City: 1986.

"Poll Illustrates Voters' Opinions in Wilson Case." *Houston Chronicle* (April 23, 1987).

Presley, James. *A Saga Of Wealth.* New York: G.P. Putnam's Sons. 1978.

"Rag-To-Riches Saga Ends as Medders Dies in Texas." *Memphis Press-Scimitar* (November 15, 1975).

"Residents Sue For 'Spindletop Fortune.'" *Beaumont Enterprise* (May 25, 1985).

"Self-styled Heirs of Spindletop Cash Lose Another Battle." *Houston Chronicle* (June 20, 1990).

"Sentencing Decision Delayed for Mrs. Medders." *Memphis Press-Scimitar* (May 6, 1977).

"71 Testify in Change of Venue Hearing." *Beaumont Enterprise* (April 17, 1987).

"Socialite, Accused in Killing, Apparently Overdoses." *Houston Chronicle* (January 29, 1987).

"Socialite Called Shooting Accidental." *Houston Post* (August 20, 1987).

"Socialite Charged in Caretaker's Killing is Hospitalized in Apparent Drug Overdose." *Houston Chronicle* (January 29, 1987).

"Socialite Found Guilty in Killing." *Houston Chronicle* (August 26, 1987).

"Socialite Gets Probation, Five." *Houston Chronicle* (August 27, 1987).

"Socialite Says Sound of Gunshot was Shock." *Houston Chronicle* (August 26, 1986).

"Socialite Wilson Gets Five Years Probation." *Houston Chronicle* (August 28, 1987).

Solberg, Carl. *Oil Power.* New York: Mason/Charter. 1976.

"Spindletop Case Moves to a Federal Courtroom." *Beaumont Enterprise* (September 21, 1982).

"Spindletop Heir Case Will Be Decided Here." *Beaumont Enterprise* (September 15, 1984).

"Spindletop 'Heir' Gushes Only with Frustration." *Houston Chronicle* (February 26, 1989).

"Spindletop Heirs Drill Dry Hole in Courtroom." *Houston Chronicle* (August 30, 1991).

"Spindletop Heirs Drill Dry Hole in Federal Court." *Houston Chronicle* (August 30, 1991).

"Spindletop 'Heirs' Press Dreams of Untold Riches." *Houston Chronicle* (December 1, 1986).

"Spindletop Lawsuit Hit by Setback/$20 Billion Claim Killed." *Houston Chronicle* (September 16, 1989).

"Statute of Limitations Held Expired in Oil Suit." *Beaumont Journal* (September 2, 1964).

"Taking Stand Widow of Gunshot Victim Testifies at Trial." *Houston Chronicle* (August 19, 1987).

"Tennessee Judge Rules Against Purported Spindletop Heirs." *Houston Chronicle* (January 26, 1991).

"Testimony in Socialite's Trial Closes." *Houston Chronicle* (August 22, 1987).

"Texans Must Come Home With $800,000 to Save Ranch, Banker Believes" Associated Press (February 22, 1967).

"Texas Indicts Ex-Memphian." *Memphis Press-Scimitar* (January 29, 1977).

"Texas Jury Convicts Mrs. Medders." *Memphis Press-Scimitar* (May 14, 1977).

"Texas Oil Field Back in Court/Spindletop Claimants Trying Again to Get Case to Trial." *Houston Chronicle* (April 18, 1989).

"Texas: Son of Billie Sol." *Newsweek* (March 20, 1967), pp. 33-35.

"The Heirs of Pelham Humphries." *Southern Magazine* (May/June 1989), pp. 31-35, 58-64.

"The McFaddin Family: Lands, Cattle, and Oil on the Texas Gulf Coast." *The Texas Gulf Historical & Biographical Record*. Vol. XVI, No. 1. Austin, Tx: 1980.

"The State of Texas vs. Rosine McFaddin Wilson Cause 47503."

"Thousand Stake Claims to Spindletop Riches/Wealth of Rumors/Heirs Belatedly Pursue Royalties From Famous Oil Field." *Houston Chronicle* (February 12, 1989).

"$3 Million Later, Medders Life is Simple." *Memphis Press-Scimitar* (January 27, 1975).

"Title Bolsters Claim to Oil Fortune." *Beaumont Enterprise* (July 19, 1985).

"Trial of Socialite in Caretaker's Death is Transferred to Houston." *Houston Chronicle* (May 19, 1987).

"Two Land Suits are Dismissed." *Beaumont Enterprise* (March 22, 1960).

"2 Lawsuits Seeking Part of Spindletop Fortune Apparently Failing." *Houston Chronicle* (May 25, 1989).

"2,500 People See Oil Fortune Dreams Fading." *Beaumont Enterprise* (November 2, 1985).

"Two Men File Suit to Claim Part of Relatives' Spindletop Fortune." *Beaumont Journal* (August 4, 1982).

"Two Men Sue Over Spindletop Riches." *Beaumont Enterprise* (August 4, 1982).

"2 Men Unfazed by Dismissal of Their Spindletop Lawsuit." *Beaumont Enterprise* (September 10, 1982).

"Two Rag-To-Riches Stories Echo in Courts." *Memphis Press-Scimitar* (April 7, 1967).

"2 Suits Seeking Billions in Royalties from Spindletop Field Back in Court." *Houston Chronicle* (September 11, 1986).

"Untitled." *Beaumont Journal* (March 17, 1964).

"Untitled." *Memphis Press-Scimitar* (November 1, 1978).

"Unusual Events Cause Wilson, Perkins to Meet." *Beaumont Enterprise* (September 5, 1986).

"Victim's Family Suing Socialite." *Houston Chronicle* (September 6, 1986).

"Who Has the Goods on Whom?" *Memphis Press-Scimitar* (May 18, 1967).

"Wilson Guilty of Involuntary Manslaughter." *Houston Chronicle* (August 26, 1987).

"Wilson Murder Trial Begins Tuesday." *Beaumont Enterprise* (August 16, 1987).

"Wilson Shows Improvement After Overdose." *Beaumont Enterprise* (January 31, 1987).

"Wilson Testifies Shooting Accidental." *Beaumont Enterprise* (August 21, 1987).

"Wilson Trial Delayed." *Beaumont Enterprise* (August 25, 1987).

"Wilson Trial Told of Bid to Blame Victim's Wife." *Houston Chronicle* (August 20, 1987).

"Woman Testifies Wilson Shot Husband After Arguing." *Beaumont Enterprise* (August 19, 1987).

"Woman Who Killed Ranch Hand Has Ties to Early Beaumont." *Houston Chronicle* (August 26, 1987).

"Would-be Heirs Sue for Accounting of Group War Chest." *Houston Chronicle* (November 14, 1989).

"Would-be Spindletop Oil Heiress Gets a New Husband." Associated Press (September 22, 1976).

Yergin, Daniel. *The Prize.* New York: Simon & Schuster. 1991.

Interviews with the author

Shirley Cochran, West Tennessee Humphries Heirs Association, June-September 1995.

Mrs. Graves, Panola County Historical Society, December 1996.

Thomas Humphries, March 1996.

Mary McClanhan, West Tennessee Humphries Heirs Association, June-September 1995.

Christy Marino, Curator Spindletop Museum, September 1996.

Mr. and Mrs. James Petty, numerous 1994-1996.

Dan Profitt, April 1994.

Geraldine Perkins Roberts, December 1996.

Cynthia K. Timms, Esq., November 1996.

Lieutenant Jan White, Jefferson County Sheriff's Office, September 1996.

Index

Other Books From Republic of Texas Press

100 Days in Texas: The Alamo Letters
by Wallace O. Chariton

A Cowboy of the Pecos
by Patrick Dearen

A Treasury of Texas Trivia
by Bill Cannon

Alamo Movies
by Frank Thompson

At Least 1836 Things You Ought to Know About Texas but Probably Don't
by Doris L. Miller

Battlefields of Texas
by Bill Groneman

Best Tales of Texas Ghosts
by Docia Schultz Williams

Civil War Recollections of Jemes Lemuel Clark and the Great Hanging at Gainesville, Texas in October 1862
by L.D. Clark

Cow Pasture Pool: Golf on the Muni-tour
by Joe D. Winter

Cripple Creek Bonanza
by Chet Cunningham

Daughter of Fortune: The Bettie Brown Story
by Sherrie S. McLeRoy

Defense of a Legend: Crockett and the de la Peña Diary
by Bill Groneman

Don't Throw Feathers at Chickens: A Collection of Texas Political Humor
by Charles Herring, Jr. and Walter Richter

Eight Bright Candles: Courageous Women of Mexico
by Doris E. Perlin

Etta Place: Her Life and Times with Butch Cassidy and the Sundance Kid
by Gail Drago

Exiled: The Tigua Indians of Ysleta del Sur
by Randy Lee Eickhoff

Exploring Dallas with Children: A Guide for Family Activities
by Kay McCasland Threadgill

Exploring the Alamo Legends
by Wallace O. Chariton

Eyewitness to the Alamo
by Bill Groneman

First in the Lone Star State
by Sherrie S. McLeRoy

The Funny Side of Texas
by Ellis Posey and John Johnson

Ghosts Along the Texas Coast
by Docia Schultz Williams

The Great Texas Airship Mystery
by Wallace O. Chariton

Henry Ossian Flipper: West Point's First Black Graduate
by Jane Eppinga

Horses and Horse Sense: The Practical Science of Horse Husbandry
by James "Doc" Blakely

How the Cimarron River Got Its Name and Other Stories About Coffee
by Ernestine Sewell Linck

The Last Great Days of Radio
by Lynn Woolley

Letters Home: A Soldier's Legacy
by Roger L. Shaffer

More Wild Camp Tales
by Mike Blakely

Noble Brutes: Camels on the American Frontier
by Eva Jolene Boyd

Outlaws in Petticoats and Other Notorious Texas Women
byGail Drago and Ann Ruff

Phantoms of the Plains: Tales of West Texas Ghosts
by Docia Schultz Williams

Rainy Days in Texas Funbook
by Wallace O. Chariton

Red River Women
by Sherrie S. McLeRoy

The Return of the Outlaw Billy the Kid
by W.C. Jameson

The Santa Fe Trail
by James A. Crutchfield

Slitherin' 'Round Texas
by Jim Dunlap

Spindletop Unwound
by Roger L. Shaffer

Call for names of the bookstores in your area
(972) 423-0090

Other Books From Republic of Texas Press

Spirits of San Antonio and South Texas
by Docia Schultz Williams and Reneta Byrne

The Star Film Ranch: Texas' First Picture Show
by Frank Thompson

Tales of the Guadalupe Mountains
by W.C. Jameson

The Texas Golf Guide
by Art Stricklan

Texas Highway Humor
by Wallace O. Chariton

Texas Politics in My Rearview Mirror
by Waggoner Carr and Byron Varner

Texas Ranger Tales
by Mike Cox

Texas Tales Your Teacher Never Told You
by Charles F. Eckhardt

Texas Wit and Wisdom
by Wallace O. Chariton

That Cat Won't Flush
by Wallace O. Chariton

That Old Overland Stagecoaching
by Eva Jolene Boyd

This Dog'll Hunt
by Wallace O. Chariton

To the Tyrants Never Yield: A Texas Civil War Sampler
by Kevin R. Young

Tragedy at Taos: The Revolt of 1847
by James A. Crutchfield

A Trail Rider's Guide to Texas
by Mary Elizabeth Sue Goldman

A Treasury of Texas Trivia
by Bill Cannon

Unsolved Texas Mysteries
by Wallace O. Chariton

Western Horse Tales
Edited by Don Worcester

When Darkness Falls: Tales of San Antonio Ghosts and Hauntings
by Docia Schultz Williams

Wild Camp Tales
by Mike Blakely

Seaside Press

Branson Uncovered
by W. C. Jameson

Critter Chronicles
by Jim Dunlap

Dirty Dining: A Cookbook, and More, for Lovers
by Ginnie Siena Bivona

Exotic Pets: A Veterinary Guide for Owners
by Shawn Messonnier, D.V.M.

I Never Wanted to Set the World on Fire, but Now That I'm 50 Maybe It's a Good Idea
by Bob Basso, Ph.D.

Jackson Hole Uncovered
by Sierra Sterling Adare

Los Angeles Uncovered
by Frank Thompson

Only: The Last Dinosaur
by Jim Dunlap

Pete the Python: The Further Adventures of Mark and Deke
by Jim Dunlap

San Antonio Uncovered
by Mark Louis Rybczyk

San Francisco Uncovered
by Larenda Lyles Roberts

Seattle Uncovered
by JoAnn Roe

They Don't Have to Die
by Jim Dunlap

Tucson Uncovered
by John and Donna Kamper

Twin Cities Uncovered
by The Arthurs

Your Kitten's First Year
by Shawn Messonnier, D.V.M.

Your Puppy's First Year
by Shawn Messonnier, D.V.M.

Call for names of the bookstores in your area
(972) 423-0090